THE AGE
OF ARTHUR

To

C. E. STEVENS

who inspired

THE AGE
OF ARTHUR

A History of
the British Isles from 350 to 650

JOHN MORRIS

Senior Lecturer in History
University College London

Volume Two:
The Successor States

PHILLIMORE

1977

Published by

PHILLIMORE & CO. LTD.

London and Chichester

Head Office: Shopwyke Hall,
Chichester, Sussex, England

*First published by Weidenfeld and Nicolson
1973*

© John Morris, 1973, 1977

ISBN 0 85033 290 7

*Printed in Great Britain by
Unwin Brothers Limited,
Old Woking, Surrey*

CONTENTS

MAPS

INTRODUCTION

This book surveys the history of the British Isles between the end of Roman Britain and the birth of England and Wales. Its aim is to make that history manageable, like the history of other periods.

In the 420s, the government of Roman Britain enlisted Saxon, or English barbarians from Germany to strengthen their defences; but in the 440s the English rebelled. Half a century of bitter fighting destroyed the Roman economy and technology of Britain, but the British won the war, under the leadership of Arthur, who restored the forms of Roman imperial government. The empire of Arthur lasted for some twenty years and on his death fragmented into a large number of small independent successor states. The English were contained within substantial defined reservations until they rebelled for a second time, at the end of the sixth century. In a generation they subdued most of what is now England; thenceforth the independent native British were confined to the west, and were called Welsh, a word that in old English meant 'foreigners'.

The personality of Arthur is unknown and unknowable. But he was as real as Alfred the Great or William the Conqueror; and his impact upon future ages mattered as much, or more so. Enough evidence survives from the hundred years after his death to show that reality was remembered for three generations, before legend engulfed his memory. More is known of his achievement, of the causes of his sovereignty and of its consequences than of the man himself. His triumph was the last victory of western Rome; his short lived empire created the future nations of the English and the Welsh; and it was during his reign and under his authority that the Scots first came to Scotland. His victory and his defeat turned Roman Britain into Great Britain. His name overshadows his age.

Two centuries of war and of separate co-existence moulded a political society unlike that of Europe, where Roman and barbarian experience merged more easily. These centuries are a historical period in their own right, more than a transition or interlude between Rome and the Middle Ages. To be understood, a well-defined period needs a name, as clear in meaning as Roman, Norman or

Tudor. The fifth and sixth centuries in Britain are properly termed the Age of Arthur, for modern historical convention normally labels periods according to their principal rulers. In early medieval Europe it distinguishes Merovingian and Carolingian periods, so called after dynasties who took their names from individuals. The Carolingian age extends from the grandfather of Charles the Great to his grandchildren's time; but the substance of history does not turn upon the personal ancestry of rulers. Though he had no royal father and founded no dynasty, Arthur was the heir of the emperors before him, and the kings who followed knew themselves to be 'heirs of great Arthur'. He straddles two centuries, and names them as fitly as Charles the Great names the eighth and ninth centuries in Europe.

The Arthurian age is the starting point of future British history. Thereafter, Britain has comprised England, Wales and Scotland; previously, these three countries did not exist. Their later history is harder to understand if their formative years are overlooked; for nations, like people, tend to form habits in infancy that their adult years harden and modify. But the early history must be seen in its own context; if its evidence is superficially raked over in a search for the origins of later institutions, then it is as uninformative as an archaeological site plundered by treasure hunters.

These centuries have often been termed the 'Dark Ages'. They are not dark for lack of evidence. The quantity of evidence is immense and unusually complex, hard to understand. Therefore it has been neglected, abandoned to a small number of specialists, who have often been obliged to limit their studies to their own particular patch. The specialist in pagan English pottery or brooches is rarely conversant with the literature of early Ireland, with late Roman administration, with Welsh or Germanic law, with Italian theology or old Welsh poems, with the techniques of the farmer and the shipbuilder, or with a dozen other disciplines that must be brought together, and related to the history of Europe, if the age is to be understood.

No one can be master of all these trades. The historian must be content to be the pupil and interpreter of many of them. But he must do his best to bring them together, for the evidence seems obscure only because its modern study is inadequate and fragmented. The significance of excavated objects cannot be perceived until they can be related to the written record of the people who used them. Yet most of the texts are made up of half truths, for they are abstracts derived from lost originals, distorted by the ignorance or interest of their compilers. They await the kind of critical scrutiny that centuries of scholarship have lavished upon the texts of other periods. Because that work has not yet been undertaken the historian of the fifth and sixth centuries has special problems. He has no main 'reliable' narrative witness, like Tacitus or Bede, to justify him in dismissing other evidence as 'unreliable' or 'forged'. He must borrow from the techniques of the archaeologist, and must uncover a mass of separate detail, most of it encrusted and corroded by the distortion of later ages. He must clean off as much of the distortion as he can, try to discover what the original sources said and then relate their statements to one another, and to the rest of the evidence.

The aim is modest, and has been well expressed by Professor Ludwig Bieler.

> according to a widely accepted view, it is the historian's task to find out 'what actually happened'. . . . This, I believe, is impossible. The historian cannot do more than collect, assess and interpret evidence.

He has to sum up like a judge, and decide like a jury. He may not blankly refuse to decide, but he cannot proclaim certainty. He must give an informed opinion on what is probable and improbable, and return an open verdict when the balance of evidence suggests no probability. He may not insinuate like an advocate, whose plea that evidence falls short of absolute proof covertly invites his hearers to disbelieve the evidence. It is irrelevant for him to assert his personal belief or disbelief. There is a reason for every statement in every text, and for the place where every archaeological object was found. His business is to ferret out the reasons. He may conclude that an author lied or misunderstood; but falsehood must be demonstrated as carefully as accuracy, and may not be casually implied by labelling a statement 'dubious', without argument. But, unlike the verdict of the jury, his conclusion is constantly subject to appeal, and he must therefore clearly distinguish between what his evidence says and what he deduces from it, that others may easily correct his inferences in the light of new evidence and deeper understanding. If he fails to offer clear conclusions from the evidence he knows, he infects his readers with false beliefs and woolly notions; if he leaves no conclusion to correct, the importance of new evidence is easily missed. He must acknowledge his own sympathies as openly as a Tacitus or a Bede, for the historian who rashly pretends to be free of bias unconsciously surrenders to the superficial assumptions of his own day; and is therefore always misleading, and usually dull.

The evidence must first be collected. Most of the main texts are printed, but many are to be found only in large or specialist libraries. They cannot be studied unless they are assembled for constant reference and comparison; and this book could not have been written without the exceptional facilities generously provided by librarians, especially of University College London, and of the London Library, who permitted rare volumes to be retained on loan for years at a time. The difficulty of getting at the sources is one of the main reasons why the period is so poorly understood; for any historical study is lamed if it can only be undertaken by a few experts, whose judgement their readers cannot easily criticise. If the Arthurian period is to be studied seriously in the future, the first need is to make the sources accessible, no longer the secret lore of the learned. The first steps have been taken. The most important single texts, *Gildas*, *Nennius* and *Patrick*, will shortly be easily available, in text and translation, with comment; the rest of the main evidence is collected in my *Arthurian Sources* (forthcoming), where the separate texts of Annals, Genealogies, Saints' Lives and other sources are collated, and the scattered information about people, places and problems is assembled and assessed in detail. The study of this collected evidence prompts the conclusions here expressed, some of which are bound to seem abrupt and dogmatic until these publications appear.

The Age of Arthur interprets this evidence. It places most weight on contemporary statements, for in any age the contemporary cannot outrageously falsify the knowledge that he shares with his readers; for the same reason, texts written within living oral memory of the events they relate command respect. A modern writer may distort the actions and motives of contemporary individuals or distant peoples, but he could not assert that modern Britain is immune from war or ignorant of electric power; he might bamboozle an illiterate audience with a story that Napoleon fought Marlborough at Minden, but he could not pretend that Gladstone lived in the eighteenth century, for many men are still alive who know that Gladstone lived in their fathers' time. So when Gildas told his readers that theirs was an age of civil war and external peace, and that Vortigern and Ambrosius Aurelianus had lived in their fathers' time, he could not have done so if these matters of public knowledge were wholly untrue. But once the threshold of living memory is passed, after about a hundred years, the antiquity of a text is of small moment; many that were written a thousand years later follow their sources more closely than others written two or three hundred years after the event.

Interpretation rests upon bringing the evidence together, once the superficial deposit of later fancy has been removed, for it is no use discussing the meaning of the sources, until we know what they do and do not say, as exactly as we can. The history is narrated and described by bringing their separate statements together. Not much faith can be placed on a single statement by a single source; confidence grows when a number of independent sources each tell something of the same story. The proof of the pudding is in the eating. The evidence hangs together, and tells its own story. Innumerable separate details combine into a plain and credible tale, more coherent than any that an ingenious later historian could devise.

The tale is plain. But any account that is built up from a mass of small items of evidence seems complex at first sight. It is doubly difficult to explain the age of Arthur simply, for most of the names are unfamiliar. The historians of later periods, whose kings are conveniently numbered, may assume that their readers know that Henry VII reigned before Henry VIII; and many well known tales make it clear that Elizabeth ruled after and not before the Henries. But in the fifth and sixth centuries even the names of persons of comparable importance are known only to specialists, and their relation to each other in time and place is often clouded, compelling examination of the evidence. In order that the unfamiliar names, dates and events may be more easily understood, a short Summary of Events and a Table of Dates is provided.

The story that the sources tell raised a difficulty that was not at first foreseen. It had been intended to start from the relatively firm ground of the late Roman Empire, and to end in the middle of the seventh century, whose events Bede recorded within living memory. But it soon became apparent that much that has been written in modern times about the seventh and eighth centuries jars awkwardly against the earlier evidence. The reason is evident. Many of those who studied the early English were well acquainted with later medieval history, and looked back from the standpoint of Norman or Plantagenet England. But the processes of history move forward in time; men are influenced by the experience of their forebears, but they know nothing of their descendants' problems; and history looks different when viewed the right way up. It has therefore been necessary to discuss some later problems, where misconceptions about the Arthurian period and its immediate sequel have caused misunderstanding. This discussion does not set out to contradict what others have written; rather, it deals with different questions, for much that looked puzzling from an eleventh-century standpoint seems no problem at all in the context of the sixth century, while some of the assumptions that seemed natural to historians of the middle ages prove alien to thinking of earlier ages. It has also been necessary to discuss some aspects of barbarian and medieval European history that have not been systematically explored; and therefore to disregard some modern notions entertained about them. Such differences of approach do not assert greater wisdom or understanding; they are the result of fortunate chances that have given me the opportunity to read and sift more varied sources than most other individuals.

It has only recently become possible to attempt an overall history of the Arthurian age, thanks to a number of important publications that have pulled together several sections of the evidence. They rest upon much detailed work, whose conclusions cannot always be discussed within the limits of this book. It has proved necessary to stick to the principle expressed by H.M. and N.K.Chadwick in the preface to their *Growth of Literature*:

> if we had read more widely, we would not have completed this book ... which might have been the better course. The amount of time at our disposal is limited; we have preferred to give as much of it as possible to the primary authorities.

It is therefore necessary to apologise to the very many scholars whose work is not here acknowledged, and has often not been adequately assessed. It is also impossible to acknowledge the many scholars whose kind advice has been freely offered on many details; my expressed gratitude must be limited to those whose unfailing patience my many queries have most heartily exploited, notably Professor Kenneth Jackson and Professor Idris Foster; Mr J.M.Dodgson and Professor D.M.Wilson; and Professor Christopher Hawkes; to Michael Gullick, who drew the maps to my specification, with limitless patience; and to Dr John

Wilkes, Dr Ann Ward and Miss Vivienne Menkes, who have kindly read and commented upon the typescript. None of them of course bear any responsibility for the way in which their advice has been treated. I am also grateful to the indulgence of the publisher, since the mass of unfamiliar names and concepts has made it necessary to use capitals, figures and punctuation for clarity and emphasis, in disregard of convention; and I am particularly indebted to the advice and help of Julian Shuckburgh and Sue Phillpott.

The interpretation here given of the Arthurian Age can be no more than a preliminary attempt to open up questions, and to make it easier for future specialist studies to relate their conclusions to a wider context. The book is therefore published in the confident expectation that many of its conclusions will soon be modified or corrected. It will have served its purpose if it makes such correction possible. It would be kind if readers who detect figure mistakes or errors of fact, in the text or the notes, would notify the author, via the publisher.

This reprint includes some corrections of substance. It has not yet been possible to correct minor misprints, spelling and punctuation which do not mislead.

John Morris

The aim of this book is to make the Arthurian period manageable. The term describes the years between the Romans and the English in the British Isles. The account is prefaced by a description of the later Roman Empire, and followed by a brief examination of the effect of English conquest. Understanding depends on how you use your sources. If you search for 'reliability' or 'forgery', 'truth' or 'falsehood', you will make no sense of this or any other period of human history. Almost all our sources are half-truths, distorted by interest or error; and in the rare instances of tales wholly untrue, woven from nothing, what matters is why the lies were told and believed. The business of source criticism is to find out why every word was written, and how each object got into the place where the archaeologist found it. That is how the interest and error or the ancient or modern writer is detected. As with any other kind of evidence, we are then left with no certainties, but with varying degrees of probability. Probability increases when two or more sources say the same thing in different ways from different standpoints. When the probabilities are assessed and put together, they outline an overall sequence of events that can be described and understood. Once an intelligible outline exists, others may in the future correct the detail and adjust the outline.

John Morris

THE
SUCCESSOR
STATES

CHAPTER EIGHT
PAGAN IRELAND

The history of the fifth century is the story of the destruction of Roman Britain, and of Arthur's unavailing efforts to rebuild its ruins. Men who lived within the former frontiers could still regard themselves as fellow-citizens of a single state, distinct from Irishmen and Picts beyond; when Patrick determined to go to Ireland, the natural reaction among the British was to wonder that he should risk his life 'among the enemy'. The war ended the ancient division between Roman and barbarian, but it also killed the ancient unity of the Roman diocese. The southerners fought as *Cumbrogi*, and won their victory with little help from the north, while Wales fought its own Irish wars. The victors restored something of the old unified administration, and forced the highlands to acknowledge its suzerainty. So long as its authority endured, contemporaries could still see Britain as a political unit, and describe its history in a single narrative. But after the death of Arthur and the end of his empire, the several nations of the British Isles have their separate histories; neither the ancient nor the modern historian can blend these accounts into one comprehensive narrative. From the early sixth century onward, the histories of the Irish and the Picts, the British and the English, must be told separately.

The four nations deeply influenced each other; their military and political strength set the limits within which each might develop. The balance of power changed decisively and permanently during the sixth century. The peace of Badon lasted for more than two generations, and when the second Saxon revolt broke out, no one was left alive who could remember clearly the earlier troubles. The revolt began soon after the fearful bubonic plague, that wasted Europe in the middle of the century. In the south, it led to crushing victories in the 570s. In the north, it gathered strength more slowly, but in the thirty years after 580 the English armies ended British rule forever. England, Wales and the future Scotland had taken shape, though none yet had a central government of its own. The British Isles were divided between a number of separate kingdoms. They differed in their speech and in their memories, but henceforth they shared a comparable economy and political structure.

The bond that reinforced similar customs among each people was the monastic church, common to all of them. It was created and shaped by the British during the peace of Badon; the Irish welcomed it with enthusiasm, and carried it to the Picts and the English, and thereafter to Europe. Through the church, the example of Ireland deeply influenced the secular development of the other British peoples. Though the Christian religion reached Ireland in the fifth century, it first seized hold of Irish society in the decades immediately after the death of Arthur. Its impact on barbarian Ireland was explosive, for Ireland was changing rapidly, ready to pour its national traditions and morality into a Christian mould.

Irish Christianity was a major influence in the formation of the new society in Britain. Christian clerks and statesmen who had been trained in Ireland or by Irishmen were prominent among its builders; and they are chiefly responsible for the manner in which its history was preserved. The records of Britain cannot be interpreted intelligibly without an understanding of their Irish background; and that Irish background leans heavily upon the long traditional history of pagan Ireland. The story of pagan Ireland is full of fancies, its reality hard to determine; yet what mattered to the future was not the reality, but the beliefs that men of the sixth and seventh centuries held about the past; and those beliefs are more easily discovered.

The Sources

The early historians of the British, the English and the Picts learned much of their trade from the Irish. They imitated the forms in which they recorded events and shared their fundamental assumptions. Unlike most of their contemporaries in Europe, they took it for granted that both the distant and the recent past of their regions and peoples ought to be remembered and explained, and ought to be cited as a guide to present conduct.

These records took many forms. Unlike the peoples of Europe, the nations of the British Isles preserved long pedigrees of royal and notable families; they did so because they believed that a man who could claim a notable ancestor deserved honour in the present. Though some of the continental Germans had once had oral genealogical traditions, their descendants did not prize them, and most of them perished without written record; but the English genealogies reach back to the ancestral gods, and name human kings who were held to have reigned in the third or fourth centuries, long before their descendants approached Roman territory. Their form, particularly in Northumbria, follows an Irish model, and some of the kings they list were also remembered in heroic tales, that were written down in England, though their counterparts in Europe were not transcribed, and were forgotten when they ceased to be sung. The British pedigrees are more numerous than the English. Their ancestral tradition rarely extends back beyond the fifth century; but its form and content are also heavily indebted to the enormous corpus of Irish genealogy, vastly older, richer and more developed than its British or English counterparts.

The study of Irish genealogy has also become easier since the publication of the first volume of O'Brien's *Corpus Genealogiarum Hiberniae* (1962), whose index names 15,000 to 20,000 persons who were held to have lived before the tenth century, with many more thereafter. The scattered texts of the Welsh and English pedigrees are also nearly all in print. Like all genealogists, their authors sought to connect living patrons with heroes of the past, so that, apart from remote and fanciful origins, the beginning and the end of each line normally copy original record, but the links between are often corrupt. The principal difficulty in their study is superficial; most of the important lines are preserved in a number of different versions, many of which leave out, insert, or duplicate an entry or miscopy their original, so that no single text preserves the whole of the tradition it reports. That tradition can be discovered only by critical comparison of the several manuscripts. All the English and Welsh early texts, and the more important Irish lines, are therefore collated in *Arthurian Sources*.

The British and the English owe a still greater debt to the Irish Annals. The Christian Irish set down a detailed account of their pagan past, and to do so they adapted the form of Roman Christian annals. Their Roman model had been shaped by Eusebius of Caesarea in the early fourth century. When the Christian Constantine conquered Rome, Eusebius set himself the task of synchronising the historical tradition of Rome with the legends of Greece, of the Near East, and of the Old Testament; and thereafter his chronicle of world history was continued by many other writers. The Irish set themselves a comparable task, of synchronising the stories of their own pagan past with the world chronicles of Eusebius and of his successors. The earlier surviving versions preserve many of the European entries that were used to fix the dates of native events, but later recensions omit them, copying only the native entries.

The Irish Annals survive in half a dozen main versions, drawn up between the 11th and the 17th century, and published in good, bad and indifferent modern editions. All the surviving texts are collations of earlier lost texts, and each makes its own selection, so that some entries occur in all, some in several, some in one only. They list events under years, but the AD dates printed in the margins are all the work of late editors, from the 14th century to the 20th. The later editors, and their lost sources, used different dating systems, so that reference to the separate texts gives a bewildering superficial impression of discordant and uncertain alternatives; and confusion is increased because the editors of all extant texts themselves faced conflicting dating systems in their originals, and therefore often enter the same event two or three times, under different years, either naming their source, or commenting 'as others say'.

These are technical problems, awkward only because they have not yet been sorted out. The manuscripts of the European chronicles abound with comparable difficulties, that have been resolved by the labours of nineteenth-century editors. The study of Irish dating has been made much easier by Mac Airt's exact and critical edition of the *Annals of Inisfallen* (1951), which has made it possible to collate the several versions in *Arthurian Sources*, permitting each event to be referred to a single year, according to its position within the Inisfallen series of dates. Collation does not resolve all problems; but it makes them manageable, by distinguishing the real historical problems from unreal apparent difficulties, that are created only by a faulty manuscript tradition.

The study of the Irish Annals does not concern Ireland alone. The English and the Welsh Chronicles derive both their form and their earlier entries directly from their Irish exemplars. The 'Cambrian Annals' are, for the fifth and sixth centuries, a transcript of the Irish Annals; of the first 22 entries, 18 are copied from the Irish, and only four British notices are inserted among them; and Irish entries still form a majority of the seventh-century notices. The Saxon Chronicle also follows the Irish form; in its earlier entries, concerning the first century, it makes the same selection as the Irish make from Bede, or from his source, and shares with the Irish half a dozen items not found in Bede. But from the 5th century on, it copies only native entries, as in the later texts of the Irish Annals; for it is preserved in a relatively late version, edited in Wessex in the 9th century.

The Irish Annals are also a direct source for the history of Britain. They preserve some hundred and fifty notices of events in the British and English kingdoms in the 6th and 7th centuries, many of them not recorded elsewhere. But the influence of the Irish historians bites deeper than its form, its example and its additional information. It also underlies the interpretation of its imitators, sometimes implanting in their texts an arbitrary date, that deeply influences later historical thinking, but cannot be explained until its Irish origin is examined; for example, the Irish plague entry of 551, wrongly interpreted as 547 in the Welsh text, was there used to date the death of Maelgwn of Gwynedd, and the Saxon Chronicle in turn used the Welsh notice of Maelgwn to give a date to Ida of Northumbria, whom it therefore entered at 547. Nor is the influence confined to dates. It extends to the Chronicler's judgement of what he should enter, how he should record it, and how the moral should be pointed, often by the Irish technique of inserting a long vivid tale into the bald list of events, in a manner alien to European practice.

The English and Welsh derivatives have fewer textual difficulties. The Welsh or 'Cambrian' Annals are preserved in two main versions, that do not substantially disagree, save that one of them leaves out about one-tenth of the entries. Half a dozen versions of the Saxon Chronicle survive, but they have been many times published, with critical commentaries, and have long since been collated. The narrative of the Chronicle however preserves three serious confusions; as in the Irish texts, the marginal AD dates are inserted by later editors into earlier notices, and, since their starting-point is too late, all events earlier than 550 are placed some twenty years later than the original version intended; the notices of the origins of Wessex are entered three times over, in the manner of the duplicate entries in the Irish Annals; but, unlike the Irish, the 9th century West Saxon authors of the Chronicle thoroughly misconceived the early history of the north.

The Lives of the Saints constitute the third main source for early Irish history. They chiefly concern the 5th, 6th and later centuries, and are an important source for the history of the British and the English as well as of the Irish. Their information about places and regions is supplemented by the evidence of so-called ancient dedications. The modern word has occasioned some confusion; a peculiar 'Celtic' custom of 'dedication' has been alleged, and refuted. The arguments exist only on word play. There were no 'dedications'. The Christians of the British Isles continued to name churches after the fashion of 4th century Europe, long after Europe had changed its practice. Churches were 'dedicated' to God alone; but they were distinguished from one another by the name of their founder, or of a teacher whom he honoured. In Rome the Basilica of Liberius was so-called because it was built by pope Liberius; it did not receive its lasting name of S. Maria Maggiore, in honour of the Virgin, until the 430s, a quarter of a century after political separation from Italy had hindered the spread of religious and political novelty to Britain. The first church in Tours was known as the Church of Litorius, after the bishop who built it; when Martin died in 398, his pupil and successor built a new Church of Martin above his tomb. At the same time in Britain another admirer of Martin, Ninian, gave Martin's name rather than his own to his church at Whithorn. Thereafter the churches, chapels and monasteries of the British Isles were regularly known by the name of their founder or of the teacher he admired, or by their geographical location.

From the later 7th century the English, but not the Irish or the Welsh, began to adopt the new European custom of naming churches after long dead Christian leaders, notably Saints Peter, Paul and Martin. The Normans introduced the more recent names of Michael, All Saints and others, and energetically imposed them, together with the name of Mary, upon churches known by older names. Sometimes local and national tradition re-asserted itself, especially in Scotland during and after the time of David I, and prompted new dedications to ancient saints; but such dedications are recorded only in regions where the old saint was already widely honoured, and are confined to a few major national saints, Ninian and Kentigern, Patrick and Brigit, David, Samson and Arthmael. No instance has yet been observed of the importation of a local saint in Norman or later times into a region where he was not previously honoured. The study of the names of churches, wells and other holy places is therefore a useful guide to the expansion of the monastic movement in 6th century Ireland, as in Britain.

Most of the main sources are to some extent affected by the art of the story-teller. In any land and in any age, the story-teller is not supposed to submit to historical accuracy. The early Irish scholars strove to keep history and story-telling apart; they could not wholly succeed, especially in their account of pagan Ireland, when other record was weak. The Annalists transcribe the substance of some ancient stories, often with expressed distaste and apology, and the genealogists traced their patrons to a few of the shadowy heroes of early story. But because the effort was made, the influence of romance is easily discerned, and often acknowledged. These main sources are supplemented by others, notably King Lists, that give the length of each reign; in the Irish, though not in the Pictish lists, the figures are usually wildly corrupt, contradicting each other and other evidence.

The evidence clings together. Annals and Genealogies, Lives and Lists name the same people over and over again, nearly always in the same regions at the same times, without serious disagreement; and from the middle of the sixth century, their story receives increasing confirmation from the history of Bede and from continental authors. Inferences are seldom wisely drawn from a single statement in a single source; they are founded upon a combination of scattered notices from different sources. The records of each people commonly note their own nationals; but the church linked them. Sixth-century Irishmen are prominent in Welsh accounts, Welshmen in Irish tradition; in the seventh century, Englishmen are frequently remembered by the Irish, Irishmen by the English, and both begin to attract the notice of Europeans. The collapse of Roman Britain and the expansion of monastic Christianity brought barbarian Ireland fully into the company of the peoples of the British Isles, and the Irish contributed as freely as the Welsh and English to the moulding of their new society. The history of the British and the Welsh is therefore lamed if Irish experience is ignored; for, in a trite truism, the Irish Sea became a bridge, not a barrier, and a bridge that was much in use, by traffic in both directions.

Prehistory

The story of Ireland's impact upon Britain and Europe cannot begin with Christian Ireland; for the monks who made that impact were soaked in the learning, the customs, the social outlook of their own historical tradition. It extended back to the Creation, to the Flood, and to the first arrival of mankind in Ireland. It began with the legends classified among the Mythological and Heroic Cycles by the story-tellers, which the Annalists tried to link with Roman dates for Hebrew, Greek and Roman history. The legends are woven around the names of imaginary kings and wondrous battles, that the early Irish historians thoroughly distrusted. One ancient Irish verse protests

> Though antiquaries record it
> The Just Canon does not;

and subsequent writers plead

> I like not to have the labour of writing this section imposed upon
> me; wherefore I beseech you . . . not to reproach me for it,

warning that what they record is not 'genuine history' but what they 'found written in old books'.

Nevertheless the nonsense conceals an underlay of 'genuine' tradition, whose reality could not be discerned until modern archaeology established something of the main outlines of Irish pre-history. The legends preserved by the early Christian Irish writers discuss and reject the notion that men lived in Ireland before the Flood; and there is as yet no proven palaeolithic, or Old Stone Age habitation in Ireland. The artefacts of mesolithic food gatherers have been observed, and tradition remembers the first inhabitants as men who 'lived on fishing and fowling till the coming of Partholon'. Partholon's people were the first agriculturalists; at about the time of Abraham, reckoned at 2016 BC in the chronology of Jerome, they came to Ireland from Sicily and southern Italy, bringing with them the first ploughs and oxen, dairy farming, husbandry and houses, and they buried their dead in 'long graves' in 'stone heaps'. The first farmers in Ireland arrived in the neolithic, or New Stone Age, in the third millennium BC, or some centuries before; they buried their dead in long stone chambered graves in long barrows, ultimately derived from the rock-cut tombs of Sicily and southern Italy. The legends recall later colonists of the same economy, who included Nemed, 'the holy man', whose children also peopled Britain, and others whose names are paralleled in Gaul, who also established themselves on the coasts and islands of western Scotland and in the Hebrides.

Several centuries later came quite different peoples, who used metal, including the bronze cauldron, the sword and the spear, and brought with them the smith and the wright, the carpenter and the doctor, and also druidry, learning and the gods, including Nuada Silverhand, or Nodens, Lug, Ogma and Dagda, the Good God. They buried their dead 'not in stone heaps' but 'in the *sid* mounds', round barrows; some of them are called a 'people of ships' who 'drank from beakers'. These particulars closely correspond to the excavated remains of middle Bronze Age peoples in Ireland, in the second millennium BC; even the improbable route assigned to them, from Greece to Ireland by way of Scandinavia, is matched by the distribution of some types of Bronze Age cauldrons.

Some 200 years later a more important metal-using people followed. The sons of Mil, ancestors of the later Gael, migrated up the Danube and down the Rhine, sailing thence to Spain through the Channel, plundering the coasts of Britain on their way. From Spain their descendants came to Ireland, adding riding horses, royal forts and tombs to the arts and crafts of their predecessors. Their fourth king first smelted gold in Ireland, and introduced brooches of precious metals. A century or so later king Muinmon, the 'Neck-decorated', caused kings and chiefs to wear collars or chains of gold about their necks, and his successor added rings and bracelet arm bands of gold. The gold *lunulae* of Ireland, crescent shaped collars of gold, sometimes solid, sometimes composed of separate chains, were not clearly recognised until modern times, more than a thousand years after this tradition was first committed to writing.

The next decisive immigration is dated to the 'time of Darius', around 600 BC, or later, early in the Atlantic Iron Age. Labraid the Exile regained Leinster with the aid of the 'Black Gauls', armed with the terrible new broad green spear. The adventures of Labraid anticipated the fatal opportunism of another Leinster king who reigned 2000 years later, the exiled Diarmait mac Murchada, who recovered his throne with the aid of Strongbow's Normans and the terrible new weapon of heavy Flemish horses, and thereby opened Ireland to lasting foreign rule.

Labraid's allies help to explain a linguistic puzzle posed by the earliest Roman accounts of Ireland. Irish is distinguished from other known Celtic languages by a number of peculiarities, of which the most striking is the general use of a K sound, designated in the vocabulary of modern philologists by the letter Q, where British, Pictish, Gallic and related speech used a P sound; so that the word for children, *plant* in Welsh, is *clanna* in Irish, and the name of Patrick was heard by 5th-century Irish ears as *Cotriche*. Throughout Ireland, and wherever the Irish settled in northern Britain, Irish place names are almost without exception preserved in a Q Celtic form; and there is virtually no trace of any P Celtic names. But when the Roman geographer Ptolemy listed the names of Irish peoples and of their principal forts in the 2nd century AD, most of the names are in P Celtic, the language of Britain and Gaul. Ptolemy's source probably dates to the beginning of the 1st century AD. But its informants were not academic philologists who troubled to transliterate Irish names into their appropriate British forms; they gave the names as they were then pronounced.

At that date, a number of the ruling peoples of Ireland were known by British or Gallic names. The background of some of them is precisely indicated; the Cauci and the Manapii, whose name the modern Irish transliterate in Fermanagh and Monaghan, were offshoots of peoples who dwelt upon the coasts of Flanders, while the portions of the Brigantes, the Gangani and others also lived in Britain. Irish tradition remembered something of these British and Gallic peoples, who were in later times treated as subject aliens. They include the *Galioin* or *Gailenga*, originally settled in Leinster, and the numerous peoples known as *Cruithne*, whose name is a simple transliteration into Irish Q Celtic of *Pritani*, the oldest P Celtic spelling of the *Britanni*, the British. The Irish used the word to describe the Picts, the northern British who had never been conquered by Rome; in north-eastern Ireland one large and important group of Cruithne retained their name and identity, though not perhaps their language, into the 7th or 8th century AD, and several other groups elsewhere, who were earlier absorbed, have left ample traces of their existence. Irish tradition was acquainted with a legend of conquering foreigners, armed with powerful weapons previously unknown, who were introduced by an exiled prince some centuries before the Romans conquered Britain; and also of peoples who lived on in Ireland, and were still known as British, throughout the Roman period and for some centuries thereafter. The Roman record confirms that peoples with British or Gallic names were dominant in parts of Ireland at about the time of the Roman conquest.

From the remotest prehistoric times to the threshold of the historical period, Irish tradition records a number of basic details that coincide with the discoveries of modern archaeology, and with contemporary Roman observation. These coincidences are too many and too marked to be the result of chance. They are real details remembered. Story-tellers richly clothed them with legends of insubstantial people and dramatic events, as the story-tellers of later Britain clothed the meagre memories of Arthur in imaginary glories; but a solid tradition remains when the gaudy clothing is removed. Its substance has the same significance that Kenneth Jackson detected beneath the stories of the Heroic Cycle:

> The characters ... and the events ... are ... unhistorical. But this does *not* mean that the traditional background, the setting ... is bogus. .... In the same way, Agamemnon and Helen are doubt-less not historical, ... but the Mycenean world dimly depicted in Homer was a real one.

Modern prejudice tends to impose an arbitrary limit of three or four centuries upon folk memory, without argument or evidence; for the narrow experience of literate Europe is unacquainted with the long memory of illiterate societies, and easily condemns uncritically what it does not understand. But the few faint details of their past that the Irish remembered through several thousand years are neither unusual nor remarkable. The oral Homeric tradition itself preserved accurate background detail for the best part of a thousand years; and Tacitus reports that the Silures of Roman Britain still remembered that their remote ancestors had come from Spain, though four centuries of literate Roman civilisation soon obliterated their oral recollections. Similar traditions have lasted far longer in Asian countries where widespread literacy developed later. The precise syllables of Vedic verse accurately report that the worship of the phallus and the humped bull belonged to the indigenous religion of pre-Aryan India in the second millennium BC; and despite centuries of Brahminical insistence on Hindu teetotal and vegetarian observance, tradition remembers that the early Hindu gods drank deep and feasted on roast beef. There the background setting has persisted in oral tradition for something over 3,000 years; the furthest recollections of Irish legend claim no greater antiquity. They are remarkable only because they were written down before they were forgotten.

The tales told in the Mythological Cycle help to show what is real and what is unreal in the legendary history of pagan Ireland; modern excavation and a Roman description demonstrate that the background setting, the main stages in the evolution of Irish society, were accurately remembered in broad and general outline; they do not confirm the reality of the people and events. The stories that concern the Roman centuries must be assessed upon the principles revealed by the earlier tales, for no later Roman descriptions survive, and the archaeological evidence is not closely enough dated to offer useful comment, except in rare individual particulars. These later tales depict an Iron Age society that had inherited powerful living influences from the Bronze Age past, and say something of its relations with the Roman power established across the Irish Sea in Britain. As the narrative draws nearer to the time when it was committed to writing, the possibility that some of the events were accurately remembered grows stronger. Many cannot sensibly be confirmed or denied; but the reality or falsity of the events and names is not important. What matters is the evolution of Irish society, and the impact upon it of the Roman government in Britain in successive generations.

The stories of the Heroic Cycle are set shortly before the coming of the Romans to Britain. Thereafter the Annalists and Genealogists are increasingly emancipated from the influence of the story-tellers, and concentrate upon attempts to relate Irish people and events to the history of Rome. The principal warriors of the Heroic Tales were the Ulaid of the north, who name modern Ulster. They were aristocrats, akin to Homer's heroes, with their chief centre at Emain, Navan, near Armagh. Their enemies were the northern *Cruithne*, and also the southern *Erainn*, the 'men of Erin', from whose name the Greeks and Romans called the island 'Ierne'. Tradition does not allot to the southerners chieftains comparable with the northern heroes. It celebrates the triumph of the northern heroes, who reduced their enemies to subjection.

Tuathal

Legend ends the old order with a successful rising of the *Aitheach Tuatha*, the subject peoples, dated to the reign of Domitian (81–96). Exiles found refuge in Britain, and early in the reign of Hadrian (122–138), one of them, Tuathal, returned from Britain 'with a great army'. He destroyed the Dumnonii of Ireland, the *Fir Domnann*, mastered the Ulaid and then the rest of Ireland. The nobility of all Ireland agreed to 'accept him as their king, since he delivered them from slavery to the serfs and subject people'. He created the central province of Meath out of pieces detached from Ulster, Connacht, Leinster and Munster, and established a fortress in each part of Meath; and he imposed upon Leinster the *Boruma*, the cattle tribute.

Tuathal is treated as the restorer of a monarchy immemorially old. But its earlier traditions are nominal and sketchy. In relating full and precise detail of Tuathal, the story makes him the effective founder of the central monarchy of Ireland, the ancestor of the future dynasty of High Kings. The initial basis of its power is said to have been a military force raised by an exile in Britain and employed to destroy the political structure of an older Ireland, that had been divided between numerous independent peoples, in the manner of Britain before the Romans. Tradition thenceforth regarded these older peoples as subjects; in treating their former independence as the short-lived result of a recent rebellion, it asserted an immense and misty antiquity for the institutions of its own day, and reduced the significance of the intervention of the army from Britain to a casual detail.

The colourful native legend must always be compared with the scanty prosaic notices that Roman writers give of Ireland. In 81 AD Domitian's legate Agricola entertained an Irish prince, exiled *seditione domestica*, by internal conflict, and thought of sending a Roman army to restore him. The Roman date coincides with the date Irish legend gives for the exile of Tuathal's family. It does not confirm the detail of the legend, for there were doubtless numerous other exiles then and later who found shelter with the Romans in Britain; and successive Roman legates must, like Agricola, have considered whether Roman interests were served by helping them. When Hadrian built the Wall from Tyne to Solway in the 120s he continued the fortified line down the Cumberland coast. He feared attack by seaborne enemies, and those enemies clearly included the men of north-eastern Ireland. The record of his reign is not full enough to say whether or not his legates adopted the proposal that Agricola rejected, and used their armies to install in Ireland a native ruler, bound to Rome by treaty, charged to restrain his subjects from raids on Roman territory. He might have done so, for the early empire frequently imposed such kings, and tried to keep them strong enough to control their subjects, yet not so strong that they could threaten Rome. The evidence of Roman fortifications shows that it would have suited Hadrian to intervene if opportunity arose; but it does not show whether he did so. Irish tradition believed that he did. The legend is not confirmed, but the story it tells is far from improbable.

The story precisely formulates the social basis of Tuathal's rule. He was the ally of a warrior nobility, whose main strength lay in the north, against their social inferiors, and also against the older peoples of Ireland, some of whom were held to be of British origin. The gist of the story is that Tuathal imposed a

---

Map 9

·—·—·	Approximate boundaries of the main kingdoms
·····	of internal divisions

≡≡≡ Northern Ui Neill territories

|||| Southern Ui Neill territories

Districts contested by the Ui Neill are shown by broken lines

■ Royal centres

+ Episcopal centres

• Monasteries

Inset and border
the Irish National Grid

The royal centres shown were not all inhabited in the 5th century

MAP 9 5th CENTURY IRELAND

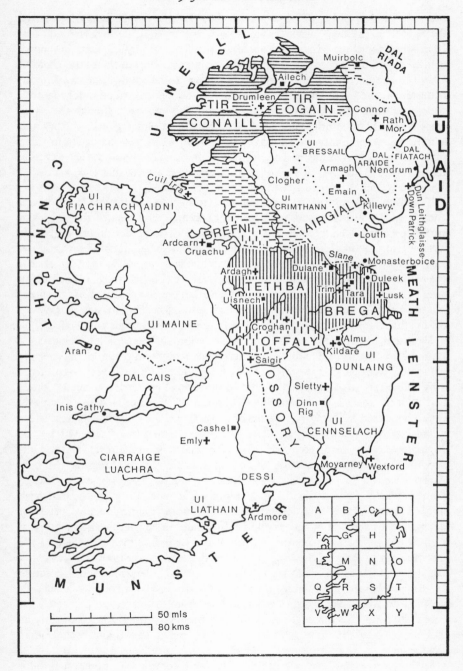

temporary unity, and tradition is precise about how he did it. He is described as the author of the five 'provinces' of early Christian and modern Ireland. The Irish word for these provinces, *coiced*, 'a fifth', itself implies that they are a deliberate administrative sub-division. The names of three of them, the Ulaid of Ulster in the north-east, the Laigin of Leinster in the south-east, and Mumu, Munster, in the south and west, argue that these regions had an older identity, and so do the traditions of Connacht, in the north and west, though the name itself is said to have originated after Tuathal's time. But regional identity and administrative definition are different things. All Gaul was divided into three parts before Caesar campaigned; but it was the Roman conquest that gave the regions defined and lasting frontiers. Irish tradition asserts that it was Tuathal who gave a similar permanence to the regions of Ireland.

Tradition does not regard Tuathal's monarchy as a lasting sovereign central authority. His successors are made to fight repeated wars against the unbroken strength of the Ulaid for two centuries, until decisive defeat reduced their territory to the modern counties of Antrim and Down; and wars against the Leinstermen lasted longer, without comparable success, while fighting against the Munstermen was sporadic and even less decisive. The story-tellers knew many tales of mighty kings who ruled these regions from the first century AD to the fifth; but the Annalists and Genealogists were unable to relate them in time to the story of Tuathal's dynasty, and different versions make discordant connections.

Connacht was treated as the peculiar patrimony of the High Kings who claimed descent from Tuathal, and there they rarely had to fight. It bears the name of Tuathal's grandson, 'Conn of the Hundred Battles', sovereign of the north. One early tradition divides Ireland into two. The north is termed 'Conn's half', but the south is the half of Mog Nuadat, the 'servant of Nodens', a god who is also honoured in Britain. The heirs of Mog, whom the genealogists treat as his grandsons, were called Eogan and Cian. Their names were assumed by the *Eoganachta*, who ultimately made themselves rulers of all Munster, and the less successful *Cianachta*, originally of central Ireland. These three are the only names that end in -*achta*; they describe not peoples or territories, but ruling families who claimed descent from a common ancestor. They are the first Irish dynastic names. This tradition portrays a significant political change, which it dates towards the end of the second century; and in restricting the territory of Conn's dynasty to Connaught, the land of the *Connachta*, it acknowledged the factual independence of the Ulaid in the north-east. The story of the division of Ireland between Conn and Mog asserted the formal independence of the south. It also proclaimed the establishment of dynastic rule over the older southern peoples, for Mog 'expelled the *Earna* (Eraínn) from Munster, such as would not submit to him'. Their social order differed, for their leader was no dynast; he was named Nemidh, 'holy', and his principal companion was known as Dadera the Druid.

Irish tradition outlines a pattern of struggle common to numerous Indo-

European and other peoples. The society of Gaul before the Romans, as of early Aryan India, also recognised distinct classes of priests, warrior nobles, simple cultivators, and craftsmen and traders. Centralised monarchy grew strong when the interest of one class, or allied classes, demanded united leadership against the rest of society, or against a foreign enemy; monarchy weakened when priests or nobles ruled without threat of challenge, separately or in combination.

In Ireland the stature of the monarchy grew when the Irish began to attack Britain. Roman evidence clearly indicates the date. In the first years of the third century the emperor Severus found it necessary to rebuild the fort of Caernarvon on the Irish sea. Irish tradition held that about 200 AD Art the son of Conn, and Eogan the grandson of Mog, were driven into an alliance of north and south in the time of Severus' son, and were destroyed by 'Benne Brit, king of Britain', who was supported by the Erainn, and installed one of their leaders as king of Ireland. The name Benne is not British or Irish, but Roman, Bennius, or perhaps Benignus. As under Hadrian, the Roman record is too thin to indicate whether or not there was such an expedition, or whether a legionary legate was so named.

Cormac

Thereafter Irish tradition fastens upon the splendid portrait of Art's son Cormac, dated from 218 to 256, who expelled the intruder. The Annals give him far more space than any other king. Though he is the hero of many romances, his portrait in the Annals and the Genealogies is clear and consistent, unembarrassed by the conflicts of time and place that surround his predecessors. In the pleasant idiom of the Clonmacnoise Annalist, he was

> obsolutely the best king that ever Raigned in Ireland before himselfe.

His first dozen years were spent in subduing the north, and, unlike his predecessors, he is made to conquer Connacht as well as the Ulaid. Then, in the 230s, his 'great fleet was overseas for three years', and he became 'sovereign in Alba', Britain. In entries dated before the middle of the sixth century, the Annalists and Genealogists normally apply the word 'Alba' to the whole of Britain, 'as far as the Muir nIcht', the 'sea of Wight', the English Channel, but thereafter Alba is restricted to Pictland, beyond Edinburgh and Glasgow. The monarchy of Cormac is represented as insecure; while the fleet was away, the men of Leinster seized Tara; Cormac was 'dethroned by the Ulaid', and enlisted the aid of the Eoganachta and the Cianachta to subdue them. In his last years he faced a revolt of the Dessi, the subject peoples of Meath; when he reduced them, the greater part migrated to their permanent home in Eoganacht territory, in Waterford of Munster.

Thus far the dry notices of the Annalists. Their Cormac was a king of Meath who mastered the north, made Leinster tributary and Munster an ally, and led the first recorded Irish attacks on Roman Britain. The tradition reported by the

Clonmacnoise Annals and by the seventeenth-century Keating gives an enthusiastic rationalised account of his civil administration; and the story-tellers built a cycle of romances thereon. He was the first lawgiver, the inventor of written record. From his great new rath, or fortress, at Tara he maintained a central administration with a hundred and fifty governors, *rectores* or *reachtaire*, and a standing army, the *Fiana*, commanded by Finn Mac Cumail, the 'slave girl's son'. Recruits, 'of very huge and tall bigness', were required to graduate in the learning of the *filid*, the professional scholars, and also to undergo a strenuous commando training and to accept a quite un-Irish discipline. They were organised in sections of nine men, brigaded by fives and tens into divisions, termed *tricha cet*, or thirty hundred, three of them in peacetime, seven in time of foreign war. The Fiana took a personal oath to their supreme commander, *Ri Feinnidh*, equivalent to the Roman *sacramentum*, and their kin were obliged to forswear claims for compensation on their death. They were paid, and were forbidden to plunder civilians; they were the 'hired warriors of the king of Ireland', their business to 'uphold justice and prevent injustice', to guard the country from foreigners, their ordinary task 'putting a stop to robbery, exacting the payment of tribute, putting down malefactors'. Abroad, Cormac was a greater conqueror; at home he was

> wise, Learned, valiant and mild, not Given causelesly to be bloody
> as many of his auncestors were; hee Raigned magestically and
> magnifitiently.

The legends of Cormac and Finn are told more amply than any other tales of Ireland in the Roman centuries. The essence of the story is familiar enough in Roman experience; the might of the imperial army impelled border barbarians to try to unite under a single centralised state, able to organise a large disciplined army under a single commander, strong enough to meet the Romans in the field. The aim and achievement that legend ascribes to Cormac is the same that Roman writers describe in the persons of the historical Maroboduus in Bohemia and of the Dacian Decebalus. Its claim, that the united Irish became strong enough to assault Roman Britain in force, is well proven; inscriptions and coin hoards show when and where the attacks fell.

Before the accession of Severus in 193, not more than 3 or 4 in a hundred of the military inscriptions of Britain were set up in the west coast forts; over the fifty years thereafter, the proportion rises sharply to one quarter; and in the next twenty years, from 244 to 264, all datable military inscriptions in Britain come from the forts of Lancashire and western Cumberland, or from Caerleon, all but one of them within the years that the Annalists assign to the reign of Cormac. The stones do not record the reasons why they were set up, but in these years it is only on the west coast that military units are known to have had reason to undertake reconstruction or to inscribe dedications.

The known west-coast coin hoards increase as rapidly as the inscriptions, but somewhat later. Those buried in the years between 222 and 260 are twice as many as in the previous forty years, but those buried between 260 and 300 are seven times as many. In Cormac's time, none are known from the rich villa lands of the Severn estuary, but nearly 50 are recorded from these lands in the next forty years. The implication of the Roman evidence is that in the years before 260 the Irish were engaged in breaking down the Roman defences of western Britain; and that in the years thereafter, assigned in Irish tradition to Cormac's successors, they were able to plunder the rich estates by the Severn Sea.

The Roman evidence does not prove that Cormac and Finn existed. It does imply that in the middle decades of the third century some power in Ireland achieved the successes that Irish tradition credits to them; the Irish were able to concentrate an effective military force against Britain on an unprecedented scale. The importance of the story in Ireland was that it was believed, and influenced the thinking of the early Christian centuries. One of the main sources that later writers cite for their account of Cormac is Amargein, who is said to have been the principal *file*, historian and adviser, to king Diarmait mac Cerbaill. Diarmait was the most powerful of the sixth-century kings of Ireland, and came nearest to realising in historical times the strong monarchy that legend ascribed to Cormac. Diarmait's adherents may have coloured the story of Cormac, but tales of Cormac are also likely to have strengthened Diarmait.

No tradition claims that Cormac's stable central government endured. His grandsons disputed the succession. Muiredach dispossessed his three cousins, named Colla, who compensated themselves by the final destruction of the ancient Ulaid power and annexed its western territories, including the old royal centre of Emain. The Annalists' date is 330, and the evidence of recent excavation tends to agree. The conquered territory was henceforth known as *Airgialla*, 'Oriel', and thence descendants of the Collas are said to have sailed overseas, to become Lords of the Isles, and of medieval Argyle.

Muiredach's son Eochaid, dated 358–365, is accorded the rare distinction of a peaceful death at Tara, and is chiefly celebrated for his wives and children; from his first wife, Mongfind of Munster, descended the future kings of Connacht, and his second wife, Cairenn, 'daughter of the king of the Saxon foreigners', was mother of Niall of the Nine Hostages, who was an infant when his father died. The second marriage rubs shoulders with reality. The contemporary Roman historian Ammian stressed that the invasion of Britain by Picts, Scots and Saxons in 367 was a *conspiratio barbarorum*, a barbarian alliance; in the late fourth century, dynastic marriage commonly sealed alliance.

Crimthann and Niall

Eochaid's adult son succeeded him as king of Connacht, but not of Ireland. Crimthann of Munster is the only southerner whom all traditions accept as king of Ireland before the 11th century. He is represented as ruler of the Cruithne of the coastlands, as the brother-in-law and ally of Eochaid against the growing power of the Eoganacht. Victory abroad secured his power at home. He was remembered as the first of the conquering kings who subdued and colonised western Britain. The Annals, austerely uninterested in Irishmen abroad, knew nothing of his wars in Britain, but other sources make much of them. He, and Niall after him, is styled king of Ireland and of Britain in the genealogies. He visited Britain and built there the royal fort of Din Tradui. Several other notices assert migration from Munster to Britain in the late fourth and early fifth centuries. Cairpre of Kerry is named as founder of the 'Eoganacht Maigi Dergind i nAlbae', the 'Eoganacht of the Plain of Derwent in Britain'; and as father of Aengus, 'ri Alban', king in Britain. Dergind is a place name wholly alien to Ireland, but Derguind or Derguenid may denote any river or place that the Roman British called Derventio, any now named Derwent, Darenth, Dart or the like. Most such places lie in hill country. But the plain of the Devonshire Dart is the likely location of a Roman *Statio Derventio*, and all its 5th and 6th century inscriptions are Irish. It may have been a short-lived Irish kingdom until the Cornovii reduced the Irish of Dumnonia in Vortigern's time.

Several sources record settlements in Britain of the *Ui Liathain*, from southern Munster. A British document preserved by Nennius reports their conquest of Demetia; they were driven out of its eastern borders, about Kidwelly, by Cunedda, in the middle of the fifth century, but both British and Irish texts prolong their rule in the rest of Demetia for another two generations, until Agricola's campaign ended their independence and their dynasty, in Arthur's time. Theirs was the longest-lived and most stable of the Irish kingdoms in southern Britain, notable enough for a late Irish tale to pirate their tradition and annex it to their neighbours, the Dessi. Nor was Demetia their only settlement, for the ninth-century Irish scholar Cormac, king and bishop of Munster, located a principal fort of theirs 'in the land of the Cornish Britons', in the same part of the country as Glastonbury. They were the best-remembered colonists, but even in Demetia they were not the only immigrants. A relative of Crimthann is said to have founded there 'the Cenel Crimthann in Britain'; and his mid fifth century grandson bore the name Eogan Albanach, Eogan of Britain. In north Wales also there are hints of settlement from Munster and from Leinster.

The armies of Cormac are portrayed as raiders, who took their booty home, but the subjects of Crimthann are described as settlers. No Irish tradition states the contrast, or even observes it. It reports settlement without comment, for the notices of the overseas exploits of both kings are few and casual. The Irish record is insular throughout, without interest in Britain. The several notices that survive are not stressed, but are minimised; what is noted is a few comments from much older records, that had ceased to be interesting long before they were copied into the manuscripts that survive. Yet these chance reports trace among the Irish the same evolution that Romans observed among other continental barbarians. All along the frontiers, the third-century enemies of Rome were raiders who went home again, however deeply their raids penetrated; but in the later fourth century and the fifth Rome everywhere faced bolder enemies, migrating peoples on the move, eager to settle within Roman territory.

Stories of Irish settlement in Britain begin with the reign of Crimthann; they extend into the time of his successor Niall, the late born son of Eochaid, whose reign is dated from 379 to 405. He was the best known of the fighting kings of Ireland, and is said to have invaded Gaul and to have been killed in the English Channel. His successor, Nath-I of Connacht, was the last of the raiding kings, and is said to have been killed in the Alps in 428. But the stories of raiders and settlers end with Nath-I. The next king was Loegaire, son of Niall, and Saint Patrick's arrival is placed in his fourth year. The coming of Patrick makes a sharp break in the historical tradition, separating Christian from pagan Ireland.

Irish Monarchy

The emphasis on religion masks profound changes in Irish secular society. From the beginning of the fifth century, the ancient peoples of Ireland submitted to the authority of an immense number of petty local princes, whose trivial and bloody feuds were to impoverish their subjects for centuries to come, and to dispose them to welcome the security of Christian monastic life.

The speed and the nature of the change are obscured because the writers of early Christian Ireland were unaware of it. They took it for granted that the institutions of their own day had existed from the remote past. The evidence lies in the detail they report, not in the interpretation that they placed upon it. Yet it was in the turmoil of a rapidly changing society that Irish Christianity was moulded; its assumptions and practices were already hardened before the Irish monks journeyed to Britain and Europe; so that the conflicts within Irish society became an important influence on the peoples who responded to the preaching of the Irish, and underlay much that they found startling in the Irish outlook.

The changes that matured in the fifth century were the climax of processes that had been at work since Rome conquered Britain. The earliest account of the political geography of Ireland is the work of the Roman Ptolemy, whose sources probably date from the early first century AD. His description of Ireland differs only in detail from his account of Britain. But thereafter the histories of Ireland and Britain diverged, for Rome conquered Britain, but not Ireland. In Britain, Roman conquest froze the political boundaries of the first century by fixing the frontiers of permanent states. But in Ireland, the struggles that caused one people to wax great and another to decline went on unchecked, so that the political geography had changed out of recognition by the fifth century. In addition, the impact of the Roman power across the sea had modified the internal structure of Irish political society, and altered the relations between her several peoples.

The Rise of the Dynasties

The traditions of Ireland during the centuries of Roman Britain stress still greater differences. They mainly concern attempts to establish large centralised monarchies. One single tradition, agreed by all sources, traces the history of the ancestors of Niall. He was heir to the dynasty that Tuathal had established with the aid of armies from Britain, later consolidated in Connacht. But the traditions of other regions are not agreed. A few great names are reported from the rest of Ireland, but different Annalists and different Genealogists relate them differently in time to one another and to the Connacht dynasty. They agree that the Eoganachta and Cianachta tried without success to establish similar large kingdoms in the west and south towards the end of the second century, and were thwarted by intervention from Britain. The Cianachta never succeeded, and the Eoganacht mastery of Munster, ruled from Cashel, was not consolidated until the beginning of the fifth century, when Corcc 'discovered' Cashel, hitherto a previously uninhabited hill, situated on the borders of two ancient peoples; for the shadowy notices of Corcc's predecessors chiefly concern indecisive efforts to subdue the older populations of Munster. The traditions of other regions are even more uncertain. The several sources agree upon the succession of early Ulaid kings, but disagree chaotically about the relationship in time between these kings and later Ulaid rulers, and about their connections with the Connacht dynasty, and the traditions of the few great rulers placed in early Leinster are as confused, until the establishment of its future dynasties during the fifth century.

These are stories about attempts to establish the direct rule of regional monarchs over large numbers of separate nations, with little sign of intermediate lordships. They are matched by the parallel account of the rise of the monarchy of all Ireland, under Cormac, Crimthann and Niall, equally pictured as supreme sovereigns. These stories resemble Roman accounts of other western barbarians, who united behind military kings when they fought Rome, but rarely obeyed stable dynasties in time of peace. But the tenor of the narrative changes in the fifth century. When Niall died, Connacht and the kingship of Ireland passed to his nephew; but his sons carved out for themselves lasting small kingdoms in northern and central Ireland, and their initiative was soon followed by men great and small throughout Ireland. The mightier kings mastered the lesser, and graded them into a hierarchy of rulers.

The new departure brought with it a new system of names, of persons and of territories, that survives to the present. Tyrone and Tirconnel mean 'the land, *tir*, of Eogan' and the 'land of Conall', who were sons of Niall's sons. Collectively his descendants were known as the *avi* or *Ui* Neill, in modern spelling O'Neill. Their separate branches were styled *Cenel Eogain, Cenel Conaill,* and other dynastic families used indifferently 'Ui', 'Cenel', 'Sil', 'Clanna' (children of) and other terms to denote their members. By the middle of the fifth century, the dynasts were already numerous, for Patrick's converts included several 'sons and daughters of *reguli*, under-kings'; and by the middle of the sixth century the greater part of the Irish were ruled by such kinglets. Most of them began as lords of a particular territory, and mobilised its strength to subdue their neighbours.

Their immediate territories were treated and taxed as 'free', those they subdued as 'subject', and the favoured status of the 'free' helped to hinder their subjects from concerted resistance.

Some dynasts grew greater and mastered many lesser lords and peoples; but they were content with a tributary supremacy, and did not normally annex conquered lands into large consolidated kingdoms ruled directly, in the manner of the earlier dynasties. By the end of the fifth century, the hierarchy of kings was adapted to the older structure of the Irish regions or 'provinces', so that in Ulster, Connacht, Munster and Leinster at least two major dynasties competed and alternated in the use of the title and the revenues of the provincial king. They claimed supremacy and tribute from lesser kings within their territory, but often had to fight to enforce their claim; though they admitted the formal supremacy of the High King of Ireland, their armies commonly resisted his authority. None the less, seventh-century Ireland accorded to the High King a sovereignty to which they gave a title that they had learnt from the Roman government of Britain. Muirchu, the biographer of Patrick, writing soon after 650, described one High King as *Imperator*, and a generation later Adomnan used for another the almost equally sonorous title of *totius Scotiae regnator*, sovereign of all Ireland. These high concepts of the kingship long outlived its practical authority, so that in the 11th century the last of the great High Kings, Brian Boru, himself used the title *Imperator Scottorum*, emperor of the Irish.

The dynasties jealously guarded and limited their identity. The dynastic name was strictly confined to those who were accepted as actual descendants of the founder, while the mass of the subject population were described by their national origin. Writers of the seventh and eighth centuries self-consciously set down the social origin of nearly everyone they name, translating *Ui* by the Latin *nepotes*, grandchildren, descendants, and using *gens*, nation, for the Irish *moccu*, or giving the Irish word untranslated. Adomnan, writing about 690, himself a member of the Ui Neill, meticulously distinguishes noblemen born, like Columba 'e nepotibus Neill' or 'Cormac nepos Leathain', of the Ui Liathain, from plebeians like 'Comgellus mocu Aridi' or 'Columbanus episcopus mocu Loigse'. The main monastic tradition, principally preserved in later texts, preferred to ignore social origins and distinguish individuals by giving their fathers' names, in place of their dynasty or nation; but among laymen the use of a *Ui* name became a badge of gentility, as highly prized as a *de* or a *von* among later Frenchmen and Germans, and was one of the main reasons for the preservation of the immense body of Irish genealogy. It is not surprising that one conscientious twelfth-century genealogist complained that his documentation was corrupted by the massive intrusion of plebeian families who falsely claimed dynastic descent.

The usage of the genealogists dates the rise of the dynasties to the beginning of the fifth century; for in the main genealogical tradition no dynasties are named from persons held to have lived earlier than the time of Niall or Crimthann, and only a very few late glosses loosely apply dynastic terms to the supposed ancestors of older peoples. The date suggests why and how the dynasties arose, during and after the wars against Britain. After each expedition, some Irish captains settled in Britain, but many more came home, accompanied by young warriors enriched by slaves and other booty. The Irish word for slave-girl, *cumal*, became the normal standard of value, equivalent to three cows. War brought social difference. Men who were rich in slaves and strong in armed retainers made themselves lords; and when the overseas expeditions ended, early in the 5th century, the energy that had been directed against Britain was for the future absorbed by domestic warfare, as the dynasts fought against each other and against rebellious subjects. Though Irish writers assumed that lordship had always existed, they preserve a few stories of prolonged resistance to dynastic rule. Conall of Tirconnel was killed by 'the old peoples' in 469; in the sixth century

> the prophet Bec mc De . . . prophisied that lords would loose their Chiefries and seignories,

but his radical prophecy echoed a wish that was not fulfilled. Similar sentiments were attributed to Brigit in the late 5th century, who is said to have proclaimed that

> all subjects (*plebei*) serve the Lord . . . but the children of kings are serpents, children of blood and death, save for a few of whom God hath chosen.

Christian protest did not prevent the increase of dynastic power. Though some of the older peoples, notably the Luigne, long fought to rid themselves of their sovereigns, most submitted; and many discovered that the best way to withstand the assault of neighbouring kings was to establish their own dynasties. By the middle of the seventh century, when a changing economy brought famine and crisis, Ireland was sharply divided between nobles and plebeians; the struggles of 'old peoples' against the institutions of 'chiefries and seignories' fade from record.

Dislike of dynastic violence was a principal incentive to the sixth-century Irish. It disposed them to welcome the Christian religion of Britain and Rome, and to find in the monasteries a refuge from a disordered world. The acceptance of the new religion also joined Ireland to Britain. From the beginning of the sixth century, the history and the historical record of the peoples of the British Isles are inseparable. They hang closely together, because they were jointly exploring a new dimension in European civilisation. The Irish, the Welsh and the English were the first European peoples, since the mediterranean authors of Greek and Roman antiquity, to write in the vernacular spoken language of the people; for centuries to come, European literature used only Latin, alien to German-speakers and far removed from the spoken Romance languages. Within this common enterprise, Irish initiative was foremost; the poets and story-tellers who popularised the legendary history of pagan Ireland deeply impressed early Welsh romance and verse, and exercised a notable influence on the earliest English literature; and the impact of Irish historical and political experience worked powerfully among the British and English peoples, especially upon the notables who took political decisions; the decisions became precedents, and the men who took them shaped their still raw and malleable political institutions, often consciously. Throughout the 7th century and the early 8th, the English and the Welsh retained a warm affection for the Irish, and gladly acknowledged the inspiration that had come from Ireland.

CHAPTER NINE

CHRISTIAN IRELAND

The Sources

Christian Ireland begins with the landing of Patrick; thenceforth the older
sources are reinforced by histories of churchmen. Most numerous among them
are the Lives of the Saints, termed 'hagiography' by modern writers. Each
author's purpose is simple, to display the wonderful virtues of his hero, and his
usual method is to recite jejune miracles. He was a story-teller rather than a
historian, and his business was to edify, to exhort and to entertain. But the first
author of each Life told of a real person, who lived in particular places at a
particular time, and most later versions preserve something of the detail,
sometimes much. Serious assessment of these misty texts must start from the
shrewd assessment of the French historian, Fustel de Coulanges:

> Saints' lives are also history . . . their aim was . . . to demonstrate
> the sanctity of their hero . . . in the interest of the church or abbey
> that had taken him for patron. . . . The life of each saint was
> written by one of his disciples, or by a man who knew him, or at
> least on the evidence of his acquaintances. But this primitive version
> has hardly ever come down to us. . . . Each century recopied it,
> making changes and additions. . . . It is very difficult to distinguish
> what . . . has been added. . . . Though there are often errors of date,
> transposition of proper names, facts distorted . . . that is unimport-
> ant. What we need to look for are the . . . facts that the hagio-
> grapher had no incentive to change.

The incentive is the key to the study of the Lives. In principle, that which
serves the morality and the practical interest of the copyist in each age is likely
to be his addition; detail that serves no such interest is normally what he found
in his original. The detection of interest is not a matter of guesswork, for numerous texts show its conventions; a number of Lives survive in successive editions,
and the differences between them disclose the ways in which later editors corrupted their originals. Some boast that they have suppressed dubious morality
and doctrine, or abbreviated the tedious 'British garrulity' of their predecessors,
leaving out the 'uncouth and barbarous British names' of people and places no
longer of interest to the later reader. Such names are rarely added; when they

remain, they nearly always derive from a contemporary original, and sometimes preserve its spelling. Often the authors of surviving Lives omitted them. In their place a few great names, notably Patrick, David and Arthur, are dragged into many Lives, out of time and place; saints are made to visit places where later ages revered their relics, and any saint who visits Rome at any date meets Gregory the Great, and at Tours meets Martin. But when other popes are named, or when stories are told of obscure places and persons, they are transcribed from earlier versions, whose 'barbarous garrulity' the copyist retained. Many monks met long-dead saints in visions, and were at the time convinced of their reality; Jonas, the 7th century biographer of Columban, was personally present in the room when St. Peter visited his abbot, though, to his regret, the abbot did not wake him. Later versions of such visions leave out the dream, and make the living and the dead meet in the flesh. Many authors purloin striking miracles from other popular Lives and sometimes transfer people and places with the story. Late custom gave many saints royal fathers. These and many other conventions are the normal practice of the hagiographer, and are not hard to recognise when the texts are submitted to the ordinary processes of historical criticism.

A few surviving works, like Adomnan's Columba or the first Life of Samson, were written within living memory; but most are copies of copies. They vary greatly. Most of the Irish Lives in Latin are preserved in two main collections. Their medieval editors gave them a standard form, so that the biographies are much alike, preserving an immensity of detail, but coating the saints with a uniform sickly sweet piety. The Irish-language Lives are mainly derived from Latin originals, and are brightly coloured to suit the taste of listeners accustomed to the rugged imagination of the story-teller. But few of the Latin versions are as distorted as the 12th-century British Lives, though few are as close to their originals as the early Armorican texts.

The Lives are amplified by other evidence, by martyrologies, or calendars, that list saints according to the anniversary of their death, and by the places and churches that bear their names. The early British and Irish Christians continued the practice of 4th-century Rome, that dedicated churches to God alone, but described them by their situation, or by the name of a living or dead patron whom they honoured. Later ages dedicated churches to long-dead humans, to apostles and martyrs, to the Virgin, to All Saints or to Archangels, and these later dedications often effaced the older name. Later Irishmen and Welshmen dedicated churches to Patrick, Brigit and David; and Martin of Tours was admitted to the canon of dedication. But lesser men were not, and a church that retains the name of a local native saint or of a European ecclesiastic is usually located in an area where he was honoured in his lifetime, save on rare occasions when the name stems from the transfer of relics in later generations. This evidence, together with the statements of the Lives and Martyrologies, is summarised in *Arthurian Sources*.

Loegaire

Fifth-century Irishmen were ready to welcome protection against the growing violence of their lords. Tradition looked back with nostalgia to the golden age of Cormac, a prince 'not given causelessly to be bloody', whose royal police preserved quiet and good order for the private individual. But Loegaire and his fifth-century successors exercised no such authority. From Patrick's time onwards, some Christians were able to curb some of the violence. Soon after his death, the virgin Faencha upbraided the young chief Enda for leading his men to avenge his father's death. Enda was as startled as any honest soldier who is told that his trade is immoral; but he was converted, and thereafter Faencha took pains to send him abroad to Britain to be schooled, lest he relapse into the violence of the society whence he came. Another chief rejected conversion with a straight answer, 'I am a soldier, so I cannot be religious.'

The Christian leaders withstood wars. Ciaran of Saigir and others are said to have succeeded in preventing some fifth-century battles. They also withstood civil violence. They forced kings to release prisoners, hostages, and persons unjustly enslaved; they rebuked royal cruelty, denounced war, opposed the execution of political opponents and of ordinary criminals; and the tradition of the church makes Irish Christians play a large part in preserving the laws and the learning that were older than the princes. In the early fifth century, dynastic power was only beginning to spread. The changes that it heralded were taking shape, and the coming of Patrick was a part of those changes. He is said to have landed in 432, four or five years after the death of Nath-I. Simultaneously, the political relations between Britain and Ireland were transformed. After two hundred years, Irish raids on Britain suddenly ceased, and were never resumed, save for a brief space, in different circumstances, about the 490s. The evident reason is the superior force of Vortigern. Irish tradition reported a raid in or about 434 by Saxons, who are likely to have been his federates, and implies that his daughter married a son of Loegaire, the new High King.

These were political events. Vortigern's concern was to subdue the Irish colonists in Britain. His was the first British Government to control an adequate naval force, able to deter Irish intervention; and the report of a dynastic marriage suggests that he exacted a formal treaty. Patrick's mission was a part of this political situation. It was long discussed, approved by the Pope, by the bishops of Gaul, and by the bishops of Britain, some of whom were aghast at the risk of sending a bishop 'among the enemy'. The proposal to send Patrick could not have been realised without the agreement of both governments.

It was plainly to Vortigern's interest that as many as possible of Loegaire's subjects should embrace the religion of Britain and of Rome. The texts suggest that Loegaire was constrained to agree, and Patrick's own writings demonstrate that he was given licence to preach, but that he received little positive encouragement from Irish authorities. The earlier traditions of his life set his headquarters at Saul by Downpatrick, and put the area of his missionary work in the north-east. After his death, about 460, four or five bishops ministered to the Christians of the north and centre, but southern tradition points to the separate creation of its own sees by the papacy, in or about the 460s, at first under the guidance of the church of Britain. All early sources assert that throughout the fifth century, and in the early years of the sixth, Christians were still a relatively small minority in most of Ireland. The massive conversion of the bulk of the population is presented as the achievement of the monastic reformers, centred on the 530s and 540s.

Meanwhile, the political structure of Ireland was changing. Loegaire was restrained from attacking Britain. Leaders whose fathers had found wealth and power in plundering Britain were forced to confine their ambition to Ireland. Loegaire himself is depicted as a powerful monarch, who had no need of force to levy the tribute of Leinster, until his last years. The dynastic struggles that faced him and his successors were of two kinds. The heirs of Niall's sons and brothers were all-powerful in the north and centre, strong enough to contain the kingdoms that they did not directly rule, of the Airgialla and the Ulaid. But Leinster paid tribute only under compulsion, and none was claimed from Munster, whose kings acknowledged no more than precedence to the northern dynasty. The kings of Ireland were northerners who needed force to maintain even nominal authority in the south; but the dynasty itself comprised several branches, and each strove to secure to itself the title of king of Ireland.

Loegaire, late-born son of the great Niall, met no opposition from within his own dynasty. His wars were southern. Leinster submitted in 455, and he invaded Munster. He withdrew without a battle, but without being attacked, presumably because the Munster king formally acknowledged his suzerainty. But he did not consolidate permanent power in the south. The men of north Leinster threw up a national dynasty of their own, whose king decisively defeated Loegaire, just before his death in 461. The new High King, Aillel of Connacht, thereafter fought the Leinstermen with varying success for twenty years.

Mac Erca

Aillel was the last High King for five centuries who was not of the Ui Neill, the dynasty of Niall. He was brought down at the battle of Ocha, in Meath, in 482, by a grand alliance. The leader of the northern Ui Neill, Muirchetach mac Erca, king of Ailech, near Londonderry, united the several branches of Niall's heirs, bought the support of the Ulaid by the cession of border territory, and was joined by the king of Leinster. The battle became a landmark in Irish history, for it ensured that thenceforth all High Kings were drawn from one or other branch of the Ui Neill.

Mac Erca dominated Irish politics for half a century, and is said to have leaned heavily upon the advice of a British ecclesiastic. He was very young in 482, and the High Kingship went to Loegaire's son, Lugid. But it was Mac Erca who led the struggle to subdue the south. In Leinster he allied with a new southern dynasty, who overthrew their northern rivals, and joined him to destroy the king of Munster, in 492. In 500 the alliance ended, and Mac Erca subdued Leinster; and in 502 he replaced the king of Connacht with a nominee of his own. In the next year he succeeded Lugid as king of Ireland, and reigned in peace for nearly thirty years, with no reports of opposition in the subject provinces.

Mac Erca was the contemporary of Arthur. It is in the years of his triumph that Irish and English tradition both record renewed Irish intervention in Britain, though none is reported in the previous 75 years, since Nath-I's death, or again in the future. In the extreme north, Mac Erca's relative and ally, Fergus of Dal Riada, found his tiny state surrounded when Mac Erca ceded his borders about Coleraine to the Ulaid; many of Fergus' subjects had already crossed the seas to settle in Kintyre, on the flank of the Clyde estuary, and about 500 Fergus transferred his royal residence to his colonial territories. There his heirs fought the Picts, but long remained at peace with the British of the Clyde.

Further south in Britain the Irish were enemies, not allies. King Illan, whom Mac Erca's victories had enthroned in Leinster, is said to have fought eight or nine battles in Britain. The Laigin of Leinster named Lleyn, the tip of Caernarvonshire, and the British remembered the fierce campaigns of Catwallaun Longhand, father of the Maelgwn whom Gildas denounced. They culminated in the expulsion of 'Serigi the Irishman' from Anglesey, in the years between about 490 and about 510. The name is rare in Ireland, but Irish tradition knew a Serach as the son-in-law of a Leinster king.

It is in the same years that the Demetian Irish received considerable reinforcements, under leaders whose names were used only in south-west Munster. At a date that seems to indicate 493, their forces are said to have pushed inland to Brecon, and to have attacked towards Cardiff. It may be that they came to help their old allies the Saxons in their last effort at Badon; but they succumbed to Arthur's counter-attack, when the forces of Agricola ended Irish rule in Demetia, perhaps some ten to fifteen years later. It was also in the same years that Theodoric repelled a formidable Munster invasion of Cornwall. The last Irish assault on Britain failed when the empire of Arthur was still strong.

These armies had reason to leave Ireland. The growing power of the dynasts threatened small men, and Mac Erca's victories threatened local dynasts. When he subdued Munster, the men of the west coast sought lands and adventure overseas; and Leinstermen too weak to fight the king of Ireland also turned to foreign war. But theirs were local enterprises. There is no sign that Mac Erca backed them or dreamt of reviving the overseas ambitions of Crimthann, Niall and Nath-I. He respected the power of Arthur, and lived at peace with Britain, content to consolidate his sovereignty in Ireland. The Ui Neill ruled unchallenged. Their security was disturbed only by an internal rift, when Ardgal, of the southern Ui Neill of East Meath, rebelled in 518. The rebellion was repressed, but it was a portent, the first recorded conflict between members of the dynasty. It became a precedent, for Mac Erca was succeeded by Tuathal

Maelgarbh, of the West Meath line. He began his reign by exiling Ardgal's nephew and heir, Diarmait mac Cerbaill, and thenceforth the throne of Ireland was in dispute between the several branches of the Ui Neill dynasty.

Diarmait

Ireland was dramatically transformed when Mac Erca died, in 532. For a hundred years, since Patrick's coming, there had been a Christian church in Ireland, governed by bishops; but it had not yet seized hold of Irish society. It is in the reign of Tuathal that ecclesiastical tradition placed the mass conversion of the Irish to monastic Christianity. An important section of the early monks maintained the earlier Christian antagonism to the princes. One of the greatest of them, Ciaran of Clonmacnoise, whose plebeian origin is deliberately emphasised by his constant description as the 'artisan's son', confronted and confounded Tuathal. He is also said to have sheltered the exiled Diarmait, who used Clonmacnoise as a base while he organised the assassination of Tuathal, whom he succeeded in 548.

A year or two later the great plague devastated Ireland, and Ciaran died. Monastic tradition did not endorse support for Diarmait. Brigit is made to foretell that he would be 'bloody, cursed by his birth', and to many monks one new tyrant was no better than an old one dead. But the movement was none the less sucked into the struggles of the dynasties. The most forceful among the younger monks who survived the plague years was Columba. He was a royal prince, of the Tirconel branch of the Ui Neill, now Diarmait's principal dynastic rivals. His father was second cousin to Mac Erca, and two of his own first cousins became High Kings. His powerful personality made as deep an imprint on the history of mankind as any man of his century in Europe, and he overshadows all Irishmen of his day. There is little doubt that if he had not been a monk, he rather than his cousins would have been chosen king. His birth and his outlook sharply contrasted with Ciaran's and later tradition expressed the realities of his time when it made an angel warn Ciaran that

> what you have surrendered for the love of God is nothing but the tools of your father's trade; what Columba has forgone is the sceptre of Ireland, his by ancestral right.

Columba was a prince and a monk. Both his career and Ciaran's served to fulfil the judgement of the doyen of the older monks, Lasrian of Devenish, that 'in the end the saints must prove stronger than the kings of Ireland'. Both men were pupils of Finnian of Clonard, but when they left him, at much the same time, about 545, their ways parted. Ciaran withdrew to the seclusion of the Lough Ree area, where the borders of the great provinces meet, as far as possible from the courts of great kings; but Columba established his first major monastery at Derry, in his own family territory, on land given to him by his cousin Ainmere, then king of the northern Ui Neill. The saints who opposed the dynasts and their wars cannot have looked kindly upon Ainmere, who in the same year killed the aged king of Connacht, and began a career of military aggrandisement, on the model of Mac Erca, that was ultimately to win him the throne of Ireland, and must from the outset have been seen to have had that end in view.

Diarmait stands out as one of the great kings of Irish tradition, as memorable as Cormac, Niall and Mac Erca before him, not again equalled in stature before Brian Boru in the eleventh century. He is Adomnan's sovereign *regnator*. With an almost Thucydidean insight, the Irish historians select two dramatic events, his quarrels with Ruadan and with Columba, to illuminate the critical conflicts of his reign. The Life of Ruadan and the Annals of Clonmacnoise recount at length the dispute over the punishment of Aed Guaire, dated to the year 558. The Ruadan account is sympathetic to Diarmait, despite the saint's hostility, and calls him a 'powerful peaceful king' who 'upheld the peace so strongly in his realm that no man dare even strike another's face in anger'. Other traditions agree; an Ulaid poet, allegedly his contemporary, is made to sing of 'Diarmait the Good, a ruler without slackness; no robber can escape the speed of his death sentence'. His stern justice executed his own son, convicted of stealing a nun's cow; he overawed the provincial kings; he married a Munster princess; the army of Leinster withdrew before him without daring to fight; and the king of Connacht gave his son as hostage.

Diarmait's efforts to enforce the king's peace embroiled him with Ruadan. He ordered that the gates of the raths, or castles, of all the local lords throughout Ireland should be no narrower than a spear's length, and sent his officers to inspect them and to destroy those that were not wide enough. As the royal officer made his rounds among the Ui Maine of Connacht, 'boasting of the king's authority in lands not his own', he reached the rath of Aed Guaire when its lord was absent. Aed's men obeyed the royal order, broke down the gate, and entertained the king's officer to dinner. During the meal, Aed returned. Enraged at the broken gate, he killed the officer, and then, 'for fear of the king', fled for protection to a relative who was a bishop in Munster. But the Munster bishop, 'not strong enough to shelter a man guilty of killing a royal officer', directed him to Ruadan at Lothra, in the monastic enclave near Clonmacnoise. Diarmait sent men to arrest him, but Ruadan smuggled him out of the country. He sought refuge with a British king, but Diarmait's arm was long, and his envoys demanded the criminal's extradition, under threat of invasion. 'Not daring to stay in Britain', Aed returned to Ruadan, who hid him in a cellar. Informers told the king, whose men arrested him in the monastery, took him prisoner to Tara, and condemned him to death.

Ruadan was outraged at the violation of the sanctuary, and resisted the death penalty. With his near neighbour, Brendan of Birr, and a company of monks, he went to Tara. The saints rang their bells in the streets, calling for a fast, or hunger strike, against the king. The king 'refused to relax the law of the land', and met the saints' fast by fasting himself. 'The saints could achieve nothing, while the king fasted and prayed', for the king was a 'peace-loving defender of his country, who helped the churches and the poor, was truthful, just in judgement and absolutely trustworthy'. So the saints tricked him, by pretending to break their fast. The king was deceived, and ate. That night he dreamed that he saw a great tree, whose shadow overspread all Ireland, felled by the sharp axes of a hundred and fifty clerics; the fall of the tree portended the end of his life, and the handing over of the kingdom to the saints of God. The king went out to upbraid the saints who were keeping vigil, protesting

> I have made the country secure. I have established the rule of law in all places, so that the churches and peoples live securely in peace everywhere. I defend the right according to Christ's law, but you do ill to defend a murderer. Much may follow from small beginnings.
>
> Turning to Ruadan, the king said, 'Ruadan, for what you have done, the Holy Trinity will punish you. Your monasteries shall fail in Ireland'. . . . Ruadan replied, 'Your kingdom shall fail, and none of your seed shall ever reign. . . . This your royal town of Tara, whence the kingdom of Ireland has been ruled these many years, shall be left empty.'

After a considerable further exchange of prophetic curses, the king turned to the other saints and addressed them.

> You, Fathers, are protecting evil. But I am defending the truth in Christ's name. You may kill me, and you may ruin my kingdom; God may love you for your merits more than me, but I place my hope in the loving kindness of my God. So go. Take the man away free. But you will render a price to the kingdom for this man.

The tale is unique in Irish historical record, utterly out of keeping with the unctuous uncritical praise that normally reduces every incident to the background of a routine miracle. It is cast in the rational narrative form of an earlier age, skilfully narrated to illustrate a major crisis through the detail of a single incident. But the Ruadan story excels in one rare gift, the ability to communicate intelligibly the motives of both contestants, to depict a conflict of two rights, rather than the victory of right over wrong.

Ruadan fought for a principle, and found himself the champion of an unruly local dynast against the central monarchy. He campaigned in the streets in full publicity, and his victory humbled the king. Diarmait's troubles multiplied. The Cruithne overthrew the dynasty of Dal Araide, and Diarmait intervened in vain. In 560 he summoned the Royal Feast of Tara, the last recorded, and began his conflict with Columba. The story is told in full in short versions and long, and its details recur in a great number of documents, Annals, Saints' Lives, tales and verses. The clash centred on two distinct issues, but rests on a deeper antagonism. Columba was not only abbot of Derry. The enormous vitality of the royal abbot attracted disciples in numbers far greater than the followers of other monks, and

Columba is credited with the foundation in Ireland of some twenty to forty houses, who looked to him as their chief and ruler. He was as mighty as a king. Religion and the world combined to make him Diarmait's enemy, for he inherited the resentment of the monks against the great king, the head and protector of the whole body of lesser rulers, and also the antagonism of the northern Ui Neill to the kings of Meath, Diarmait's own territory.

The first quarrel arose over a book. The monk Finnian of Moville visited Pope Pelagius, who reigned from 555 to 560, and on his return 'first brought the whole Gospel to Ireland', evidently a Vulgate text. Columba borrowed it and transcribed it, 'working day and night, remote from the noise and sight of other men who might have hindered him'. Finnian was 'furious that the book was copied secretly without his permission', and claimed the copy as his of right. The dispute was referred to Diarmait, and Finnian argued that it was as though Columba had cut his corn without permission. Columba replied

> I admit I copied the book, but it was with my own labour and in my own time. Finnian's book is none the worse for being copied. . . . Whatever I find in any book, I have the right to copy and to place at the disposal of other men, for the glory of God.

But Diarmait decided for Finnian, 'either because he wrongly weighed the arguments, or because he was influenced by private interests'. He delivered his judgement

> in a phrase still famous in Ireland, 'As a calf is to the cow, so is the copy to the book.'

Private interest there was. The monks were the king's enemies, and Columba was Diarmait's dynastic opponent; Finnian was bishop of the Ulaid of Dal Fiatach, who were hereditary enemies of the northern Ui Neill, but were Diarmait's allies against the Cruithne. But it is a tribute to the reputation of Diarmait that even the Columban tradition admits that his mistake might have been honest. Columba himself denounced the decision as 'irrational, manifestly wrong, and untenable'.

Finnian's visit to Rome is dated to the years just before the Tara Feast of 560. A still graver conflict came in the year of the Feast, evidently during it. The king of Connacht's son, Curnan, a hostage with Diarmait, killed the son of a royal steward in a quarrel at the games. The offence was worse than Aed Guaire's; homicide in the royal household, on the occasion of a rare and solemn festival, was unforgivable. For a less offence, the king had executed his own son. The young man fled to Columba for protection; the king overrode his right of sanctuary, enforced royal justice, and had the boy executed.

The breach was beyond healing. Columba was outraged. He went home to Tir Connel, raised his cousins of the northern Ui Neill, king Ainmere and the sons of Mac Erca. The king of Connacht, father of the dead boy, joined him in 561.

> They gave battle to Diarmait and his army at Cuil Dremhni.
> Columba was present with his forces . . . and besought God by
> prayer and fasts to grant victory over the insolent king without loss
> to his own men. . . . At the king's request, saint Finnian . . . prayed
> for the royal army. . . . But the royal army was dispersed in flight,
> losing 3,000 men, their opponents losing one man only. . . .
> Columba made peace with the defeated king . . . and kept the book.

Diarmait survived for three years more, but his strength was gone. The issue
decided at Cuil Dremhni was weightier than those that had occasioned earlier
battles. They had merely determined which individual should rule. But if
Diarmait had routed the combined armies of the north and west, and with them
the greatest of the monks, then the authority of the king of all Ireland would
have been firmly vindicated, the independence of provincial kings and lesser
dynasts curbed, the political power of the monks broken. When he failed, it was
not one king who fell, but the monarchy itself. In an age when all Europe saw the
hand of God in each earthly decision, victory could not be ascribed to the
superior generalship of king Ainmere. Columba and Finnian had both invoked
God with conflicting prayers, and God had made a clear decision. Columba had
gone to war to vindicate the independence of the church, upholding the right of
sanctuary against royal justice, denying the right of the king's law to forbid the
free circulation of the word of God. Finnian was a bishop who served his king.
God had decided that the church was stronger than the king.

The great tree had fallen, and Ireland was changed. The quite different
western traditions of Brendan of Clonfert, remote from the central conflict, echo
the same view. The king's wise men, interpreting a different dream, are made to
tell him:

> Your kingdom is taken away, and is to be given to holy churchmen.

The judgement was sound. No later king attained anything near to the authority
that is credited to Diarmait. He was succeeded in 564 by Mac Erca's two elderly
sons, who reigned jointly. When they were killed, a year later, division increased.
Several simultaneous rulers are accorded the title of High King, but only
Columba's cousin Ainmere and his son Aed earned record, beyond their name
and date, in the memory of later ages.

Their successors are better documented. From Columba's time onward Irish
local political history is remembered in considerably greater detail than that of
England, Wales or Scotland. Its meaning cannot be disentangled until the
extensive documentation is scrutinised, for the record of the Annals is a dreary
tale of mounting slaughter, with battles ten times as numerous as before, fought
for no greater cause than the aggrandisement of individual families. The com-
batants are increasingly lesser kings, fighting each other on their own account in
disregard of the High King, and the High Kings' wars are principally fought in
defence of their own individual dynastic territories. The High Kings continue

to receive some tribute and to give gifts, to preside over conferences and to settle ecclesiastical disputes; but they are no longer credited with the power or the will to discipline provincial or lesser kings. Those bold enough to claim the cattle tribute of Leinster perished in the attempt, and their successors ultimately remitted the impost. The title remained with the descendants of Niall, but their effective power was limited to their own dominions, scarcely noticeable in the south, weak in Connacht.

The Church Triumphant

The squalid secular violence of seventh-century Ireland is matched by the splendid vigour of its church. Columba's war had been as much a crisis for the monks as for the king. The military victory of an all-powerful royal abbot brought with it the danger of a divine monarch. The threat was real. In contemporary Britain Cadoc was held to have ruled as both abbot and king, and several later rulers of Munster were to combine the offices of king and bishop; in Italy, the disastrous invasion of the Lombards was thrusting local temporal responsibilities upon the head of Christendom, and the phenomenon of the prince-bishop was to appear in several parts of Europe. In Ireland, there is little doubt that if Columba had been free to wear a crown he would have been the obvious successor to Diarmait. One late tale asserts that he was actually offered the throne. Whether it were so or not, the story expresses a situation. The danger was conceivable, for the autocratic abbot who ruled far more monks than any other cleric might have imposed upon Ireland an authority stronger than Diarmait's. There is no sign that Columba was tempted by such ambition, or that the monks or laity of Ireland were disposed to submit to it. But the possibility warned that the monastic church, designed as a withdrawal from political force, might find itself transformed into the instrument of an all-powerful clerical state.

The monks of Ireland faced the danger. A synod condemned Columba's intervention in the wars, and excommunicated him. The sentence was stayed, on the proposal of Brendan of Birr, and gentle Lasrian, most senior of the monks, advised Columba to leave Ireland for ever, in voluntary exile, that he might 'win as many souls for Christ as he had caused to die in battle'. Columba accepted the sentence and sailed away to Iona. He too was transformed by the fearful shock of the crisis. In Britain, he steadfastly refrained from becoming the national saint of his Irish fellow-countrymen, and made it his business to convert their Pictish enemies. He remained the spiritual adviser of their king, Bridei, as well as of the Irish, and his stern authority earned him the reputation of the 'dove of peace'. So long as he lived, Irish Dal Riada remained at peace with Bridei, and also with its British neighbours.

The future history of Ireland was to be the history of its church. The crisis that had sent Columba to Iona compelled the Irish monasteries to seek and find a new direction. The traditions of Ireland, Britain and Brittany agree that they summoned the aged Gildas to visit them and advise upon the ordering of their future. They were already strong. Victory over the secular government had given them unchallenged independence, and a considerable moral authority. They used it to restrain the violence of kings. They failed to stop it, but in the end they curbed it. In 697 a conference of the principal bishops and abbots endorsed a code of war. The principal initiative was attributed to abbot Adomnan, the biographer of Columba, who named the law, known as the *Cain Adomnan*, and to his English friend, Egbert of Iona; their notable southern allies included Muirchu, the biographer of Patrick, and his patron, bishop Aed of Sletty. War crimes were defined, and severe ecclesiastical penalties were enacted for offences against non-combatants, especially for the killing of women, children and students. Governments were not consulted. Adomnan's law was imposed upon them, and fear of the monks' spiritual authority commonly deterred soldiers from perpetrating atrocities against civilians until the coming of the Scandinavians.

The power of the monks put bounds upon the licence of rulers, but they did not reform Irish political society. They withdrew from it, and built an enduring alternative society. Lay violence continued, but the learning and the art of Irish monasteries won the admiration of Europe and of future ages. The continuing disorder of secular politics attracted new recruits in each successive generation, men who welcomed escape from the conflicts of kings. Some sought new lands beyond the Atlantic, but many more carried their piety and learning to known peoples. They converted the northern English, and spread their monastic life throughout England; thereafter, the English and Irish inspired the Franks and Germans with their monastic fervour. At home, they wrote down the traditions of their forefathers while they were still remembered, and gave a Christian blessing to the legends of the pagan past; in so doing they preserved a unique record of the manners of barbarian society in western Europe, that remains essential to the understanding of the excavated remains of illiterate peoples elsewhere.

The Ireland that the scholars describe evolved with few sharp and sudden breaks, but in definite stages. From the second century to the middle of the fifth, its history is the story of a single dynasty, of the Ui Neill and their ancestors, told consistently and with coherent dates; to it the scholars attached fragments from the debris of other traditions, though their valiant attempts to 'synchronise and harmonise' these outside stories were unsuccessful, for the unchecked imagination of the story-tellers contradicted each other, and confused the sources of the annalists and genealogists. But from the middle of the fifth century, annalists and genealogists agree and record settled traditions from the different regions of Ireland, that concur with each other. The history of the sixth century is told in increasing detail, and is supplemented by the Lives of the earlier saints. Few contemporary documents survive, but the quantity of information preserved in medieval texts is immense, complex, and consistent. A full account of the sixth and seventh centuries, whose local conflicts are reported more profusely than in any other European land, would fill a large volume on its own.

Until the monastic upsurge of the mid sixth century, Ireland was still barbarian, its customs little affected by the impact of Christian and Roman ideas. The accounts of its last generations, in the years between 480 and 560, describe in detail a still unmodified Iron Age society. The records of the next century describe the struggle of the Roman religion to transform barbarian Ireland. At first, the monks were in conflict with still powerful Druids, and deeply distrusted those baptised Druids who sought to marry alien worlds. But later the abbot and the bishop replaced the Druid, whose title devolved upon lowly intellectual craftsmen. On the initiative of Columba, the arts over which the Druids had formerly presided were accommodated within the structure of Christian Ireland. It was that compromise which enabled the scholars to write down the records, laws and customs of the past, adapting them to the outlook of Rome and Christendom. The monasteries were also enabled to perpetuate in durable materials the artistic skills of their ancestors, and to apply their uninhibited energy to the learning and theology they found in Europe.

Early Christian Ireland, like the Hellenistic Age and the Italian Renaissance, is numbered among those societies which combined enormous intellectual and artistic vitality with the extremes of irresponsible violence, cruelty and insecurity. Its faith stemmed from Britain, and its strongest impact was returned upon the peoples of Britain. Its political direction was determined by the new-found strength of fifth-century Britain, which ended the earlier raids and defeated the renewed attempts at expansion in Mac Erca's time. The Irish Christians were themselves convinced that they owed their inspiration to Britain, their initial conversion to Patrick, their mass monastic movement to the reformers who grew to manhood in Arthur's lifetime and in the generation thereafter. Monasticism brought Ireland into a common polity with Britain. No longer aliens, the Irish also were included among the heirs and successors of Arthur, who shaped the common future of the British Isles. A monk of Columba's Iona moulded the church of Northumbria; Bede grew to manhood in a monastery fostered and protected by a king born and bred among the Irish, who was honoured in both countries as the most learned Irishman and most learned Englishman of his day.

The great age of Ireland lasted some three centuries. The victory of the monks equipped the Irish to become the intellectual inspiration of Europe. But the cost was heavy. The monasteries absorbed the energies of the ablest Irishmen, and spent them in the service of all lands. Emigration remained the natural outlet of the liveliest minds; for in breaking and rejecting the structure of secular society the monks left it unreformed and robbed of reformers. Lay society was left leaderless, with no tradition of secular national strength, never able to rally round a native equivalent of a Hereward, a Llewellyn or a Wallace, in time to become the easy victims of an invader. Eight centuries of bitter national humiliation were endured without rational hope of liberation until our own day. In the idiom of the story-teller, the monks who destroyed the early national monarchy entailed upon their successors a great price to be paid for the freedom of a lawless chieftain.

CHAPTER TEN

THE DAL RIADA SCOTS

Geography

Modern Scotland owes its name to immigrants from Ireland. But they were only one among the many peoples whom the medieval and modern kingdom united. The present-day border lies virtually upon the same line as the frontier of the Roman empire. It is a frontier dictated by geography and by the convenience of armies. The high unpeopled moors of the Cheviots run north-eastward from the rivers that water Carlisle to the richer lands of the Till and Tweed. They are the feasible limits of a northern power, based on York, that controls Tyne and Solway, but cannot subdue the enormous open spaces beyond. Yet the border did not last continuously from Roman times, for it is only a military and geographical line. It was not and is not a clear national boundary that separates one language and one culture from another. When the centralised power of Rome disintegrated, it was eclipsed by the political frontiers of smaller peoples, and the old line was not permanently reasserted for more than six hundred years, after the Norman conquest of England.

The frontier, and with it the identity of Scotland, took long to establish because the population beyond it was mixed. The English, the Irish and the Welsh were each a coherent people, bound together by language and tradition. Northern Britain was peopled by portions of these nations, and also by the Picts, the Atecotti and the peoples of the islands, to whom later centuries added Scandinavian settlers. The medieval kingdom was not united by language or by a common culture, but by the compelling demands of geography, the seas that enclose it on three sides and the military frontier of the Cheviots on the south.

Scotland comprises three large regions, the lowlands, the highlands, and the north-west. Each of them is sub-divided by nature. The southern lowland is a rectangle, marked by the two Roman walls, from Forth to Clyde, and from Tyne to Solway; and was in the fifth century British in speech, culture and political allegiance, bound by its past to the Roman south. It is cut diagonally by the Cheviot frontier, that is most easily controlled by the rulers of Northumbria and the lower Tyne. Beyond the Cheviots, the Pentland Hills divide the Lothians from the western lands that lie open to the rulers of the Clyde. In the centuries after Arthur, the English proved able to conquer and absorb the British of the Lothians, but they never overran the Clyde.

Beyond the Forth and Clyde the main mass of Pictish territory is bounded by the Great Glen, from Inverness to the Firth of Lorn. It includes the Grampian mountains, the highlands that reach the sea just south of Aberdeen. They separate two fertile regions, the coastal plain of the northern Picts from Aberdeen to Inverness, with its extension to the nearer firths of Beauly, Cromarty and Dornoch; and the southern Pictish country about the long valley of Strathmore, from Perth to Kincardine and Stonehaven, south of Aberdeen.

The long narrow triangle of the north-west is a wilder and emptier country. Its internal communications distinguish its northern and southern portions. In the north, half a dozen narrow roads radiate from Inverness like the fingers of a hand, with no cross routes between them, except the winding coast road. To the south, communications are poorer still. There is no coast road, and only two roads run from the coast to the Great Glen, their outlets dominated by Forts

---

Map 10

ROADS

The modern roads follow and indicate the ancient and natural routes. The roads are shown as classified by the Ministry of Transport (MoT) and by the Automobile Association (AA).

SOUTH OF THE CLYDE AND FORTH ESTUARIES the map shows only

=   Trunk Roads (A 1, 7, 8, 9; 68, 70, 74)

NORTH OF THE CLYDE AND FORTH ESTUARIES the map shows

=   Trunk Roads (A 9; 80, 94, 96)
▬   Main Roads (all other roads classified by the MoT with two figures)

NORTH AND WEST OF THE GREAT GLEN AND DORNOCH FORTH

all roads and vehicle tracks are shown
—   Roads over 12' wide
--- Roads classified by the AA as 'narrow or rough surface, with passing places', by the MoT as A
··· Classified by the MoT as B, or unclassified

HILL AND MOUNTAIN RANGES

1   The North West Highlands
2   The Grampian Mountains
3   The Sidlaw Hills
4   The Ochil Hills

5   The Campsie Fells, and Lennox and Kilsyth Hills
6   The Pentland Hills
7   The Southern Uplands
8   The Cheviot Hills

THE TWO ROMAN WALLS are shown

MAP 10 SCOTLAND, COMMUNICATIONS

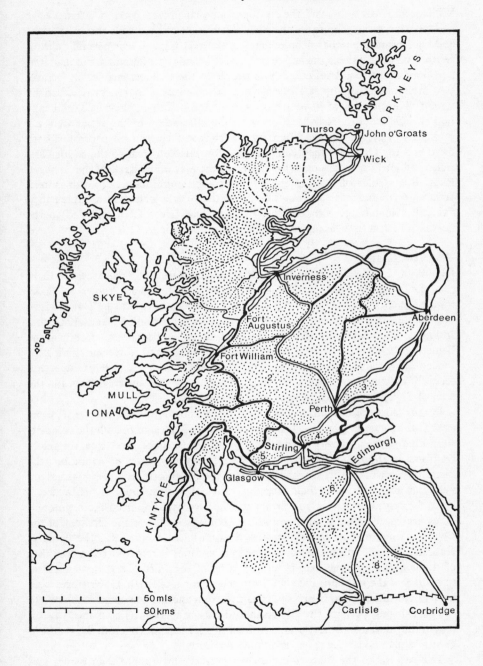

ORKNEYS

Thurso
John o'Groats
Wick

SKYE

Inverness

Fort
Augustus

Aberdeen

Fort William

2

3

MULL

Perth

IONA

4

Stirling

5

Edinburgh

Glasgow

6

KINTYRE

7

8

50 mls
80 kms

Carlisle
Corbridge

William and Augustus, and the fortifications that preceded them. This precise and exacting geography made the early inhabitants of the north and west aliens and enemies to the richer peoples across the Great Glen. Their natural political centres were at all times the larger and nearer islands that dominate the scattered harbours of the mainland coast. The people of the Orkneys may easily control Caithness, the fertile tip of Britain, unless the power of Inverness is unusually strong. The peoples of Skye are masters of the mainland they face, and may raid the Great Glen at will, to retire behind the safety of the sea if they are pursued by stronger forces. Whenever a warlike seafaring people controlled both Skye and the Orkneys, they constituted a formidable threat to the south. The richest and nearest prizes open to Orkney seamen lay in the lands of the northern Picts. But a ruler of Skye might sail his coracles unhindered to north-eastern Ireland, or might reach Dumbarton across the Argyle lochs with no more than five miles marching, with coracles carried. The Great Glen afforded to the northern Picts a route almost as easy towards the Clyde.

The Scot Kings

Islands and headlands screen the Clyde from Inverness and Skye. It was in them that the Irish, or Scots, of Dal Riada settled. Irish legend, known to Bede, recalled extensive settlement long before the 5th century. But the Dal Riadans became a formidable people when their king Fergus forsook Ireland about 500, and made Kintyre the centre of his kingdom. He evidently came as the ally of the British of the Clyde, and the Clyde king was well-disposed to Ireland, giving his son an Irish name and marrying him to an Irish wife. His interest was well served if the ambition of the new kingdom was directed against the Picts and the men of Skye, shielding the Clyde from their attacks.

Fergus' successors built a powerful military monarchy, and turned its arms against the Picts. It grew slowly at first; and there is no sign that all the colonists submitted to the authority of the dynasty in Fergus' time. Two texts, originally set down in the middle and the later seventh century, trace its evolution; the district dynasties (*ceneil*) are made to derive their authority from Fergus, and are neatly arranged in pairs, their founders artificially represented as his brothers. Only the central territories are firmly attached to royal line from the beginning. They are named after Fergus' grandsons. Kintyre itself was the territory of the *Cenel Gabrain*, and its nearest westward extension, Cowall, bears the name of Gabran's brother and predecessor, Comgall. Gabran is remembered as the first of the conquering kings. He is termed 'king of the Forth', and in the central territories of the southern Picts, in Strathmore, north of Perth, Gowrie preserves his name, while beyond it Brechin is named from another Irishman, unknown to the genealogies, perhaps the ally or subordinate of Gabran. The names suggest that in the middle of the sixth century Gabran's Irish armies overran the southern Picts and planted lasting colonies on their territory.

The records of the Picts, though they preserve little more than names and dates, also suggest that their kingdom was in disarray in Gabran's time. But they recovered their strength. About 556, they took the novel decision to choose a foreigner for their king, and selected Bridei, brother of the most powerful ruler in Britain. Bridei restored their fortunes. He defeated and killed Gabran in 560, and recovered some territory from the Irish, perhaps much; for when Columba reached Britain in 563, Iona is said to have been granted to him not only by Conall, the new Dal Riada king, but also by Bridei.

Columba

Columba was foremost among a number of Irish monks who brought their religion to northern Britain. Conversion was slow, but it opened new possibilities. Iona was centrally placed to reach the Picts, the Irish of Dal Riada, the men of the north-west and of the Isles, and to influence the British of the Clyde. It served them all, and became the burial-place of the Pict as well as the Scot kings. It retained its pre-eminence. Though Ninian, Kentigern and very many Irish monks were honoured locally and regionally, only Columba was honoured in all parts of the future Scotland.

Columba's pre-eminence gave the northerners a common ecclesiastical centre, in an age when kings heeded clerics. But his principal impact was upon his fellow-countrymen in Dal Riada. When he arrived, neither they nor their monarchy were yet consolidated, and they had proved unable to withstand the Picts. Dal Riada grew strong in Columba's lifetime and under his guidance; but not until he had lived many years in Iona.

Wars against the Picts were not renewed, but in 568 Conall and the king of Meath undertook a joint expedition to the Western Isles. In striking up the coast, Conall of Kintyre necessarily assumed the leadership of the Irish settlers on his northern borders. They may not have welcomed his intervention, for he was killed in 574, and with him 'many of the allies of the sons of Gabran'. When the enemy is not named, and when the casualties are described as the allies of a dynasty, the language suggests that the battle was fought between different groups of Irish colonists. But its outcome taught them to unite. Their tradition asserts that it was the next ruler, Aedan, son of Gabran, who became 'king of the separate portions of Dal Riada'. The sovereignty of the dynasty was thenceforth accepted by all the Irish colonists, and the genealogies drawn up half a century after his time contrive to represent all the local lords as heirs of cadet branches of the royal house. The contrivance implies a conviction that all Dal Riadans ought to unite behind a single monarch.

Aedan

Conall had failed to unite the Irish, but Aedan succeeded. No tradition suggests that Conall received or listened to advice from Columba; since the stories of Columba abound with the names of kings who heeded him, their silence about Conall suggests that he did not. But it was Columba who selected and appointed the new king. He is said to have preferred Aedan's brother Eogan, but he was visited three nights running by an angel with a 'glass book of the ordination of kings', who ordered him to consecrate Aedan, lashing at him with a whip until he obeyed. The curious story comes from abbot Cummene, who wrote within sixty years of Aedan's death, and adds the saint's promise of continuing political success so long as the king remained faithful to Iona, and refrained from war against the Ui Neill dynasty of Ireland. Aedan came to Iona, and was consecrated by Columba.

Whatever the reasons for Columba's preference, whatever the pressures brought upon him, the central assertion of the story is that the choice of a successor in practice required his consent, and the story was believed while men who had known Aedan were still alive. It was a quite extraordinary power in an ecclesiastic; no abbots in Ireland and no bishops in Europe commanded such authority. In Europe, Ambrose of Milan had sternly reminded the emperor Maximus that the Old Testament priests had appointed kings, but no Roman emperor had owed his throne to bishops. The authority of Columba was exercised in the name of heaven, but it was accepted in deference to his own strength. His imperious personal force was inseparable from his birth; and it prevailed with his cousin, the High King of Ireland.

Columba took Aedan to Ireland. King Aed m Ainmere had summoned a Convention at Drum Ceat, 15 miles east of Derry, probably in 588, and the tradition of Columba records those decisions wherein his views prevailed. Disputes between north and south were assuaged when he interceded for a son of the king of Ossory, then Ainmere's prisoner; he achieved a concordat between the church, the state, and the secular scholars of Ireland, thereby legitimising and baptising the preservation of ancient legend in Christian Ireland; and he negotiated a lasting agreement between Dal Riada and the Irish monarchy. The colonists in Britain were exempted from normal tribute, but agreed to contribute their quota to the High King's army, and to send no aid to his enemies.

Columba's authority prevented war between the Dal Riada Scots and the Picts of Inverness, the men of the Isles and the king of Ireland. It also preserved the long-standing peace with the British of the Clyde. At almost the same time as Aedan's accession, Kentigern returned to the Clyde from long exile in Europe. He is the only major monastic reformer of the British north, credited with an authority in his own land as eminent as Columba's in Dal Riada. He is said to have met and worked with him, but whether or not they were ever able to meet personally, their outlook was similar, and they had common concerns. Adomnan reports that King Riderch of the Clyde sent a secret mission to secure peace through one of Columba's most trusted and experienced diplomats, and obtained his request. Columba's emissary to Dumbarton must have been accredited to Kentigern the bishop rather than to the king, and Kentigern was plainly as concerned as Columba to negotiate agreement. Their efforts succeeded, and Aedan remained at peace with the British, at least until after Columba's death in 597.

Aedan's power grew. In 581 he attacked the Orkneys; their king had earlier submitted to Bridei, giving hostages, and Aedan's attack is more likely to have been made on Bridei's behalf than against him, perhaps after an Orkney rebellion. No wars against the Picts are recorded until the last year of Bridei, who was killed in 584 by southern Pictish rebels. In 583 Aedan won the battle of Manaan, probably on the borders of the southern Picts and the Lothian British; at that date, the southern Picts, apparently already in rebellion under a separate king, were Bridei's enemies as well as Aedan's. After Bridei's death they ultimately asserted their supremacy, for future Pictish kings whose territory is recorded ruled from Fortrenn, about Stirling and Perth, not from Inverness.

Aedan fought to recover the conquests won and lost by his father Gabran. All his recorded wars were fought eastward. Leithrig, fought in 593, was perhaps near Stirling. About 591 he is reported to have joined with the Ulaid from Ireland, to help the British against the English at Bamburgh. In 599 his army suffered heavy losses at the hands of the southern Picts in Strathmore, but the enemy fled. In 603, reinforced by the King of Ireland's brother, he was able to lead a large force to help the British for a second time against the English, at 'Degsa's Stone'. The place has not been identified. The allies went down in crushing and decisive defeat. Thenceforth 'no king of the Scots ever dared to meet the English in the field' for centuries to come. The British dynasty of the Lothians foundered without trace, and their territory was opened to unimpeded English settlement. But Aedan's kingdom survived, and so did some of his annexations in Pictish lands. His son was styled 'king of the Picts' as well as of the Scots, and the Scots retained the upper Forth; they were still able to penetrate the main territories of the southern Picts, until the disastrous reign of Aedan's grandson, Domnall Brecc.

Aedan's heirs

Domnall fought his neighbours in turn, and earned the reputation of a splendid warrior. One Dal Riada tradition credits him with establishing colonies under his sons in Fife, deep in Pictish territory. But enemies unnamed, presumably Picts, defeated him in 636, probably very near to his royal fortress of Dunadd. He then directed his energy and his armies towards Ireland, in support of an exile, and was defeated by the High King at Mag Roth in Ulster in 639. The battle was celebrated in splendid tales, but Domnall earned the enmity of Iona, for he had defied the precept of Columba and broken the agreement between Dal Riada and the Irish monarchy, that the colonists should never make war upon the kin of Columba; for the king he attacked was the grandson of Columba's cousin. His contemporary Cummene, subsequently Abbot of Iona, ascribed his death soon after to divine vengeance, exacted for his disobedience to Columba.

Domnall was no more fortunate in Britain. He was again defeated in 640, at Glenn Mureson, perhaps Mureston, a few miles south-west of Edinburgh, and the next entry in the Annals records a siege of Eitin, Edinburgh. Who besieged whom, and who beat Domnall, is not stated; but the locality suggests his ambition. Lothian wars were a dangerous gamble for high stakes. The English power was recent and not yet secure. Pict, Scot and Clydeside British might still hope for rich prizes. Their opportunity came when Penda of Mercia killed Oswald of Northumbria in 642 and advanced as far as Bamburgh. The Annals enter two battles under the next year, 643. The British killed Domnall Brecc; and they also attacked Oswy, the new king of Northumbria. Whether their attack succeeded or failed is not reported; but their intention was evidently to recover the Lothians. Domnall may well have had the same aim. But both failed. The Lothians were not recovered; and Domnall's ambition ended in disaster.

Domnall's repeated defeats cost many lives, and wasted the limited fighting strength of a small kingdom. His failure ended the power of his people and the authority of his dynasty. The Picts passed from defence to attack. It was some twenty years later that abbot Cummene recalled Columba's warning; if Aedan's heirs attacked the sovereign dynasty of Ireland, they would 'lose the sceptre of their kingdom from their hands', for 'the hearts of men would be taken from them'. He saw its fulfilment in the misfortune of the Dal Riada Irish, for

> from that day till this they are in subjection to foreigners; which fills the heart with sad sighs.

The monarchy of Dal Riada disintegrated. When it was restored, at the end of the seventh century, the new king of the 'separate portions' was not a descendant of Aedan. He was Ferchar the Tall (680–696), chief of the Cinel Loarn about Loch Linnhe, to the north, who were further and safely removed from the Pictish armies of Fortrenn, but were also ill-placed to challenge them. Although the Cenel Gabrain ultimately returned to power, it was to be almost two hundred years before Pictish military supremacy was overcome; and victory was not clear-cut. In 844 a Scot king with a British name, Kenneth mac Alpine, established a dual monarchy wherein the king of the Scots was also king of the Picts; but though the dynasty and its language were Irish, its seat was established in Pictland. Along with the neighbouring nations that they subdued, its inhabitants ultimately consented to be known by the national name of their Irish monarchs; but when they did so, they submitted, not to Irish military conquest, but to the cultural superiority of the Irish Christian religion and of the literate Irish language.

These were the ultimate consequences of the faith that Columba preached, and of the political conduct he imposed upon the Irish immigrants. He died in 597. As a monk he had founded a potent church rooted not on organisation, but on a particular concept of Christianity, that was to hold 'the hearts of men' for centuries, uniting the kingdoms of northern Britain, and also most of England. But his eminence also made him a political leader, his policy grounded on the knowledge that kingdoms, like churches, are maintained by the hearts of men. Apostle to the diverse peoples of northern Britain, spiritual counsellor of the

Picts, of the men of the Isles, and of his fellow Irishmen, friend and ally of the British, he was the first architect of the later Scotland. So long as he lived, he held the four nations together at peace, and his own Irish king was accepted as their joint leader when they had to face a common English enemy. The time for permanent political unity was not yet. But the processes that were to combine these several peoples into the Scottish nation were already at work.

CHAPTER ELEVEN

THE PICTS AND THE NORTHERNERS

The Picts

Half a dozen different peoples inhabited northern Britain in and before the fifth and sixth centuries. They are easily confused with one another, because Roman and Irish writers used the same words with different meanings. Earlier Roman writers regarded them all as British, because they lived in the island of Britain. Late Roman writers distinguished the British, who lived south of the Antonine Wall, between the estuaries of the Clyde and the Forth, from the barbarians beyond. They described the barbarians as they saw them, as the *Picti*, the 'painted people', because they tattooed their bodies, but they had no distinct word for the distant peoples of the north and west, whom they rarely saw.

The Irish were better informed and used more exact words. They restricted the Latin word *Picti* to the nearer neighbours of Rome, who called themselves *Albani*, inhabitants of Alba or Albion, the oldest name of Britain; and in Irish called them British, *Cruithne*. Their language, known only from the names of people and places, was akin to British and Gallic. Their ancestors had reached Britain long before the Roman period, and their principal archaeological relics are some thousands of forts, very numerous in their territory, and also south of the Antonine Wall. A scatter of forts beyond their borders, many of them destroyed by fire, witness their failure to subdue the far north-west. They were simply the British peoples whom Rome never conquered, who therefore remained barbarian.

Their language preserved a few Gallic words that are not known to have survived among the Roman British. But it was never written. The scanty records of the Picts are set down in Latin or Irish, and form no more than a small subsection within the immense body of Irish documentation. The most informative of their texts is a King List, that survives in several versions. It begins with made-up names. 'Cruidne, Father of the Picts' is 'Briton', transliterated into Irish, and his 'sons', Fib, Cat, Circin, Fortrenn, and others are the names of districts, Fife, Caithness and the rest of Pictland. Real names begin in the Roman centuries, when one king, vaguely dated to about the 3rd century, is given a name that is attested in a Roman inscription of the early 3rd century. Real people begin early in the 5th century. The first king of whom anything but the name is reported is Drust, son of Erp, who 'reigned 100 years and fought 100

MAP II THE PICTS

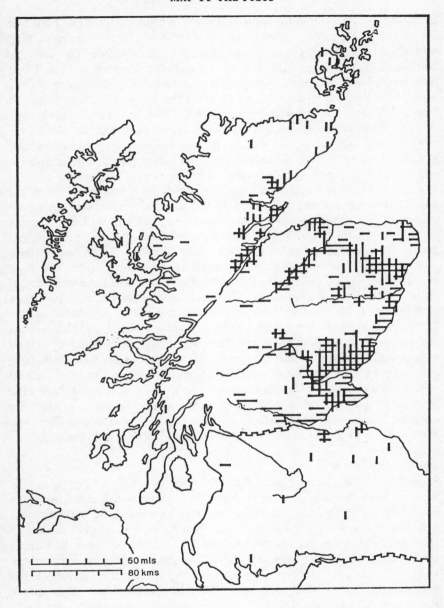

50 mls
80 kms

— Pictish Place Names   ❘ Memorial Stones

battles; in the 19th year of his reign St. Patrick came to Ireland'. The Irish date for Patrick places his accession in 414, and the Irish Annals also name him, putting his death at 458, after a reign of more credible length. The 'hundred battles', as in Irish usage, mean that he was regarded as a great warrior. These dates make him Vortigern's contemporary; and Gildas reports the audacious intention of the Picts to conquer and settle the rich lands of southern Britain in Vortigern's time. The name and precise dates of Drust are not elsewhere confirmed; but in his time some Pictish leaders organised a large and daring expedition on an unprecedented scale. Had it succeeded, Britain might have become Pictland. It failed; but it was the enterprise of the Picts that caused Vortigern to enlist English aid, so that in time southern Britain became England.

The territories of the Picts are well defined. They were the people of the eastern coasts and glens, not of the north and west. Their place names are confined to the lands that their ancestors had fortified and held, between the Forth and the firths about Inverness; their archaeology and their pictorial inscriptions are concentrated in the same region. But they did not form a single political unit. Their own tradition names seven principal provinces, but these provinces are a late simplification, listing the regions over which the later kings of Albany claimed suzerainty, from the ninth century onward. First-century Romans loosely described the whole of the barbarian north as Caledonia; but the Roman geographer Ptolemy recognised their dominant nation, the *Caledones*, as the people who dwelt by the Great Glen and Inverness, one among several named peoples. Later writers, from the 3rd century to the 8th, distinguish between the northerners, whose capital lay in or near Inverness, and the southern *Meatae* in Fortrenn, about Stirling, in Circinn, or Strathmore, and in Fife. Though the stronger rulers were able to command the obedience of both, the separate identities of north and south long outlived the name of Pict, and remained a powerful political force in the medieval kingdom of Scotland.

Brochs and Duns

Beyond the Picts lived several other peoples. Long before the Romans came, the western coasts and islands were inhabited by a people whose small defended strongholds are nowadays called *duns*. They may have been Irish in their speech and their remote ancestry, but they were alien to the peoples of Ireland, who knew their country by the simple geographical name of *Iardomnan*, the western lands; and they were perhaps the unnamed raiders who savaged the northern coasts of Christian Ireland in the years from 617 to 619. But the people who mastered the Orkneys built more formidable castles, called *brochs*. They are tall round towers, swelling at the base, with their habitable rooms within the thickness of the wall, that encloses open space. They were the castles of conquerors, for, on a few sites where excavated evidence outlines their history, their inhabitants moved out after a few generations, to live beside their ruins in more convenient houses that no longer needed such defences.

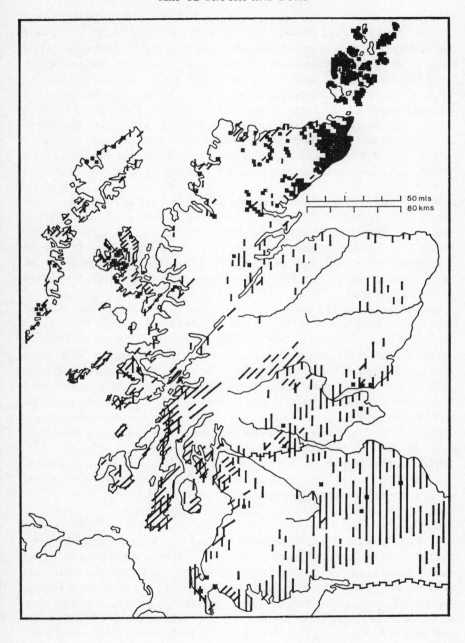

MAP 12 BROCHS AND DUNS

50 mls
80 kms

■ Brochs   / Duns | Forts

Orkney conquest spread. More than a hundred brochs held Caithness, and guarded the valleys and estuaries beyond, on the west and south. In the early Roman centuries, brochs in numbers controlled Skye and the nearby coasts and islands, subduing the duns of the northern *Iardomnan*. A few reached further. Half a dozen penetrated southern Pictish lands on the upper Forth and the Tay estuary, and another half a dozen extended into the Lothians and Galloway. But they did not survive the Roman conquest of the lowlands, to Forth and Clyde, in the second century; and they were never able to invade the northern kingdom of Inverness, or the main southern Pictish regions. Nor were they ever established in the south-western headlands, the future Argyle, where the Dal Riada Scots erected their kingdom in Arthur's time, in a land where the *duns* are many.

By the time of Drust and Vortigern, in the fifth century AD, the brochs, the duns, and most of the forts had long been ancient archaeological ruins. But the descendants of the men who built them still lived beside them. Centuries before, the ancestors of each had come as invaders. Time had dulled the memory of whence they came and when, but the divisive geography of north Britain had perpetuated their separate identities and their different national languages.

In the fertile east and south the Picts retained their ancestral Gallic tongue. But in the north and west, burnt forts and the rarity of their place names attest the failure of the Picts to settle the lands beyond the Ness and the Dornoch region. There, in the land of the duns, almost all place names are Irish. Their numbers and extent are too great to be explained by recent immigration from Ireland; they imply that for many centuries the language of the north-west had been Irish, a barrier to peaceful communication with the Gallo-British Picts.

The people of the brochs were evidently the most recent invaders. Their location, backed by a few other indications, suggests that they may have come from Scandinavia, but gives no clue to their language. It may be that they, like some other conquerors, accepted the speech of the conquered, perhaps of the Irish, perhaps of their predecessors; for some signs suggest the survival of an indigenous population, older than any of the invaders.

Atecotti

The national names of the builders of brochs and duns are not remembered. But the name of one people is known, whose exact location is not recorded. Late fourth-century Romans encountered a peculiarly savage nation, called the *Atecotti*, who lived near the Picts and the Scots. The word is British or Pictish, not Irish, and means the 'very old people', the aborigines; and there is no trace of such a name among the richly documented peoples of Ireland. It is therefore probable that they lived in northern Britain. Their name is matched by a few traces of an aboriginal language. Columba met one old man who came to Skye and spoke a tongue that was neither Irish nor Pictish. Speakers of an older language also seem to have survived in Pictish territory. The Picts themselves carved many memorial stones; and incised them with pictures or symbols, not with letters. But in and near their borders are also a small number of stones inscribed in Irish Ogam characters. Yet when they are transliterated, most of their wording is gibberish, apart from a few personal names. If the characters had the same sound values as in Irish, the language is neither Irish nor Pictish nor any form of Celtic. It is an unknown language, still undeciphered, whose speakers made a brief unsuccessful attempt to express its sound in Irish characters. It is unlikely to concern the peoples of the brochs or duns, who left little trace of settlement where the stones are found. It may be the language of the aboriginal peoples who dwelt in northern Britain, before the coming of the British, and before the builders of brochs and duns, who found a brief separate identity when the barbarian nations combined to assault the Roman frontiers in the 360s, and inscribed a little of their language centuries later, when they were familiar with Pictish memorials and the Irish alphabet.

Christianity

The records of the Picts and Scots alone are preserved. They are easily misinterpreted if the existence of their neighbours is overlooked. To Roman historians, the Picts were an undifferentiated mass of northern barbarians, to be fought and feared. But the attitude of the army was not the outlook of all Romans; a significant trend in late Roman Christianity advocated that barbarians be tamed, absorbed and assimilated by baptism. Not many missionaries preached beyond the frontiers, but some worked among the Picts. Patrick, writing in the 440s, denounced Picts who were apostate from Christianity. Someone, some time before, had converted a considerable number of Picts, but in the intervening years Christianity had died out or been suppressed. The date of the mission cannot have been less than a generation before Patrick's time, nor later than the first years of the fifth century.

Native tradition adds detail to Patrick's generalised statement. Bede reported that Ninian of Whithorn in Galloway had converted the southern Picts, under the inspiration of Martin of Tours. Local legends date the beginning of Ninian's preaching to Martin's last years, in the late 390s; and the places where his name was venerated extend into southern Pictland. Ninian's work was undone when Patrick wrote, in the time of Vortigern and Drust; for when the Picts combined in a national effort against the Roman south, those of them who had embraced the Roman religion are likely to have been submerged. But Christianity regained its hold. Bede knew nothing of the apostasy, and remembered only that the southern Picts, unlike the northerners, had become a Christian people well before 560. Pictish tradition gives detail. Nothing is known of Drust's shortlived successor, but the next king, Nectan Morbet, who reigned from 462 to 486, is held to have revived Christianity, receiving the missionary Boecius from Italy, and entrusting Abernethy on the Tay to Brigit of Leinster.

Nectan was a southerner, but he is styled 'king of all the provinces of the Picts'. Throughout the fifth century the King Lists acknowledge only one ruler at a time. But early in the sixth century, after the establishment of the Scot monarchy in Dal Riada, their record is troubled. It suggests that the kingdom was divided about 528; and the evidence of district names argues that the southern kingdom was overrun and colonised by Gabran of Dal Riada, between 540 and 560. Four kings are said to have died in the years 553 to 556, when Gabran's power was great.

Bridei

It was then that the Picts took an extraordinary decision. They preserved an ancient custom, long since extinct in Europe, that passed the inheritance of property and of political sovereignty through the mother rather than the father, so that no Pictish king was ever succeeded by his son. Hitherto, all their recorded kings had been sons of Pictish fathers, but about 554 they chose a foreigner, Bridei, son of Maelgwn, the mighty king of north Wales, whom Gildas had attacked. He was evidently eligible, for Welsh tradition gives Maelgwn a Pictish grandmother.

When the Picts chose Bridei, they knew who he was. His father, recently dead, had been the strongest king in Britain, 'dragon of the island'; they could reasonably hope that the son of such a foreigner might unite their own strength and draw upon outside resources to mend their fortunes. Bridei justified their choice, and proved himself the greatest of their kings. But he was not at first universally accepted. He ruled in the north, and for the first two years of his reign he is said to have shared power with another king. Welsh legend suggests what happened. At about the time of his accession, his brother Rhun, the new king of north Wales, is said to have marched a vast army to the Forth and beyond. The Welsh remembered the expedition for its unprecedented size and duration, and though they knew nothing of why it marched its context makes plain its purpose and achievement. Rhun's campaign avenged his own wrongs; but when the armies of Bridei's brother crossed the Forth, they entered the southern Pictish lands, that the Dal Riada Scots had recently invaded and colonised. Bridei was doubly strengthened; the rival Pictish king disappeared; Bridei was acknowledged for a generation as sole ruler; and in 560 his armies decisively defeated the Dal Riada Scots.

Bridei's reign brought deeper changes than reunification and the recovery of lost lands. For nearly a hundred years, religion had divided the Pictish kingdoms. The southerners were Christian, the northerners still pagan. Bridei was a prince from a Christian kingdom, and many among the northerners who invited him were disposed to accept the new king's religion. Christianity came, but later ages simplified the manner of its coming. The brief entries of the Pictish lists telescope the conversion into a headline, that

Bridei was baptised by St. Columba in the 8th year of his reign, and northern legend envisaged the speedy conversion of the king's subjects by wholesale baptisms in Loch Ness, much as the pagan English were converted in later times. As early as Bede's day, in the 8th century, tradition had hardened into the simple belief that 'Columba converted the Picts', and had come from Ireland to Britain for that express purpose. But the stories told by Columba's biographer, Adomnan, in the 7th century, give a more exact account. Columba spent his life among his fellow Irishmen; in thirty years, he made three or perhaps four missionary expeditions to the Picts. Nothing is said of the baptism of the king, who was already Christian. Columba received the king's support, and needed it. On his first visit to the royal fortress by Inverness, he was denied entrance; when the outer gates were opened by a miracle, the king and his 'senate' came forth from the 'house' within the fort, to meet the saint with respect. A powerful faction in the Council of the Picts was clearly reluctant to admit the emissary and the faith of their Irish enemies; and acceptance was a personal triumph for the king over the conservative elements among his subjects. But for the rest of his life, on each visit, Columba faced bitter resistance from the *magi*, the established pagan priests. He engaged with them in wonder-working contests, like St. Paul in Cyprus, or St. Patrick in Tara; he confounded the heathen by sailing against the winds, and magnified the God of the Christians in the eyes of 'pagan barbarians', when his curse repelled a monster that dwelt in Loch Ness and had overturned a boat.

The conversion of the Picts was achieved over many years by many men. Even in his old age, Columba laboured to convert individual lords, while their fellows remained pagan. He could not speak the Pictish language, and he was but one among many Irish monks whose labours among the Picts and their neighbours are reported. But he towers among his fellows by reason of his personal eminence, of the lasting vigour of his central monastery at Iona, and of his spiritual and political guidance, which the Picts and the Scots heeded, and the Clyde-side British respected. In keeping the peace in the North for thirty years, he gave a new generation time to grow up free from the scars of former hatreds, able to accept the new religion, even though it was the faith of their enemies.

Bede calls Bridei an 'exceptionally powerful king'. He had no need to fight wars after the victories of his first years. The king of Orkney was his tributary, and gave him hostages. The once formidable power of the islanders was curbed, and was not again reasserted until the Norse invasions. A few Pictish monuments, in Orkney, Skye, and their adjacent coasts, with a few Pictish place names on the mainland opposite Skye, suggest that the Pictish kings installed some colonists, prefects or advisers when they subdued the islands.

Art

Secure sovereignty and the spread of Christianity gave a new stability to Pictish society, that found expression in their art. The imagination of their craftsmen devised memorial stones, depicting bold and splendid designs of abstract mathematical figures and vividly impressionistic animals. The designs plainly convey a meaning, and amount to an attempt to develop from scratch a form of pictographic writing. The attempt is itself a considerable intellectual enterprise. The artistic concepts are as original as the idea, and their execution is precise and beautifully ordered; some of the designs are also found in Irish and Northumbrian manuscripts, from the 7th century onward; and though some are imitated from Irish originals, others are more likely to be Pictish innovations that the Irish manuscripts copied. Though their beauty is shrouded by the unexciting modern description of 'symbol stones', they rank among the notable achievements of Celtic art in any age or land. The stones are difficult to date. The earliest might possibly be as old as Bridei's time, but it was under his successors that they became fashionable and frequent. They indicate the emergence of a class of notables, eminent and rich enough to acquire permanent memorials; they derive from the stability that his government engendered, and emphasise secular change. But they coincide in time with the establishment of numerous monasteries, both among the Picts and among their subject neighbours. The monasteries gave new cohesion to a people who had previously known no centres but the residence of a chief or king; they soon recruited native converts, and with the Irish language they brought literacy to a people who had hitherto known nothing of writing. The more convenient symbols of an alphabet based on Latin limited the pictorial script to the memorials of great men, but in imposing a single written language upon diverse peoples who spoke different tongues, it brought into being another powerful force that was to unify the north.

Bridei's heirs

Bridei's wide sovereignty did not endure unchallenged. In 581, twenty-five years after his accession, the Irish Annals record both the brief reign of 'Cennaleth, king of the Picts', evidently a rebellious rival among the southern Picts, and also 'Aedan's expedition to the Orkneys'. More than 200 miles of Pictish territory and Pictish waters separated Aedan from the Orkneys; if he had fought against Bridei, he could not have assaulted the Orkneys without first defeating the Picts, in a war that the full record of the Irish Annals could not have ignored. It is more probable that Aedan helped Bridei to suppress an Orkney rebellion. But the troubles in the south persisted. In 583, Aedan won a battle in 'Manaan', probably the Stirling area; his enemy may have been British, or southern Pictish, and he is again likely to have fought as Bridei's ally, for in 584 Bridei was himself killed by the southern Picts. Thenceforth, the Pictish kingdom was more loosely organised. The King Lists of the next half-century recognise only a single succession of kings, all of them sons of Picts. But the Irish Annals also record a series of notable Picts, whom they do not describe as kings; they may well have been independent lords of Inverness.

These are the years in which the Northumbrian English grew from a tiny people clinging to their coastal strongholds into the most powerful kingdom in Britain. The British, the Dal Riada Scots, and the mainland Irish combined in vain efforts to check them, but no account involves the Picts in their alliances. They appear to have made short-term gains when the English weakened their southern neighbours. The British kingdom of the Forth is not again recorded after the English victory of 603; and English settlement began to spread English place names all over the Lothians. But when the English reached Edinburgh, they knew its nearby hills by the name of 'Pictland', or 'Pehtland', now Pentland; and Bede believed that the native name of Abercorn, at the eastern end of the Roman Wall on the Forth, was its name 'in the Pictish language'. The Picts had evidently subdued the lands on both banks of the upper Forth, and annexed the former British kingdom of the Manau of Gododdin.

For fifty years more, the Picts were little troubled. The power of the Dal Riada Scots was dispersed by the incompetent ambition of Domnall Brecc, and the main effort of the English was directed against their own fellow-countrymen in the south. In 617 the Picts and the Irish received the numerous refugee sons of Aethelferth of Bernicia, exiled by the victory of Edwin of Deira, and taught them Christianity. When the British and the Mercians killed Edwin in 633, one of the sons, Eanfrith, returned for a brief inglorious reign, perhaps with Pictish help. His brothers Oswald and Oswy soon restored their dynasty, but for 20 years their authority was circumscribed by the power of the Mercians and the British on their southern borders.

The ambition of the Picts revived. In 648 they fought the chiefs of the Kintyre Scots, heirs of Aedan and Domnall; and in 652 they chose an English king, the son of Eanfrith. Their choice was a challenge, for their new king had a better ancestral claim to the throne of Northumbria than Oswy himself. But Oswy soon triumphed. In 655 he overthrew the Mercians, and in the next year the English king of the Picts died or was killed. Then Oswy overran southern Pictland. Bede reports that he

> conquered the greater part of the Picts and Scots, who hold the
> northern parts of Britain, and made them tributary.

The impositions of the conqueror were not limited to tribute. The Northumbrians installed an English underking, and the main territories of the southern Picts in Strathmore are thick with English place names, witnesses of heavy colonisation; the place names have not yet been studied, but their most probable origin begins with Oswy's conquest.

Beyond the conquered territory, the Picts chose an Irish king. But when Oswy died in 670, they attacked his son Egferth, and also expelled their Irish king, choosing another Bridei. The second Bridei was the son of a British king of the Clyde, and was first cousin to Egferth. A contemporary Northumbrian complained of the bestial nations of the Picts, who despised subjection to the Saxons, and gathered innumerable peoples from the cavities of the north.

Egferth surprised them and overwhelmed them, but Bridei survived, and strengthened his kingdom, recovering control of the Orkneys in 681. When his power grew Egferth again attacked, and in 685 set out to 'waste the provinces of the Picts'. This time, he was defeated and killed at Nechtansmere, near to the southern Pictish capital. The Northumbrians, influenced by their clergy, who were well-disposed towards their fellow monks among the Irish and the Picts, chose Aldfrith as his successor, a pacific prince, trained at Iona to esteem both Scots and Picts, who shared the clergy's dislike of Egferth's military aggression. Bridei restored an ancient kingdom. He also created the core of a larger state. He and his successors were known as 'kings of Fortrenn', and the Stirling region remained the centre of government for centuries. For, though the monarchy of Dal Riada was also reconstituted, Fortrenn long remained the dominant northern power. Unlike the kingdom of the first Bridei, it was a multilingual state, for though the English government was expelled, the English colonists and their language remained; but the continuing expansion of the literate Irish church also taught men to read Latin and speak Irish.

By the middle of the seventh century, the other nations of the British Isles were set upon their future courses, within borders that have not greatly changed thereafter. But there was as yet no likeness of the future Scotland. Both Pictish territories obeyed a single king, who held their northern and western neighbours in subjection. But the name 'Scot' was still restricted to a weak and alien Irish kingdom, and the British and the English still ruled south of the Forth and Clyde.

Yet the pressures that were to create Scotland were already felt, and the origin of the nation seems obscure unless their growth in the succeeding centuries is outlined. The Picts long retained their military supremacy, containing the Scots and breaking their armies. They were reduced, not by military conquest, but by their own archaic institutions. They did not learn to write their own language; their monumental pictographs delight the eye, but were unsuited to ordinary communications. A stronger state had greater need of written paper, and the Irish and Latin languages of its clerks and court overlaid the native speech. The new monarchy was more than a national institution of the Picts; it ruled subjects who spoke half a dozen tongues, and was increasingly tied to an Irish church that also served its neighbours.

The alienation of the monarchy from the Pictish people was accelerated by their antique inheritance custom. Powerful kings married their daughters to foreign princes; and since inheritance passed through the woman, more and more kings were sons of British and Irish fathers, born and bred abroad. The old tradition snapped in 843, when victory in civil war enthroned Kenneth Mac Alpine, by the right of female descent. Through his father, he was king of the Dal Riada Scots, and he determined that his brother and son should succeed him in both kingdoms. Though for a few generations the patrilinear dynasty of the Scots was challenged by the heirs of the daughters or sisters of past kings, it maintained its hold.

Albany

The dual monarchy permanently united the Scot and Pict kingdoms. The dynasty retained the name of Scot, but made its principal seat in Fortrenn. Its ancient home of Dal Riada became a province, known in later times as Argyle. But to Fortrenn itself, the Irish kings brought Irish political concepts and Irish notables. The king became a high king, suzerain over regional dynasts termed *mormaers*; the provinces of the northern Picts obeyed a dynasty that named its founder Morgan, and placed his lifetime soon after the foundation of the dual monarchy. His name proclaims his origin, for it is British, at home south of Forth and Clyde, whence it had passed by marriage into the usage of the Dal Riada Scots. The tradition is that Kenneth or his son installed an Irish Scot dynasty in Inverness; but continuing northern wars bound the dynasty to its subjects, and later rulers asserted the title of king of Moray, ruling the lands west of the Spey in virtual independence.

In the south, the name of the Picts passed from use. It had always been a Latin term, alien to native speech; and Latin henceforth elegantly adapted the ancient name of Britain, Albion, turning it to Albania, or Albany. The descendants of the southern Picts long declined to be known by the name of their foreign Irish dynasty; and as late as the 12th century, their battle cry was 'Alban!', not 'Scot!'. But pressures from abroad tied them to their dynasty. From the outset the dual monarchy faced fearful enemies. Six years after Kenneth's death the Norse of Dublin overran Albany; Orkney and Skye were also lost, and the Great Glen again became a frontier. Beyond, the half-Irish, half-Norse kingdom of the Isles was not securely reunited to the mainland crown until the later middle ages.

The conquests of the Norsemen revived the divisions of the Pictish past; geography imposed upon the *mormaers* of Inverness the obligation to defend Albany against the foreigner, and it compelled them to rely principally upon their own resources. But it also damped down the occasions of conflict between Inverness and Stirling. The northerners were too busy to attack the south, and the ambition of the Albany kings saw easier opportunities to the south. The Scandinavian inroads upon the English enabled the Clydeside British to extend their borders deep into the Northumbrian Pennines and also permitted the Scot kings of Albany to push far beyond the Forth into English lands. They acquired Edinburgh about 960, and the Lothians in 1018. In the same year the last British king of the Clyde died or was killed; and the grandsons of the Scot king succeeded to the government of the British and the English south of Forth and Clyde.

Scotland

The medieval kingdom of Scotland was in being; King Malcolm 11 of Albany was suzerain of Inverness, Glasgow and Edinburgh, and ruled well to the south of the later border. But the new kingdom was insecure, and its dynasty was destroyed by the intemperate ambition of Malcolm's grandson and successor, the young Duncan of Cumbria. He assembled the forces of his vast dominions, and asserted his authority over the king of Inverness, but was disastrously defeated by the Orkney Norse. He marched south to besiege Durham, but the English dispersed his army in an even greater disaster. The victorious North-men invaded and wasted Albany itself, where their arms had not been seen for two centuries. The triple catastrophe drove Duncan's subjects to rebellion, and he was killed 'in youth by his own people' in 1040, six years after his accession. His infant sons went into exile, leaving none of his dynasty to succeed him. His notables offered the vacant throne to the able king of Inverness, Macbeth, whose irms had driven back the Norse invaders.

After nearly twenty years of strong and peaceful rule Macbeth was overthrown in 1058 by an English invasion. The conquerers installed the exiled son of Duncan, Malcolm 111, termed Canmore, 'Big Head'. He owed his throne to foreigners, and kept it with their help; and their obsequious historians transformed Macbeth into the villain whom Shakespeare immortalised. Malcolm married Margaret, an English princess reared in Hungary, who could not stomach native manners and highland custom. Her English companions received lands and authority; the king's residence was transferred to English Edinburgh, and the Queen's English became the language of court and government. When the Normans destroyed the English monarchy in 1066, Malcolm revived his father's ambition, and sought to extend his borders by repeated unprofitable invasions of England. But he was no match for the Norman kings, and he lost his ancestors' southern conquests. In 1092 William Rufus fortified Carlisle and colonised Cumberland; when Malcolm lost his life next year in another ill-organised invasion of Northumbria, the eastern border was permanently fixed upon the Tweed, and the old Roman frontier of the Cheviots was at length re-established.

The Normans gained more than a serviceable frontier. Malcolm's subjects expelled his heirs, but they were again restored by English arms. The kings of England were now Normans, who had learnt how the castles of foreign lords might subjugate a hostile nation. Numerous Norman freebooters arrived to bolster the king they had imposed, and were rewarded with lordships that permanently fringed the lowlands, and overawed the highlands. Notable among them was Walter of Oswestry, grandson of an Armorican British adventurer who had accompanied William the Conquerer. Walter's brother William was the ancestor of the Fitzalans and Howards of Arundel and Norfolk, and Walter himself became Steward of the Scottish kingdom in or about 1136. In office for forty years, through four reigns, he moulded the form and practice of the Norman English monarchy of medieval Scotland. He was succeeded by his son. The office became hereditary, and its title became a surname, until his 14th-century descendant, the Steward Robert, acquired the throne as the first of the Stewart kings.

The monarchy was transformed into an instrument of English supremacy. Its efficiency was limited, for the conventions of Norman government encouraged vassals to defy their lords when they had the strength; and the narrow bounds of the sea and the Cheviots bred a national sentiment that warmed to kings who renounced English suzerainty. But their independence was half hearted, for they ruled by English methods and by English consent. Native lowland lords resented the new Norman nobility, but their strength was curtailed by the spread of the English language, already deeply rooted in the lowlands. English clergy were thrust upon the church, and the Irish language, once the vehicle of a superior culture, became the uncouth speech of highland barbarians. When highlands and lowlands were sundered by language, lowlanders were easily taught to fear and hate highland ferocity; and within the highlands earlier identities dissolved when the peoples of each district were subjected to the rule of foreign dynasts, and were encouraged to massacre each other in the name of artificial local loyalties. The English suborned the allegiance of king and noble by generous grants of estates, that were easily forfeit by rebellion.

But though successive kings dampened the growing national cohesion of their subjects, they could not destroy it, and could not permanently withstand its power. In spite of the kings and nobles, the peoples of the north persisted in building a common Scottish nationality, that the modern world accepts as on a par with English, Welsh and Irish nationhood. The medieval historians of Scotland ignored or denied popular feeling, save when it served the interest of authority; and have successfully kept the modern Scots indifferently aware of their own early history, still prone to clothe it with legendary romantic nonsense. But though the nation took longer to create, and has been denied a proud clear record of its origins, its unity none the less derives from the men of the sixth and seventh centuries, above all from Columba of Iona, who first taught Picts and Scots to live at peace, and fired the imagination of ordinary men, who dimly perceived a future nobler and kinder than the wars of local dynasts.

CHAPTER TWELVE

BRITISH SUPREMACY

British tradition is preserved in the same kind of sources as Irish tradition, especially in Annals, Genealogies and Saints' Lives. But the texts are fewer. The Cambrian Annals insert no more than a dozen entries of the 5th and 6th centuries, into a short transcript of the Irish Annals. The Genealogies list some scores of names from these centuries, instead of thousands. The Saints' Lives are in worse shape. Those that are preserved in Armorica conserve much 6th-century material, but most of the mainland British texts are reconstructions of the 11th and 12th or later centuries, put together after long oblivion, in which no one had cared to read or copy ancient lives. Several of their authors complain that they have had to research among illegible decayed manuscripts, and others boast that they have drawn upon sources written barbarously, of unsound morality and doctrine, and have replaced them with new works adapted to modern standards, phrased in elegant Latin. Some reproduce recognisable sections of their originals, but others modernise or omit the names of people and places.

British tradition is weak, and archaeological evidence is still slight, but contemporary evidence is strong. Gildas' invective is directed against authorities whom he and his readers knew at first hand. His judgement and his interpretation are his own, but the reality of the men, the institutions and the events is not to be gainsayed. His notions of the past are full of misunderstandings, and similar incomprehension pervades many of the texts that Nennius assembles. But they aim, in the Roman manner, to give a factual record. They too apologise for faulty sources; but they do not replace them with polished moral tales. The sixth- and seventh-century British also have a great deal of poetry. It is great literature, much of it heroic verse. Some of it is contemporary with the events it concerns, some composed not long after; some of the later poems are modernised versions of older tales, and others are rich in oblique allusion to lost poems. These principal sources are supplemented by a number of specialised documents, notably the charter memoranda of Llandaff and Llancarfan, that illuminate disconnected incidents, and have much to say of the structure of their society. The record of the early history of Britain is more uneven than that of Ireland, a torch that lights isolated patches amid the surrounding obscurity.

Gildas' Kings

Gildas first attacks the secular authorities, thereafter the churchmen. His carefully ordered paragraphs balance the enormities of kings and judges in alternating sentences, whose force is clearer when his reproaches are set forth in pairs.

> Kings Britain has, but they are tyrants; judges, but wicked ones. They terrorize and plunder the innocent; they protect and defend criminals, and robbers.
>
> They have wives, but they are whores; they swear, and perjure themselves. . . .
>
> They make war, but wars civil and unjust; they zealously chase thieves throughout the country,
>
> yet they love and reward the thieves who sit at their table; they sit on the seat of judgement, but they rarely seek the rule of right justice.
>
> They despise the humble and the harmless, but they praise to the stars . . . their military companions, bloody arrogant murderers and adulterers, enemies of God, who should . . . have been altogether rooted out, together with their very name; they keep many prisoners in their jails . . . more often the victims of intrigue than of their just deserts.
>
> They hang about the altars, taking solemn oaths, and soon after scorn them as though they were dirty stones.

The alternation contrasts the function of the king and of the judge; Gildas is outraged because the king has usurped the function of the judge, or made him his passive instrument.

The invective is a bold frontal assault upon a system of military government, maintained by *duces*, generals, who have become *reges* and *tyranni*, kings and tyrants. Critics of Gildas, then and now, might protest that he exaggerates; but they could not deny the existence of the generals and the judges, the companions and their wives, the wars, the jails and the altars. Gildas' tirade establishes beyond question the general form of the government in the generation after Arthur's death, for no man complains that the wrong people are in prison, unless there are prisons and prisoners inside them. The armies that had won the war had not been demobilised thereafter; on Arthur's death, they had become independent warbands. They, the *commanipulares*, the fellow-soldiers or military companions of the generals, were in Gildas' eyes the main cause of political disorder; and they ought to have been abolished. But the warbands persisted. Their evil conduct looms large in the tradition of the Saints' Lives, several of which categorise the notables of early sixth-century Britain as 'the kings, their companions, and the nobles'. Later, nobles and 'companions' fused into a single class; but in Gildas' day, as in the late Roman empire, they were distinct and antagonistic. Military tyrants and their retainers overbore the civil authorities.

Not all tyrants were of military origin. There is no reason to suppose that the dynasties of Honorius of Gwent, Constantine of Wroxeter, Vitalinus of Gloucester owed their origin to military commands. When central government is weak, hard-pressed cities easily accept the rule of one overmighty citizen in place of an aristocratic senate; many Italian cities did so before Rome regulated their government, and did so again in the Renaissance. Other Roman cities submitted to tyrants as the power of the imperial government weakened in the fifth century. One incident is typical. In the summer of 444, the imperial chancery was shocked at recent events in Emesa in Syria: its edict reads

> it would not have been necessary to issue this ruling, if the effrontery of miscreants were restrained by fear of the laws or respect for the imperial authority. . . . Valerianus, a councillor of the city of Emesa . . . invaded the offices of the governor of the province, with a large force of barbarians, and had the audacity to claim the fore-most place for himself, sitting at the right hand of the man in whom we have invested jurisdiction, and to whom we have entrusted the fortunes of the provincials. . . . Being as rich as he is criminal, he summoned the other councillors to his own house, and, to defraud the public revenue, imposed a servile garrison of his own on the revenue officials, causing great loss to the Treasury of Our Serenity. . . . Wherefore we sentence him to be deprived of the military belt and of the rank of *Inlustris* (Most Honourable).

In fifth-century Britain, several of the magnates who lived in Cotswold mansions were great enough to bear Most Honourable rank, and to wear the *cingulum*, the richly ornamented belt that marked high military and civil office. Their wealth and eminence made them the social superiors of the governors and gave them enormous local influence. As in Syria, some may well have openly usurped political power. In Syria, the imperial government was still strong enough to prevent a Valerianus from founding a hereditary dynasty, and Gildas attributes a like authority to the government of Arthur. But when 'all the con-trols' of good order were swept away, many generals and some civilian potentates openly asserted the sovereignty latent in their actual power. In Gildas' time, the local despots were a recent evil, a serious menace only in the last ten years or so. He spoke out because the governors of Britain and their staff were as hopelessly overwhelmed as the constituted civil authorities of fifth century Syria.

Gildas follows his general invective with a denunciation of five named kings, who between them ruled the west country from Chester to the Channel. Their criminal violence is not unparalleled, for it recalls the licentious brutality of the sixth-century Frank kings in Gaul, that Gregory of Tours chronicles with no less horror. Political violence was no novelty in Britain, for some of the kings are rebuked for crimes committed 'many years ago'; what was shocking was that these outrages had recently become the normal practice of governments who ruled large regions.

The kings had met resistance and beaten it down. Constantine of Dumnonia, while 'clad in the garb of a holy abbot', had recently murdered 'two royal youths', in a church and in the presence of their mother. 'Many years before' he had put away his wife; he had sworn 'never to harm our countrymen', and Gildas urges him to 'come back from your far-off haunts of sin', for 'I know full well that you are still alive'. Gildas refers to recent events well known to his readers; his allusions are not clear enough to reveal the details, but they suggest their outline. When Gildas wrote Constantine was no longer a reigning king; his whereabouts were unknown, and men might doubt whether he still lived. He had reigned years before, but had lost his throne, entered a monastery, and sworn to abstain from violence. He broke his oath; and the murder of the princes and renunciation of his wife explain the context of his offences, the bitterness of dynastic conflict.

Gildas names next Aurelius Caninus (Conan), perhaps of Gloucester, whose 'hatred of the country's peace' and 'thirst for civil war, and unjust and repeated booty' has shut the doors of heaven to his soul. He is left alone 'like a withering tree in the midst of the field', forgetful of the 'vain ambition of your father and brothers, of their death in the immaturity of youth', and hell awaits him. The third king is the greying Vortipor, tyrant of Demetia, whose life's end is now near; the evil son of a good king (Agricola Longhand), he too was 'sunk in murder and adultery', and now, after his wife's virtuous death, he had 'violated' his daughter. The charge may mean that he had married his step-daughter; other kings married heiresses, and, if his wife had a daughter by an earlier marriage, a motive is clear for so sharp an affront to the laws of the church.

Cuneglassus of north Wales had fought against man and God. Like Constantine he had put away his wife, and now he sought to marry her 'pestilential sister', though she had promised to God the 'everlasting chastity of widowhood'. Again dynastic marriage with an heiress is likely. Cuneglassus was first cousin to Maelgwn, the

> last in my list, but the first in evil, mightier than many, and mightier still in malice, profuse in gifts and in sin, strong in arms, but stronger still in what kills the soul ... greater than almost all the generals of the British in the size of your kingdom, as of your physical stature.

Maelgwn was the 'dragon of the island', who had 'deprived many tyrants ... of their kingdoms and their lives'. His story is told more fully.

> In the first years of your youth, you crushed the king your uncle and his bravest troops with fire and spear and sword. ... When your dream of violent rule was realised, your longing for the right road pulled you back, perhaps because your sins then bit your conscience;

day and night you pondered . . . the life of the monks, and then
publicly proclaimed that you would vow yourself a monk for ever,
before God Almighty, in the sight of the angels and of men with no
thought of going back on your promise.

You seemed suddenly to have broken through the vast nets that
normally entangle fat bulls of your kind, the chains of royal power,
of gold and silver, and, what matters more, of your own overweening will . . . when you came to the caves of the saints. How
great the joy of the church our mother, if the Enemy of all mankind
. . . had not snatched you from the Lord's fold, . . . with no very
vigorous resistance on your part . . . to make you a wolf like himself. . . . For the rejoicing at . . . your conversion to the good fruit
was as great as the grief . . . at your reversion to . . . your frightful
vomit. . . . Your excited ears heard no more the praises of God, sung
by the gentle voices of Christ's soldiers, nor the melodious chanting
of the church, but your own empty praises, shouted by lying
thieves . . . shrieking in frenzy.

Maelgwn killed a kinsman, left his throne to turn monk, and later returned to
the world. The earlier events of his reign recall those of Constantine's in
Dumnonia; and they happened for similar reasons. It was the custom of many
British kingdoms, as of the Franks in Gaul, to partition a dead king's territory
among his sons; the genealogists explain that on Cunedda's death his son
Ceretic and his grandson Marianus inherited and named Cardigan and Merioneth;
the north passed to another son, Einiaun, and on his death it was subdivided
between his sons, Maelgwn's father, Catwallaun Longhand, and Cuneglassus'
father, Ewein Whitetooth, whom Maelgwn killed. Where such partition prevailed, each strong ruler was constrained to hack his way to power through
numerous uncles, brothers and cousins, before he could found any considerable
state; and if he succeeded, the kingdom built on dynastic violence must again
be partitioned when he died, inviting a renewal of the fratricidal wars. This fatal
practice prevented any one among the generals or kings of the British from
mastering his fellows and uniting his people, and was to split Wales for centuries
into impotent and quarrelsome lordships, rarely able to combine against the
English until one among them had first subdued his neighbours; so that success
itself destroyed the loyalties to which a national leader must appeal.

The evil was new in Gildas' time. He foresaw its consequence, and repeatedly
warned that the anger of the Lord would raise up the heathen against kings
whose civil wars and dynastic murders sinned against man and God. The heathen
English were not raised up until the year of Gildas' death, but the fatal violence
of the British kings already filled their subjects with foreboding. Gildas deplores
the familiar evils, repeated in Maelgwn's second reign.

Like a lively foal, to whom any unknown place seems inviting, your
boundless fury carried you over wide plains of crime, adding new

> sins to old. You renounced the proper wife of your first so-called marriage ... and sought not a widow, but the beloved wife of a living man, not even a stranger, but your own brother's son. This uttermost limit of sacrilege bent your stiff neck ... from the lowest crimes to crimes still lower, by an audacious double murder, the killing of the husband and of the wife you had once held yours. Then you publicly married the woman whose collusion and encouragement had swelled your crimes ... and the lying tongues of your parasites cry ... that the marriage is legal, because she is a widow!

Gildas spends more words on Maelgwn than on the other four kings put together; and these words express a more intimate personal feeling, the bitterness of hope deceived that reveals some trace of former affection. There is no doubt that he had been genuinely moved when the great king seemed to have put aside his earthly power and his overweening will, and the simile of the young animal roaming wide plains touches a note of sympathetic understanding. His conclusion is also personal. The other kings are formally exhorted to repentance; not so Maelgwn, for his redemption is a possibility that might have been, a chance now lost beyond recovery. To Gildas, the hope of the British people, their moral and spiritual salvation, their religious and political strength and unity, lay in their acceptance of the new teaching of the holy men, the saints or monks. The genuine conversion of the greatest prince of the age, the example of his high station and the energy of his powerful personality, could have helped that movement to transform society, to create a Britain of a new substance, strong and confident in itself, an example to the world. These were not idle hopes, for, a few years after Gildas wrote the conversion of an Irish prince, Columba, no less eminent or able than Maelgwn, was to become a principal influence in the transformation of his society. Maelgwn's defection was a bitter sorrow; Gildas continues:

> Is there a saint whose bowels do not weep at such a tale? ... Nor had you any lack of counsel, for as your mentor you had the finest teacher of almost the whole of Britain.

The greatest teacher of the age, remembered in the accounts of several of his pupils, was Illtud; and the best remembered pupil of Illtud was Gildas himself. Gildas was much the same age as Maelgwn, and might have been his fellow pupil. Past personal friendship may well underlie his words. But Gildas had now abandoned hope of salvation through the conversion of kings, and reluctantly appealed to the people over their heads, after long hesitation,

> constrained by the religious prayers of the brethren

among whom he evidently already had some standing. He called his work

> the history of the evils of this age, written in protest and with tears.

His readers found heart and courage in an attack fearlessly directed against the 'proud and stubborn princes of this age', that concentrated upon the greatest of them all, the leader who had first inspired the reformers and then betrayed them. The book was a formal renunciation of obedience to the authority of established kings and bishops, a denial of their right to rule, delivered on behalf of the reformers. It made Gildas their leading thinker, and he retained their respect; he became the arbiter of their disputes, the architect and apologist of the theory behind their practice.

Gildas ends his attack on Maelgwn, not with a vain appeal to repentance, but in sorrow at his fate. Repentance of course is urged upon the people.

> Despise not the unspeakable mercy of God, who said 'I shall speak to the nation and the kingdom, to . . . destroy and ruin it . . . but if the nation repent . . . I too will repent of the evil that I said I would do unto it.' (*Jer.* 18, 7–8)

But Maelgwn himself is almost beyond hope. Gildas thunders

> if you listen with deaf ears, you despise the prophets, spurn Christ, and spurn me too. I am a man of little standing, and you may count me of no weight, but at least I keep the word of the prophets with a sincere heart. . . . But you have set your course, and that dark flood of hell shall roll its bitter waves fatally around you, always torturing and never consuming, for it will be too late and useless when your eyes recognise the punishment, and repent of evil.

Maelgwn was not only the greatest of Gildas' kings. Wherever the traditions of the British are remembered, he dominates his age. Lawyers credit him with judicial reforms, and the stories of the monks abuse his government. Poets who knew nothing of Gildas report the fear that his arm inspired; and his heirs prolonged his power. His son Bridei created the strongest kingdom of the north, and his other son, Rhun, who succeeded him in Wales, was able to march his national army unopposed throughout the Pennines; and a century later, the national army destroyed Edwin of Northumbria. Medieval poets called it the 'host of Maelgwn' and complimented later heroes who seemed 'of the calibre of Maelgwn'. The middle ages knew him as the *Gwledic*, the supreme 'ruler of the land', before the Welsh forever lost 'England and the crown and sceptre of London'. In his own day, he came nearer than any other of the successor kings to achieving primacy over his fellows; he failed, because his society could not revive the institution of a sovereign emperor, or even evolve a high kingship on the Irish model.

Gildas lived in the west, and named only western kings. But he mentioned others, who did not share their vices, and constituted a pious threat to evil kings.

> What are these ill-starred generals now to do? Those few among them who have left the broad way and are finding the narrow are

forbidden by God to pour out their prayers for you, so long as you persist in evil. But if, on the contrary, you had sought God again with your hearts, it would have been impossible for them to punish you, for . . . even the prophet Jonah could not punish the Ninevites, though he greatly desired to do so.

The threat is plain, real and political. The few good rulers who cannot pray for bad kings will not punish them if they repent. The converse is implied, that they will punish unrepentant wrongdoers. With God's blessing, good kings might dethrone the wicked. The good kings are not named, but since they were not to be found among the westerners, they are to be numbered among the rulers of the north and east.

The threat did not mature. Men listened to the second part of Gildas' denunciation, directed against the clergy, and in fact reformed the church. But the praiseworthy *duces*, heirs of the last generation when men had kept their station, did not overthrow the arrogant highland tyrants. In the event, the dynasties of the western kings lasted for centuries, but the states of the rest of the country were destroyed soon after Gildas' death. The language of the British kingdoms survived in Wales and the north-west, and therefore something remains of their tradition. Elsewhere, their language died with them, and almost nothing is recorded of the sixth-century rulers of lowland Britain.

The Lowlands and the West

The political frontiers of sixth-century Britain emerged from the *civitas* states of the Roman past, sometimes swollen and sometimes dismembered by the impact of the wars and of the break-up of Arthur's empire. Most of what is known concerns the west, and its evidence must help the interpretation of the few hints that suggest the political organisation of the lands that in the end became England.

South Wales

The culture of the Roman lowlands extended into south Wales. There, two major Roman states are known, the Silures, whose capital was Caerwent in Monmouthshire, and the Demetae of Carmarthen and Pembroke. The boundary between them is not known, but it is commonly assumed, probably rightly, that the fertile vale of Glamorgan was Silurian. The name and identity of the Demetae survived; their country is still called Dyfed in modern Welsh. The state was colonised and ruled by the southern Irish while Rome still governed Britain; in Vortigern's time, Cunedda recovered Kidwelly, south-eastern Carmarthenshire, but the rest of Demetia was not subdued until Arthur's time; thenceforth the dynasty of Agricola and Vortipor ruled the kingdom for centuries.

But the name of the Silures died with Rome. During the fifth century the dominion of Caerwent, known as Gwent, was reduced to a strip of land between the Usk and the Wye. Its ruler was named Honorius, Ynyr, and the city is the only *civitas* capital of Roman Britain where the ordinary incidents of urban life are reported in texts that concern the sixth century. The future Glamorgan was known as Glevissig, and at the end of the fifth century was partitioned between several local lords, whom tradition collectively named the 'sons of Glivis'. Most of them are figments, coined from the district names of later times, but a few have tangible human names, and are named in other texts. Marcianus ruled westward from the Thaw, at the southernmost point of Wales, perhaps as far as Gower. On his east, Paulinus ruled Penychen to the neighbourhood of Cardiff, whence Gwynlliw's small territory extended towards Newport, with Etelic established in the Usk valley. These tiny lordships were detached from Gwent, and from the early sixth century they appear to have acknowledged the suzerainty of Demetia, perhaps after Agricola's conquest; for a late sixth-century writer who knew the country well gave Demetia and Gwent a common border, on or near the Usk, and a hundred years later the Englishman Aldhelm of Malmesbury equated all south Wales with Demetia. Ecclesiastical tradition concurs, for in the first years of the century bishop Dubricius ministered in both Gwent and Glevissig, but a generation later Teilo of Carmarthenshire is reported as both bishop in Demetia and in Glevissig.

These small territories amalgamated during the sixth century. Gwynlliauc and Penychen combined under the rule of the abbot-king Cadoc, and formed the nucleus of a powerful military monarchy that emerged at the end of the century, in the course of resistance to English conquest. In its later history it was several times split among heirs, reunited by strong kings who slew their uncles and brothers, and again divided; it threw off Demetian sovereignty, perhaps in 645, but it was not until the 10th century that Glevissig took its modern name of Gwlad Morgan, the land of Morgan, or Glamorgan, from an exceptionally powerful ruler.

Military monarchy developed late in Glevissig, after Gildas' time, for it was a land where Roman gentility lingered long. Medieval texts record many Roman names, and contemporary inscriptions confirm them; some old-fashioned family names persisted, like Pompeius, and Turpilius, a distinguished Italian name, rare in the provinces. Illtud inherited a mansion on a Cotswold scale, its buildings decayed, but its estates intact. The owner of another estate, near Chepstow, kept the baths of his villa in repair, and used them 'usually on Saturdays'. The stories of the monks know more of learning and letters than elsewhere in Wales, and treat of men who wined and dined in civilised comfort; Gildas' later letters defend abbots who travelled in a carriage and pair, 'because it is the custom of the country'.

North Wales

The Llandaff texts preserve the traditions of south Wales in some detail; but the history of the north rests on genealogies, supplemented by scattered

MAP 13 BRITAIN ABOUT 550
KINGDOMS, DISTRICTS AND CENTRES

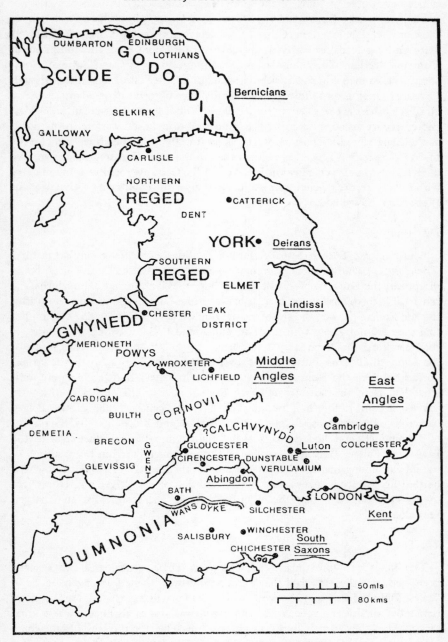

DUMBARTON   EDINBURGH

CLYDE   GODODDIN   LOTHIANS

Bernicians

SELKIRK

GALLOWAY

CARLISLE

NORTHERN
REGED   CATTERICK

DENT

YORK•   Deirans

SOUTHERN
REGED   ELMET

GWYNEDD •CHESTER   PEAK
DISTRICT   Lindissi

MERIONETH
POWYS

CARDIGAN   CORINOVII   WROXETER
LICHFIELD   Middle
Angles

BUILTH   East
Angles

DEMETIA   BRECON   ?CALCHVYNYDD?   Cambridge

GLOUCESTER   Luton   COLCHESTER

GLEVISSIG   GWENT   CIRENCESTER   DUNSTABLE
VERULAMIUM

Abingdon

BATH   LONDON

WANS DYKE   SILCHESTER   Kent

DUMNONIA   SALISBURY   WINCHESTER
CHICHESTER   South
Saxons

50 mls
80 kms

British, as BATH.   English, as Luton.

209

notices elsewhere of some of the kings they name. Only two Roman *civitates* are known, the Ordovices and the Decangi, or Deceangli, perhaps separated by the Conway. The kingdom of Powys was detached from the Cornovii of Shropshire and Staffordshire early in the fifth century, and soon the conquests of Cunedda overlaid older boundaries. Tradition also gives Cunedda many sons, some with Roman and some with native names. Other tales suggest that though Ceretic, Marianus and Einiaun may literally have been his descendants, some or all of the others are as likely to have been his subordinate district rulers. Gildas' contemporary account describes the same kind of dynastic warfare in the north as the Llandaff texts report among the kings of Glevissig. The furniture of well-to-do Roman life is much less evident than in the south, but some traces survive of civil government. One inscription, west of the Conway, roughly contemporary with Gildas, records a civil 'magistrate', and gives the country its native name of 'Venedotia', Gwynedd.

Dumnonia

South of the Severn estuary, fainter traditions outline a similar history. The *civitas* of Dumnonia is prominent in all records, but its eastern neighbours disappear, the Durotriges and Belgae of Dorset, Wiltshire and Hampshire. One remarkable earthwork suggests their history. The Wansdyke was thrown up after the late Roman period; and the name the English gave it, Woden's Dyke, implies that they did not know who made it, and found it there before they came. It runs eastward for some sixty miles from the hills opposite Bristol, south of the Avon, till it turns south to point towards Portsmouth, roughly on the former border between the Roman Belgae and the Atrebates. It defends as one unit what had been the territory of three Roman states. The stories of the wars suggest a context for their union. The late fifth-century ruler of the Belgae had enlisted barbarians, fought against Arthur and killed his ally, Gerontius of Dumnonia; and had perhaps also fought and fallen in alliance with the English at Badon. Gerontius' successor Cato is remembered in the tradition of the monks among the most prominent and loyal subjects of Arthur; it may well be that his loyalty was rewarded by the addition of the Belgae and Durotriges to his kingdom, and that the Wansdyke marks the frontier of an enlarged Dumnonia.

The South

The kings of Dumnonia were Cornovii. Their genealogies are scantily preserved, but they indicate that the kingdom was divided among heirs, as in Wales. Only the rulers of the west, where the language persisted, are distinctly remembered. But the genealogies and the Saints' Lives also name a few great kings whom they cannot locate in any part of Wales or the west. Somewhere between the middle Thames and the south coast lay the kingdom of Caradoc

Vreichvras, 'Strong Arm', who is said to have ruled on both sides of the Channel in the mid sixth century. He may have inherited some of the western territories of Cato's Dumnonia. Away from the coast, a little archaeological evidence demonstrates that in the early or mid sixth century, somebody still inhabited Silchester, the capital of the Atrebates; and dykes were dug north-west of the city, facing towards the small English territory about Abingdon.

North of the Thames, English texts record British states. In 577, the English killed three kings and took three 'chesters', Bath, Gloucester and Cirencester. The spelling of the entry is very nearly contemporary with the event. The Chronicler reports victories, and by 'chesters' he meant inhabited walled cities, not empty archaeological ruins. His words imply that the three towns were the capitals of the three kings; they may well have been heirs who partitioned a kingdom that had once been larger, including Gloucester and the Roman *civitas* of the Dobunni.

The Midlands

Further east, the English remembered that they destroyed a British army near Bedford in 571, and followed their victory by marching down the Vale of Aylesbury to the Thames. A south midland state and army existed. The Welsh poets knew a king Catraut, whose kingdom Calchvynydd, the 'hill(s) of limestone or chalk', lay to the south of Powys; one dubious text locates it between Trent and Thames; and late medieval Welshmen believed that it included the towns that in their time were called Dunstable and Northampton. Both of these towns lie within the Roman *civitas* of the Catuvellauni, whose civil capital, Verulamium, prolonged sophisticated Roman building techniques to the end of the fifth century or later; Verulamium is one of the few major Roman towns of the south-east where extensive excavation has noted no sign of fifth or sixth century English settlement; the nearest English were established around Luton and Dunstable, where the apparent signs of British military and royal power have been uncovered. If further discoveries confirm the implications of present evidence, the likely inference is that the armed forces were strategically sited near to the English villages and far from the Roman city; the magistrates of the Catuvellauni were perhaps less overawed by the power of the army than their fellows further west.

London and Colchester also show no trace of permanent English settlement before the end of the sixth century. The British of London imported a few mediterranean wares, and traded with Roman Gaul, until the Franks annexed it; and tradition gives the Roman name of Colchester to a principal residence of Arthur. Present evidence argues that both remained British. The tradition of Arthur's campaign in Lindsey implies a belief that he recovered most of Lincolnshire, and the Welsh poems prolong the independence of the Cornovii in Shropshire and Staffordshire to the middle of the seventh century. The poets sing only of their last military hero, and his warband, but recent excavation at

Wroxeter has uncovered well-built timber houses constructed in the Roman architectural tradition over the ruins of the Roman town centre, the homes of civilian British who lived in the city.

The evidence now available does little more than signal where the British lived in Gildas' time. Most of the archaeological discoveries are quite new, their meaning still uncertain; but many are the result of new methods of enquiry, that may soon show something of how the successor states were organised, and how far those in the lowlands differed from their better-known western neighbours. Already the new evidence suggests that in the lowlands men lived more comfortably than the texts make known; though Roman technology was forgotten, the men who worked in perishable materials were craftsmen of considerable skill. Their kings made war, as in the west; and the rulers of the Cornovii and of Cirencester at least seem to have garrisoned their frontiers with English federates. But, whatever the difference, all these states grew from the same political context, the final disappearance of a central imperial government and of the economy on which it had rested. Though urban life might be stronger in some towns than in others, all towns were feeble echoes of their past, full of ruins that men could not or would not repair. Though the authority of civil magistrates lasted longer in some states than in others, the power of the military was everywhere growing. Roman society was dead. The controls of ordered government were gone, and force was the only law.

The empire of Arthur had recovered and reunited almost all of Roman Britain. Though its governors, magistrates and other officials persisted into the middle decades of the sixth century, political power devolved upon military successor states, each of them small and independent, each liable to fragment by partition among heirs, each unsure of its legality and permanence, each exposed to the intemperate ambition of its neighbours. The power of each ruler depended upon his armed retinue, and upon his ability to feed his men and supply them with arms and horses. He could secure the necessary income only by extracting it from his own impoverished subjects, or by plundering other kingdoms. Since the business of an armed force is fighting, the logic of each king's immediate needs impelled him to attack his fellows. The new dynasts of Britain were as grave a threat to the peace of their countrymen as were the dynasts in Ireland. The peasant cultivator risked either the requisition of his crop and stock by his own ruler, or its seizure or destruction by the invading army of a neighbour state. Noblemen who retained some property faced the same risks, and were exposed to insult and injustice at the hands of needy rulers. Conservative opinion looked back with envy on the ancient stability of the empire, and its more recent revival by the victors of Badon. Gildas voiced their protest, calling for the overthrow of the new rulers, pleading for a change of heart among his countrymen, warning of the vengeance that the Lord would otherwise raise against them.

The North

North of the Trent, the conflicts of the late sixth century are the theme of contemporary poets, and are remembered in later English tradition. But events before the 570s are chiefly known from the genealogies. The poems identify the districts where many of the later kings ruled; the genealogies trace and date their evolution from a single Pennine sovereign, Coel Hen, Coel the Old, dated to the early fifth century. His name did not pass into living oral usage; it was transmitted in writing, and its origin is Latin, deriving from Coelius, or perhaps Coelestius. The lands ruled by his heirs comprise the whole of the region garrisoned in Roman times by the troops of the *Dux Britanniarum*; and it is possible that Coel was the last regularly appointed *dux*.

Nearly all the other people listed have ordinary personal names, and most of them are mentioned in other texts. A few are manufactured from places, but even they say something of their tradition. Coel's 'wife', Stradwawl (Wall Road) and his 'daughter' Gwawl (The Wall), named as the wife of Cunedda, confirm his date, and show that his authority was held to have extended to Hadrian's Wall.

These traditions make Coel the elder contemporary of Vortigern, ruler of the north when the English first came. Early English settlements were few in the north, confined to parts of the East Riding, to York itself, and to the forces of Octha and Ebissa, that Vortigern despatched to the 'regions about the Wall' when Cunedda moved south to Wales. One English tradition echoes a belief that the rebellion of the 440s extended to the north, and asserts that about the middle of the fifth century the Deirans, the English of the East Riding, 'separated' themselves from the rest of the north, whose only effective authority was then the British ruler of York.

The rebellion was contained, and its impact in the north was less catastrophic than in the south; the English were fewer, the wealth to be plundered was less, and the British were better armed. But it permanently disrupted one vital region. The principal English forces were stationed in the East Riding, in place of its former garrison, the 'Anticipators' of Malton, with their coastal watch-towers. They were put there because those were the rich lands that invited raiders and needed defence, the only part of the north where the comfortable landlord economy of the villas flourished. When the English rebelled, they destroyed that economy. It included almost all the known northern pottery kilns, whose products had supplied the northern forts, and Hadrian's Wall. Their production ceased, and such local wares as may have replaced them have not yet been recognised.

The rebels evidently held out for a considerable time. They were eventually subdued, for their cemeteries at York seem to have gone out of use well before the end of the fifth century, and for more than a century there is no more sign of an independent English power. The English of the East Riding stayed within the borders of two tiny regions, and the little evidence of farms and villages within them suggests that there the English and the British lived side by side, at peace after the revolt.

The first dynasty to branch off from the line of Coel is dated to the years of the revolt itself, about the 440s. The descendants of Germanianus ruled a kingdom that was probably located between Tyne and Tweed, the territory that the British knew as Bryneich, the English as Bernicia. Its Roman garrison had been overwhelmed long before, in 367, and not restored. It was replaced by a *praefectus*, commanding native forces, whose heir was Cunedda; and about the time of Cunedda's departure, English garrisons were installed. No source says whether they rebelled or not; but the appointment of Germanianus sufficed to prevent or suppress rebellion. Little more is heard of the Bernician English until the later sixth century, and their cemeteries altogether lack the grave goods of the south; no more than an occasional knife identifies a few of their graves as English, and suggests that some other similar burials and burial grounds, with no knife to prove their nationality, may also be English. Further west, not even cemeteries are known; the only traces of the early English are a few place names, several of them described as the homes of Frisians.

Germanianus seems to have been installed in the lands Cunedda left, among the southern Votadini. Their probable headquarters was the great prehistoric hill-fort of Yeavering Bell, by Wooler, inland from Bamburgh, south of the Tweed; for at its foot the English kings later established a royal centre, and the choice of so windy and uncomfortable a site is not easily explained unless it were already a centre of government. Germanianus owed his authority to Coel; and whether or not he was a blood relative, the idiom of the genealogists made him a son, because in their day authority passed from father to son. He is as likely to have been an officer commanding a force permanently detached by Coel or his successor to hold the north-east coast.

The territories of the *dux* remained intact till the end of the fifth century. Then the lands west of the Pennines became a separate kingdom, called Reged, and in the next generation it split into a northern and southern portion, roughly corresponding to the future Lancashire, and to Cumberland with Westmorland. Lancaster, or Ribchester, and Carlisle were their principal fortified towns, and southern Reged may have approximately coincided with the Roman province of Valentia. At about the same time as the division of Reged, somewhere about the 530s or 540s, the remainder of Coel's inheritance was partitioned into three kingdoms. Eleutherius of the Great Army was father of Peredur 'Steel Arm' of York; tradition characterises their armies as 'spearmen', and thereby suggests that they included a larger force of infantry than other rulers. Keidyaw was father of Gwendoleu, who ruled by the western end of the Wall, north of Carlisle, and of two other sons. Keidyaw was perhaps master of the whole line of the Wall, and divided his inheritance between his sons. The third region passed to Pabo, Pillar of Britain; one of his sons, Donatus or Dunawt, named Dent, in northernmost Yorkshire, and another, Samuel, apparently reigned in the southern Pennines. Pabo probably ruled all or most of the Pennines, and also divided his kingdom between his sons.

The authority of Coel prompted other rulers, far beyond the Roman frontier, to claim descent from him. Kynvelyn, or Cunobelinus, of Edinburgh, and Guallauc of Lennox, whose name perhaps means the 'man of the Wall region', denoting the Antonine Wall from Forth to Clyde, are both intruded into the Coel pedigrees; but the intrusion is awkward, for in both cases the generations are misplaced, and the names of districts and peoples are transformed into persons. But the intrusions may echo early tradition, for neither of these rulers derives from the dynasties established beyond the frontier, and they may have acquired their kingdoms as allies, perhaps as dependants, of the heirs of Coel. Tradition firmly groups the three armies of York, of Reged and of Kynvelyn of Edinburgh as natural allies, who ought to fight together, and were invincible when they did; it gives their armies distinct names that may translate the titles of late Roman army units. The tradition implies a belief that Kynvelyn brought an army from York to seize and hold Edinburgh.

The intervention of the Pennine powers beyond the Roman frontier has a context in local tradition. Bishop Jocelyn's unctuous medieval Life of Saint Kentigern of Glasgow claims to be an edifying modernised portrait, strained from crude originals that the author despised and could not understand. The meaning of some of its particulars is explained by other texts, in Gaul and Britain, that treat of Kentigern and his times. It preserves a story of important change about the 540s. North of the Tweed, Votadinian territory extended to *Manau Gododdin*, the 'Manau of the Votadini', whose name is preserved in Clackmannan, below Stirling, by the lowest crossing-place of the Forth, and in a few other place names. South of the Forth, the Lothians take their name from Leudonus, who was held to have reigned in the late fifth century in the northern Votadinian capital of Traprain Law, a fortress as large as Yeavering Bell; and his descent is traced from a prefect installed by the emperor Valentinian. On the Clyde Dyfnwal, the successor of king Ceretic, the contemporary of Patrick, was the heir of another of Valentinian's prefects. Wisps of memory indicate that he was a mightier king than most, and the genealogists make him succeed Germanianus as ruler of the southern Votadini, in or about Arthur's time. A Clyde king who ruled by the Tweed as well must also have made the Lothians tributary.

Dyfnwal's enlarged kingdom did not endure. In the 540s, his grandson ruled on the Clyde, and bishop Jocelyn's sources told him that the country, which he knew by the medieval name of 'Cambria', extending 'from sea to sea, like the Wall built long ago by the emperor Severus' was seized by a king called 'Morken', aided by his arrogant subordinate, 'Cathen'. Both names are listed by the genealogists. About the middle of the sixth century, Caten was the reigning descendant of Leudonus, and Morcant Bulc was the heir of Germanianus. Both names are altogether exceptional; Caten is almost unique, and though Morgan later became and remains a much-used name, Morcant Bulc is the earliest individual known to have borne it. The tradition of the genealogies hints at what happened. Dyfnwal of the Clyde had mastered both Votadinian kingdoms; in the 540s, both Votadinian kings rebelled as allies and overran the Clyde, expelled Dyfnwal's heirs and occupied his kingdom.

Morcant's conquests were also short-lived. By about 560 Riderch Hael, heir of the expelled Clyde kings, had recovered his throne; his neighbours and allies included Mordaf, uncle of Caten, and Nud, perhaps ruler of Dumfries and Peebles, on his southern border. He is also given a fourth ally, Clytno, son of Kynvelyn of Edinburgh, the ally of York. It was plainly the interest of the rulers of York and of Hadrian's Wall to prevent the consolidation of a large Votadinian state on their northern border; and Riderch evidently profited from rivalries within the Lothian dynasty, that echo conflicts between uncle and nephew, akin to those that Gildas deplored in north Wales and Dumnonia and that the Llandaff texts report in south Wales.

The story of Riderch's restoration is reported in scattered fragments, that make no sense until they are placed side by side. The story of his wars thereafter is reported in a precise, coherent Welsh account. Elidyr, a king of the Reged dynasty, probably of Lancashire, son-in-law of the great Maelgwn of Gwynedd, sought to wrest Gwynedd from Maelgwn's son Rhun, probably about 560. He came by sea to the Menai Straits, but was killed by his landing place, near Caernarvon. He is not reported to have been aided by the York or Pennine kings, but Riderch and his northern allies sailed to Gwynedd to avenge him. They had a direct motive, for Rhun's brother Bridei had become king of the Picts; the combination of the power of Gwynedd with the hereditary enemies of the British of the Clyde and Forth was a threat to the whole north. In invading Gwynedd the northern kings might hope to forestall the danger. But the allies did not succeed. They burnt Arvon and withdrew. They had shown their striking power, and it was doubtless wise not to stay until Rhun was able to concentrate his forces.

Rhun's reply was his march to the Forth. It brought aid and comfort to his brother and the Picts. It was also a powerful and decisive demonstration of strength, a threat far stronger than a naval raid. The army of Gwynedd was an infantry force accustomed to fight in the narrow space of their native hills. Their long march became a legend among their own people, for they are said to have stayed away so long that their wives 'slept with their bondservants'. A king who could raise a levy of his subjects and keep them under arms for a long time in distant lands was beyond the reach of the smaller retinues of the northern princes. His army must have marched either by York or, more probably, by Carlisle. He is not said to have met resistance and one report argues that he did not. His route necessarily passed through Lancashire. Elidyr's son and successor was Llywarch Hen, then very young. He is widely famed as a poet, greatest of the 'amateur' bards of early Wales, but is nowhere honoured as a great warrior. Instead, he is numbered among the 'passive princes', who did not assert their fathers' inheritance. He died in extreme old age, a refugee in Powys, after the English had overrun his kingdom; but the time when his father's inheritance needed to be asserted was in his youth, when Rhun marched through his kingdom. He or his advisers evidently deemed it wiser to allow Rhun free passage than to attempt vain resistance, inviting the enemy to waste their lands.

The kings of York and the Pennines are also not reported to have intervened. They perhaps reached agreement, for Rhun is said to have married the king of York's cousin. Agreement was prudent, for Rhun's march proved him to be as powerful as his father, perhaps more so. He was military master of northern Britain from the Trent to the borders of his brother's Pictish kingdom. He left a great name. The tradition of the northern poems remembered the hosts of Gwynedd and of Maelgwn as the pre-eminent military power of the past; but in his own land, the foremost of the medieval Welsh poets, Cynddelw, described Gwynedd not as 'the land of Maelgwn', but as 'the land of Rhun'; and the Roman fort that commands the two halves of Gwynedd, Caer Rhun on the Conway, bears his name and not his father's.

Rhun appears to have withdrawn undefeated, satisfied to have shown his strength. His withdrawal floodlights the political weakness of the British. Though he was militarily supreme, he did not and could not consolidate his gains into a large kingdom, like his Irish contemporary Diarmait, or like the English kings of the next century. His army was composed of his subjects in Gwynedd, and it caused wonder that they stayed away from home as long as they did. They were not professional soldiers who could be imposed as standing garrisons upon conquered territory. Nor was there any body of opinion in the lands through which Rhun marched that could constitute a government to rule for him. The dislike of kings that Gildas voiced extended at least as much to the all-powerful stranger as to the local ruler, perhaps more so, and Rhun was heir to the hatreds that Maelgwn had aroused as well as to the armies he had trained. The British had no obvious need to unite behind a powerful monarch, for there was as yet no hint of danger from the English. The tiny impoverished Bernician population of the north Northumbrian coast, and the few small Deiran communities about Market Weighton and Driffield in the East Riding, were in the 560s still insignificant, politically and militarily. No external threat prompted a sense of national unity among the cultivators who tilled the soil of the northern kingdoms. Each of them was ruled by the 'military companions' of 'ill-starred generals'. The northern poems vividly express the outlook of faithful warriors, each devoted to the personal triumphs of their own lord, their highest duty to support him against his neighbours, their deepest disgrace to desert him. No sentiment urged them to join one another in the service of a greater captain; to do so, most warbands must first betray their chief.

The new monarchies were to become the nucleus of medieval kingdoms; but in the sixth century they were recognisably rooted in the Roman past. Arthur had restored the familiar institution of a sovereign emperor, who appointed generals and maintained a centralised civilian administration. The generals remained, but the remnants of the administration were fast fading, and the centralised authority was gone for ever. Yet the kingdoms of the generals were still bunched into groups marked off from each other by the political frontiers they had inherited from Rome. Between the Walls, the descendants of the fourth-century Roman prefects knew that they were British, alien to the barbarian Picts and Scots. The Pennine kingdoms were still grouped as descendants of Coel, joint heirs of the Roman army of the north. The political boundaries of Wales, and of the south and south-west, had been chopped and changed by Irish conquest and then by reconquest, under the new dynasties of Cunedda and the Cornovii; but the chopping and changing left some of the older boundaries intact, amalgamated some states, fragmented others, and the process of fission and fusion continued. In the lowlands, frontiers were less disturbed. Even where English settlement was dense, the borders of Kent and of the East Angles, of Lincolnshire and of the Middle Angles, did not greatly differ from the frontiers of Roman Cantium, of the Iceni, and of the Coritani of Lincoln and Leicester. Further east, the midland Cornovii and the Dobunni, the Atrebates and the Catuvellauni maintained their capitals and their identity, though most of their old names passed from memory. But the lowland states now formed a compact and distinct group. The government of Arthur had cleared the independent English from many regions, but suffered them to remain, in numbers, all along the right bank of the Trent, from Derbyshire to the Humber. But no English crossed the river. The Trent became a frontier, and its English garrison in practice shielded both their own kinsmen and the British of the lowlands from the armies of the British north.

In all the British states, the military power was dominant. Theirs was the system of government that Gildas attacked. The inbuilt pressures of the new kingdoms drove them to wars against each other, and to internal dynastic struggle. The best that could be done was to limit the frequency and ferocity of their wars. In some regions they were limited. Columba stilled the far north, and after Rhun's triumphant march, there is little to record of warfare in most of Wales and the southern Pennines. But in the north-west, the Annals and the poems report successive battles. The most celebrated was fought in 573, at Arderydd, now Arthuret, ten miles north of Carlisle, near to the Roman fort of Netherby. It was the subject of an extensive group of poems, now lost, known only through obscure allusions in much later mystic verses. Though the verses are principally concerned with the consequences of the battle, the identity of the two forces is clear. It was a battle between different branches of the Coel dynasty. The kings of York combined with Dunaut of the Pennines to destroy their cousin Gwendoleu, who ruled in the Carlisle region.

Gwendoleu was defeated and killed, but it was not the victors who benefited. The armies that marched from York to Carlisle were no more able to exploit their success than those which Rhun had led to the Forth. But when they withdrew, they left a vacuum, and nearer neighbours filled it. The principal burden of the surviving poems is the sorrow of Gwendoleu's bard Myrddin, who hid in Celidon forest, in these verses apparently the upland between Dumfries and Peebles, fearing and hating a king who favoured monks and frowned on bards. But the king he feared was not Dunaut or Peredur of York, who had fought the battle, but Riderch of the Clyde. The leader of the monks whom Riderch favoured was Kentigern, who had returned from long exile abroad and now established an important monastery at Hoddam, by Ecclefechan near Dumfries. Riderch had extended his frontiers to annex the greater part of south-western Scotland. It was the first such annexation of territory that proved permanent, for Riderch's gains laid the foundation of the large kingdom that was in the future to be known as Strathclyde. Unlike most British kingdoms, it was not subdivided on the deaths of kings, and later rulers much enlarged its dominion, maintaining its independent power until it was merged with the Scot kingdom of Albany in the 11th century.

Riderch's conquests endured, but in 573 the greatest gainer was Urien of northern Reged, whose royal residence lay close to the borders of Cumberland and Westmorland. He became lord of Carlisle, and probably also secured control of much of the northern coast of the Solway Firth. Urien was immortalised by his bard Taliesin, the earliest of the Welsh poets whose works survive. His adventurous daring won successive victories over his neighbours and made him chief among the kings of the British in the few years that remained before the outbreak of the second Saxon revolt in the north, in and after 580.

British Political Society

About 540, Gildas protested at a new and growing evil; upstart generals had usurped the functions of civil government, and they and their retainers ought to be abolished. By the time he died, thirty years later, the military kingdoms had taken root, and civil government was dead. Though some sections of the old administration were to prove adaptable, the fledgling kings of Britain had no native example to teach them kingship, for the institutions of their past embodied obedience to imperial sovereignty, and failed them when the sovereign was no more. The only available model of independent kingship was Irish, for Rome had obliterated all memory of earlier British kings. The embryo courts of sixth-century Britain reproduced something of the manners of the Irish kingdoms. Ceretic of the Clyde in the fifth century, and Maelgwn of Gwynedd in the sixth, maintained court musicians, as Irish kings kept poets and harpists, to celebrate their deeds and to embroider legends of the mythological past; and the mythology that survived into medieval Welsh tales is chiefly Irish, for little of the Celtic legends of Britain had outlived Roman civilisation. The kings housed their warriors in halls and in Roman and pre-Roman forts in the highlands; but in much of the lowlands Roman town walls afforded the equivalent of the great raths of Ireland. In south Wales and parts of Dumnonia small defended homesteads match the accounts of the little lordships of Glevissig; and one small stronghold, near Dinas Powys, by Cardiff, still bears the name of one sixth-century local lord; its thorough excavation, clearly reported, offers the best evidence yet available of how the smaller *duces* lived.

The structure of Irish kingship was hierarchical. Some of the greater British kings seem to have achieved a short-lived overkingship; Maelgwn and Rhun in Wales and the north-west, Dyfnwal and Riderch between the Walls, the Demetian kings in south Wales exercised a kind of supremacy, for which the later Welsh coined the word *Gwledic*, ruler of the country; such authority might have matured into a superior kingship, if successive generations had had time to consolidate it; and it may be that some of the kings of Dumnonia and of York exercised a similar regional supremacy. But its growth was hindered by the custom of divided inheritance. The Irish royal hierarchy turned upon their practice, similar to that of the Goths in Europe, of passing an undivided territory to one member of the dynasty; and some of the Irish kingdoms passed from father to son in many successive generations. British practice varied. Some of the greater kingdoms most open to Irish influence, Demetia, the Clyde, and Gwynedd after Maelgwn, adopted the Irish model, but in most of the smaller kingdoms British heirs, like the Franks in Gaul, divided their inheritance, and with the same result; a king who tried to bequeath or to inherit an undivided realm was liable to be challenged to battle by outraged relatives, whose claims were approved by public opinion. The consequent repeated changes in the size and power of lesser states prevented the formation of any regular hierarchy below the greater rulers; though some came near to the status of Irish provincial kings, they could acknowledge no sovereign superior, and could not organise the local kings below them.

But the British kings did not acquire their revenues in the manner of the Irish. The Roman past offered a better model. Like the Irish kings, Maelgwn and other British rulers levied a tribute of cattle, corn and other dues. In Ireland each lesser king was required to deliver dues to his superior, and to receive gifts in return. Payment depended on continuing loyalty, and loyalty was enforced by obliging the lesser king to deposit one or more of his sons as hostages at the court of his superior. The British kings found more efficient means of levying tribute; the stories of the Welsh monks are stuffed with dramatic miracles whose occasion is the visit of royal officers demanding tribute and maintenance for their men.

The laws of medieval Wales detail the functions of such officers, and some of them are recognisably Roman. Late Roman military commanders were entitled to receive fixed quantities of *annona*, supplies and maintenance, whose collection was supervised by *erogatores*, armed with warrants authorising the requisition of stated commodities from named villages. In fifth-century Gaul the Goths were billeted on landowners by Roman law, and received *annona* also collected by *erogatores*. In Gaul and Italy, the title and the function of the *erogator militaris annonae* long outlasted the days of the emperors; and in fifth-century Britain

Gildas describes the supplies due to the English federates by the technical term *annona*. There is little doubt that in Britain too they were collected through *erogatores*.

In medieval Welsh law the revenue officers were termed *Cais*. The word is formed from *ceisio*, to ask, seek, search for, and is the linguistic equivalent of the Latin *erogator*, 'a person who asks' for revenue on behalf of the state. Like the *erogator*, the *cais* visited each district in turn to collect its stated tribute, in a circuit called *cylch*. The tributes were those which the Saints' Lives condemn, a 'cornage' of miscellaneous foodstuffs, with a cow payment, and *dofraeth*, billeting and maintenance. But the Welsh system is not confined to Wales; it persisted until the 12th century throughout northern England from Cheshire to Northumberland and Durham, and in the Clyde kingdom, and was accompanied by much Welsh land tenure. The term *cais* was commonly Englished as *Keys*, or was translated by 'serjeant'; and the serjeant made similar circuits, collecting cornage, cowgeld and maintenance.

The elements of the system are simple, and might naturally arise in a simple society. But they differ radically from the practice of the rest of England; and when identical customs and identical terms are found in Wales, northern England and southern Scotland, then it is evident that their origin dates back to a time before these territories were separated from each other by English conquest, in the late sixth century. They already existed within a hundred years of the days when *erogatores* collected *annona* for the army that Coel commanded in northern Britain. It is probable that Coel and his heirs continued the fiscal system of the late Roman army, and thereby provided a model for other British kings to imitate.

The pale image of a Roman financial administration was no new burden to the north, for the north had always fed an army. But in the rich lands about the lower Severn something of the sophisticated life of Roman country gentlemen had escaped the furnace of the wars; there the imposition of tribute by an arrogant military tyrant from the mountains of Snowdonia seemed outrageous. Gildas spoke for civilised men who were disgusted by the theatrical violence of unrestrained military rulers. Protest was keener in south-east Wales, and across the estuary in north Somerset and beyond, areas where Roman practice lingered, and where the new monarchy was still weak and undeveloped. Demands for tribute turned a generalised resentment into a personal grievance. The stark brutality of the kings destroyed even the remnant of ancient virtue that Arthur's victory had salvaged from the wars. Royal exactions hit landowner and tenant alike; royal corruption of justice threatened the liberty of both, and royal control of venal bishops degraded their church.

Protest grew quickly stronger during the 530s. Its pressure impelled Gildas to write; and he explains his hesitation.

> I deplore the general dissipation of the good, and the mounting
> force of evil. . . . I have kept silent for ten years or more, aware of

my own inadequacy. . . . Can I tell myself that it is my business to withstand the violent assault of the torrent, the all-pervading rope of crimes tautened over so many years? But 'there is a time to keep silence, and a time to speak', . . . and I have yielded to the pious entreaties of my brethren.

Gildas' manifesto focused the grievances of many men, and resentment exploded into a mass movement. Gildas denounced the evils of society in the hope that men might be stirred to remedy them. But his readers did not share his optimism. In Britain, as elsewhere, there had long been a few who admired and imitated the principle and practice of the monks of Egypt, and withdrew from a corrupt society to seek personal communion in the desert with their God. In the years immediately after the publication of Gildas' book tens of thousands followed their example. Men left their homes to settle elsewhere, away from the dominion of the tyrants, either overseas, or nearer home, under the protection of holy monks; and the weight of public opinion compelled tyrants to respect those whom the monks received. The movement matured soonest and strongest in the lower Severn lands. It was not confined to those who took monastic vows. They were its centre and its impetus, but numerically they were few; the monks who moved were accompanied by men of property and standing, and by large numbers of harassed cultivators. Gildas expressed the contempt and anger that men already entertained for governments shown to be criminally irresponsible. His readers did not undertake its reform. They wrote it off as sick beyond hope of recovery, and abandoned it to its fate.

The Plague

The enfeebled economy of Britain was wasted by the great plague. The pestilence killed Maelgwn about 550, and many monks and kings in Britain and Ireland are reported to have died of the infection at the same time. It was bubonic plague and was the central disaster of mid sixth-century Europe and the mediterranean. It began in Egypt in 541 or 542, and reached Constantinople in 543, whence it ravaged 'the whole Roman empire'. Gregory of Tours, then a child in the Auvergne, narrowly escaped infection in November, probably of 544; he records its sweep through central and southern Gaul in 544 and 545, naming places that lie along the trade routes to the upper and middle Rhine, but neither he nor any other writer extends it to the lower Rhine, or to northern or north western Gaul. The Irish Annals put the first outbreak in Ireland in 544, but assign the heaviest mortality to its backlash, the relapsing fever called the 'Yellow Plague', at its worst in 550 and 551. The traditions of Brittany report it as much less severe in their land, for they have several stories of plague refugees who came to Brittany for safety, and others of earlier British immigrants who hurried home to help their distressed countrymen in Wales and Cornwall.

The geography of the plague in Europe shows the way in which it reached Britain. Contemporary notices tell incidental stories of sea-borne trade between western Britain and Europe and the eastern mediterranean in the sixth century. An Egyptian Saint's Life concerns the voyage of a merchantman that imported lead from Britain, presumably from Cornwall or the Severn estuary; central Ireland imported wine, and a ship of Gaul brought news of Italy to Kintyre; vessels of Nantes were regularly 'engaged in the Irish trade'; though many of the saints who sailed abroad are made to float on leaves and stones, others are prosaically recorded to have paid their fares to commercial shipowners. The archaeological evidence matches the texts. Several details of the style and wording of British inscriptions argue influence from central Gaul and the Bordeaux area. A number of excavated monasteries and royal residences in south-western Britain, Ireland and south-western Scotland contained pottery imported from Egypt and southern Gaul. It is evident that the ships which brought the pottery and the wine also brought the rats that spread the plague.

The plague hit the Irish and the British, but not the English. Texts and archaeology explain their immunity. Gildas emphasises that the British were altogether unable to visit the shrines of martyrs 'because of the unhappy partition' of Britain; the British did not journey into English areas. The silence of the Saints' Lives concurs. A couple of Irish stories record Irishmen who preached to pagan Saxons, both of them before the outbreak of the plague; there is little record of British monks among the English except for a single journey, placed in the 590s; and thereafter several continental writers record their astonishment, at the extravagant refusal of the British to have any dealings with the English, refusing even to dine or lodge with them in Rome, or when they met in Britain. Gildas shared their attitude; it never occurred to him that the British should attempt to convert the heathen; instead, he sighed for a Gideon to exterminate them.

The English escaped from infection from the British, because the British refused to have contact with them. They escaped infection from Europe because they did not import from plague-infected areas. What trade they had is indicated by their grave goods; their imports were the ornaments and weapons of northern and north-eastern Gaul, and of the Franks of the lower Rhine. These are the regions which Gregory omits from his account of when and where the plague was rampant. The lack of contact cannot of course have been absolute, but there is no reason to suppose that the disease ever took hold upon the main body of the English. Their simpler life offered greater immunity, for, as an acute contemporary observed of 6th-century Africa,

> plague favours war and does not harm the rough races.

There it spared the Moors and devastated the Roman population. In Britain and Ireland its impact burnt itself into the memory of later ages. It was plainly as crippling and weakening as it was in southern Gaul and in the mediterranean, and there it wasted the population on a scale that compares with the plague of 1348. In Britain it infected a people who were already enfeebled and dispirited by the decay of their political government. It was the prelude to the second rebellion of the English. But it was not the cause of the British collapse, for other societies survived fearful pestilence, then and at other times. At most, the plague hastened the dissolution of states that were already dying of a deadlier disease, the rotting of their own society.

CHAPTER THIRTEEN
BRITISH COLLAPSE

The South

The second Saxon revolt did not mature until the 570s, but its first stirrings began immediately after the plague. The Saxon Chronicle reports that Cynric put the British to flight at Salisbury in 552; in 556 he fought them again at Barbury, thirty miles to the north, near Swindon, but no victory is reported, and he is not said to have advanced further. English tradition is sharp, and sure of its names and dates, for the entries in the Saxon Chronicle begin to be confirmed by other evidence from the middle of the sixth century. The dates, though still approximate, are reckoned backwards from the living memory of a literate age and are no longer dependent upon a mistaken date for the landing of Hengest and Horsa. But tradition still had no clear idea of the meaning and context of the events it chronicled.

The Saxon Chronicle naturally took Cynric for an Englishman, and was substantially right, for his men were English. But his own name is Irish, and so is his successor's; for the same two names occur together on an Irish inscription from Wroxeter, that was probably erected a generation or two earlier in honour of other people of the same name. Cynric may or may not have been a son or grandson of his Irish namesake, but the men who served under him were not Irish. A small English population had lived in eastern Hampshire since the fifth century, and the ornaments in their graves indicate that many or most of them had come from Sussex. A few of their cemeteries came into use in the immediate neighbourhood of Salisbury towards the middle of the sixth century, perhaps some decades earlier than 550; and their ornament soon spread to East Shefford in the Berkshire Downs, 15 miles to the east of Barbury. But it did not yet reach north of the Downs to the English of the middle Thames.

The circumstances that caused an Irish general to lead the English to victory over the British are not known. But they pose no problem. The fifth-century English who had settled near Winchester were suffered to remain in Arthur's time, probably within an enlarged Dumnonia; and the British ruler of Winchester was free to entrust the command of his armies, Germanic and native, to a commander of Irish or any other nationality, and to use them against his neighbour at Salisbury when the Dumnonian kingdom fragmented like other British states in the earlier sixth century. Cynric's victory may have been gained on behalf of one

British ruler against another; or he may have overthrown and replaced his British king, as generals before and since have overturned the governments they served.

At the time, Cynric's campaign may well have seemed no more than another incident in the civil wars that Gildas lamented. But when the victorious army was English, the state soon ceased to be British; and in 560 the command passed to Ceawlin. He is remembered as the first conquering overking of the southern English, but at first he did not attack the British. In 568, he fought in alliance with Cuthwulf, or Cutha, whom the evidence of genealogies and of archaeology seems to locate as leader of the Eslingas of south-western Cambridgeshire. The allies drove back Aethelbert, the young king of Kent, who had tried to break out from his ancestral borders beyond the Medway. His objective is not stated, but it was plainly London. They defended the city against the armies of Kent, but their victory made them military masters of the London region. Yet they did not exploit the victory to establish English colonies in or near the city; for English burial-grounds of the middle and later sixth century are plainly recognisable, but none have been found amid the enormous mass of archaeological material discovered in London and its vicinity. Half a dozen chance finds suggest that a few individual Saxons from Mitcham and Croydon visited the city in the 5th and 6th centuries, some of them perhaps admitted as residents. But their territory is marked by the cemeteries placed near to their homes, and when they expanded their new homes reached south into the Downs, not northwards to the city, for they sought easy agricultural land, not to be found in the London clays and gravels. They too were numbered among the allies of Ceawlin and Cutha, for the ornamental styles favoured in their territories are common in Surrey, whose people were still strangers to the fashions of Kent. London came within the control of English rulers and English armies, but it was not yet peopled with English-speaking inhabitants.

English ambition was directed elsewhere. The Chronicle records that in 571 Cuthwulf routed the British of the midlands, at or near Bedford. His victory mattered more than Cynric's local gains in Wiltshire twenty years before, for he destroyed a once-powerful kingdom, and opened the whole of the midlands to the free movement of the English. He immediately marched down the Vale of Aylesbury to the Thames, where the English of Abingdon had lived for almost 150 years, a small isolated people, surrounded by large territories in which no English had hitherto been able to make their homes. Cuthwulf's arrival liberated the Abingdon English, but he did not become their king. The Thames-side towns that he is reported to have taken, Eynsham and Benson, lie outside their borders, on the opposite bank of the river, as does north Oxford, where he appears to have been buried. He died in the same year, 571, and was succeeded by Cuthwine, also called Cutha for short, who continued in alliance with Ceawlin, and with the Abingdon English. They were known as the *Gewissae*, 'federates' or 'confederates', but they ultimately accepted the national description of Saxon, probably because it was the word used of them by their British neighbours.

The allies marched west, and in 577, at Dyrham, seven miles north of Bath, they killed the British kings of the lower Severn, and took Bath, Gloucester and Cirencester. Badon was avenged, not far from the old battlefield. A second major British territory, formerly the *civitas* of the Dobunni and the *colonia* of Gloucester, was destroyed for ever. Cirencester became English. It had been ringed by English villages for a generation or more; but there was no longer a British king for their inhabitants to defend or threaten. Before the end of the century, not long after the battle, an English warrior was buried within the city, and a few other scraps of archaeology attest the advent of an English population. But beyond the Cotswold escarpment there are no signs of English settlement, in Gloucester or Bath or in between, for another half-century. If any government replaced the kings who fell at Dyrham, they left no trace; and it may be that there was a long interregnum between the end of British rule and the establishment of English authority. The cities are not heard of again for nearly a hundred years; then, when English kings founded monasteries within their walls, Gloucester had a population of 300 families, about 1,000 persons. Nothing is said of their language, but there is little reason to suppose that many of them yet spoke much English.

Ceawlin's campaigns did not stop at the Severn. In 584 he fought the British at 'a place named Fethanlea', and his ally Cuthwine was killed. He is said to have taken many places and much booty, but to have come home 'in anger'. There was a field called Fethanlea near Banbury, but other sites are possible, and include Hereford. But wherever the battle, a strong British and Irish tradition remembers a vigorous English campaign beyond the Severn in the years about 580; and no tradition, British, Irish or English, knows anything of English armies in that region at any earlier time, or for many years thereafter.

A number of independent stories describe the English invasion. In Leinster, in south-eastern Ireland, the Life of Maedoc of Ferns relates that when he was a pupil of David in Demetia

> the English raised a great army and came to Britain. . . . The British assembled quickly against them, and sent to David, to ask him to send them Maedoc. . . . Maedoc came . . . and, since the British were engaging battle ill prepared, Maedoc . . . prayed to God for the British against the English; the English were forthwith put to flight, and the British pursuit lasted for seven days, with great slaughter.

David's death is placed at 589; Maedoc was his pupil for some years, between about 575 and 585.

Another Irish Life recounts the active help of Finnian, a life-long companion of Cadoc at Llancarfan, in the vale of Glamorgan.

> The Saxons invaded and wasted the land of the British. When they were encamped in a valley between high hills, the British besought

> Finnian to pray to the God of Heaven against their enemies. The
> man of God . . . went to the Saxons and urged them to return home
> without attacking other peoples. When they refused, the man of
> God returned to his own side, and said to the British, 'Let us go
> round the hill tops that surround the enemy with my staff'. . . .
> The sequel was marvellous, for the high hills are said to have
> poured down upon the enemy, so that none of them escaped.

The English, unused to the terrain of Wales, were evidently not yet alerted to the
danger of falling boulders prised loose by British staffs. The story carries no
close date, save that Finnian was not greatly younger than Cadoc, who died about
580, and did not long survive him.

Cadoc was the principal saint of Glevissig, roughly identical with the later
Glamorgan; and is also said to have been the secular ruler of its eastern portion.
It had been a land of small lordships, too weak to withstand invasion, and found
itself defenceless before the armies of Maelgwn, and hard-pressed by the kings of
Brecon. In his last years Cadoc is said to have found the secular government too
much for him. He

> prayed the Lord to grant him a king, who should rule his people
> for him, and Mouric, son of Enhinti, was granted him.

Mouric is exceptionally well recorded, in the Llandaff and Llancarfan texts, and
in the genealogies. Enhinti was sister to Urien of Reged, who was then at the
height of his power, conqueror of Powys, his armies dominant from the Cheviots
to the borders of Gwent. Southern Welsh tradition links the new kingdom with
the dynasty of Budic of Quimper, in Armorica, and names Mouric's father,
Theodoric. Theodoric, son of Budic, bore the name of Arthur's naval commander,
who was perhaps his grandfather. The younger Theodoric was a contemporary
of Gregory of Tours, who reports that after spending most of his adult life in
exile in Britain, he briefly regained his throne in advanced years in 577. In
selecting Theodoric's son, Cadoc chose wisely. The new king was heir to a name
already famous on both sides of the Severn Sea, and was also nephew to the most
powerful king in Britain; but he was not a native of his new kingdom, and was
free of the jealousies that must hamper any local lord elevated above his fellows.

Mouric was installed because Glevissig was threatened by British neighbours,
but he soon faced a deadlier enemy from the east. The Llandaff texts tell the
story.

> King Theodoric . . . commended the kingdom to his son Mouric,
> and undertook a hermit's life among the rocks of Tintern. While he
> was living that life, the Saxons began to invade his country, against
> his son Mouric.

An angel bade him leave his cell to aid his people, and promised a victory, after
which the enemy

will not dare to attack this country again for 30 years, during your son's time.

Theodoric was mortally wounded at Tintern Ford, by Brockweir on the Wye, while Mouric pursued the defeated army. When it is freed from its turgid 12th century presentation, the story fits the age; Bede tells a similar tale of king Sigbert of the East Angles, who commended his kingdom to his son half a century later, and was recalled from his cell to aid his people against pagan Mercian invaders.

The Irish and Welsh tales describe the repulse of an English invasion that reached at least as far as the Wye in the early 580s. The English report a westward invasion that began with the battle of Dyrham in 577 and ended with a withdrawal 'in anger' in 584. It is likely that the two versions report the same invasion, that it was Mouric who defeated Ceawlin by Tintern; the various stories do not necessarily all concern the same battle, and there were doubtless several engagements during the course of the war. But the British victory was decisive. The Wye remained and remains the frontier, save for the administrative eccentricity that has treated Monmouthshire as part of England for several centuries. Both the English and the Welsh report no wars for a generation after 584. The Welsh prophecy, made after the event, implies a belief that there were no more attacks for 30 years. The next English report of a battle against the Welsh is dated to 614, exactly 30 years later; that battle was fought against Dumnonians, near Axminster on the Devon–Dorset border, but the Dumnonians and the south Welsh were evidently both attacked together, for the next Welsh report of English wars is an account of an English defeat between Monmouth and Abergavenny, at the hands of king Idon of Gwent, probably in the first years of the seventh century.

Ceawlin's power soon crumbled, and though the 7th-century West Saxon kings overran eastern Dumnonia, they made no inroads into Wales, and were overshadowed in England by the Mercians. But Mouric's kingdom grew great. He began as the local ruler of eastern Glamorgan, probably accepting the status of an under-king within the dominion of Demetia, whence he summoned help against the English; for when the monks sent Maedoc, their king is likely to have sent troops. The Llandaff grants trace the expansion of Mouric's power after his victory. He married the daughter of the king of Gower, and inherited her father's kingdom; towards the end of his reign, the dynasty of southern Gwent disappeared, and his son became king of Gwent, evidently under his father. Though Mouric's kingdom was partitioned on his death, it was speedily reunited by his able and ruthless grandson Morcant. In his time the dynasty of northern Gwent, known as Ercig or Archenfeld, also disappeared, and so did Demetian supremacy; the entries in the Cambrian Annals that record the 'overthrow of Demetia' in 645, and the 'slaughter in Gwent' in 647, perhaps record his victories.

In Morcant's time, control of the lower Severn passed from the West Saxons to the Mercians. Like other Welsh kings, Morcant seems to have been the ally of Mercia, and the enemy of the West Saxons, attempting when he could to recover the lost southern chalklands. In 652 the West Saxon king fought at Bradford-on-Avon, near Bath, against the Mercians or the Welsh. The Dumnonians long held much of Somerset, and when Mercian power was briefly broken in 655, they are said to have been reinforced by British refugees from Lichfield. When the Mercians regained their independence in 658, the British attacked the West Saxons, and probably reached Selwood, barely 25 miles from Salisbury, before they were driven back. The British army may have come from Dumnonia or Glevissig or both; but in 665 the Cambrian Annals record the second battle of Badon and the death of Morcant. They do not say who fought or won the battle, and do not explicitly assert that Morcant fell there. But the record of the half-century from 614 to 655, with two battles near Bath and a British advance towards Salisbury, implies a determined effort by Morcant and the Dumnonian kings to join forces and regain control of the south-west, whenever such attacks did not involve war with Mercia.

Attempts at reconquest failed, and are not reported under Morcant's successors. But the British checked the English advance. Western Dumnonia, modern Cornwall, retained its independence until the Scandinavians came. Morcant's kingdom lasted longer, and lived at peace. His son ruled it for many years without division, and without record of foreign war; though his grandsons partitioned their inheritance, they are not reported to have fought each other, and the last of them lived on until 775. Their long peaceful rule gave their territory an enduring unity. Gwent survives, under the modern name of Monmouthshire, and Glevissig received from a later Morcant its permanent name of Glamorgan. The dynasty of Mouric and Morcant retained for their people one part of the fertile lowland of Britain, the land where Roman letters and Roman manners lingered longest, where Gildas and the reformers had been bred; and their heirs preserved it from annexation by the conquering English.

The North

The story of the south is pieced together from a few perfunctory English annals, supplemented by fragments scavenged from the luxurious legends of Llandaff. The conquered vanished silently, for Ceawlin and his allies permanently destroyed the southern British states within a decade. The capture of Gloucester separated Wales from Dumnonia, and both were effectively contained from the end of the sixth century. The British of the lowlands accepted defeat sooner and more completely than their northern neighbours. Over the next few centuries they abandoned their ancestral language, and absorbed the culture and the speech of the conquerors. The memory of their defeat died with their native speech. But the northerners long retained their language, and clung proudly to their memories, crying their disaster to the heavens in the earliest and noblest vernacular verses of medieval Europe. The lands where civilised Roman life had been most deeply rooted more readily forgot that it had ever been; but the poorer hills, where the rough new monarchies grew strongest, made their defeat the proud foundation of their future nationhood.

The ruin of the northern British and the triumph of the Northumbrians in the late sixth century are described in sources of a quite different kind. The kingdoms of north Wales and of the Clyde received refugees from the Pennine states, who brought with them their poets; posterity preserved their verses in the lands that sheltered them. It is therefore the record of the British that is full, much of it written quite soon after the event, the record of the English that is twisted, broken and distorted, set down long afterwards by men who did not understand what they reported. But the Welsh poems are hard to interpret, precisely because they are contemporary, for the poets took for granted the knowledge that they shared with their readers, without explanation.

The old Welsh poems are of three main kinds. Some, notably the *Canu Taliesin* and the *Canu Aneirin*, are probably of the late 6th and early 7th centuries, and much of the surviving texts are quite possibly the work of the poets to whom they are ascribed; others, particularly the *Canu Llywarch Hen*, are in their present form not earlier than about the 8th century, but include poems that may be modernised versions of older originals; the third and largest group consists of much later poems, full of mystic prophecies, which allude obscurely to older poems that have not been preserved.

Good modern critical editions have been published of the Taliesin, Aneirin and Llywarch poems, and of a very few others, but the text and introduction, notes and commentary are usually available only in modern Welsh, not yet translated into English. Most of the other poems have been published, but only in facsimile or diplomatic form, without critical discussion. Translations of varying quality are available for a few scattered verses from some of the main texts, but none of the longer poems has yet appeared in any but a literal translation. Consequently, a number of the important problems of the texts have not yet been resolved; for a translation with adequate commentary must face historical problems that a literal rendering or a linguistic commentary in Welsh can afford to overlook.

It is therefore not yet possible to make full use of the abundant information about the last age of independent Britain that is embedded in these poems. They deserve and urgently require full study and proper publication, not only as sources of historical information, but because they are the earliest literature written in a living European language, apart from Greek. They constitute one of the chief glories of Wales; but they remain a private and neglected glory until they can be understood and appreciated by men of other speech.

The Saxon rebellion in the north begins with Ida, king of the Bernicians, who lived by the northern coasts of Northumberland. A text preserved by Nennius brackets him with Maelgwn, allots him a twelve year reign, and states that he 'joined *Din Guayrdi*, Bamburgh, to Bernicia', and was opposed by

Outigirn, who is otherwise not known. The Saxon Chronicle therefore enters him at the date the British assigned to Maelgwn, 547, and later versions explain that Bamburgh was built by him, fortified at first by a stockade, thereafter by a rampart. Revolt began with the seizure or construction of a coastal fort, probably between 550 and 570.

Urien

The praises of Outigern, and doubtless of his wars with Ida, appear to have been sung by the poet Talhearn, whose works do not survive. Late verses preserve allusions to poems that described the battle of Arthuret in 573, but the oldest extant poems honour Urien of Reged, who emerged immediately thereafter as the most powerful of the northern princes. In verse, and in the brief entries of Nennius, Urien stands out as the greatest and best-loved prince of his age, chief of the thirteen kings of the north. He is said to have fought on the Clyde, and also to have captured Solomon of Powys, who lived on to die at Chester in 613; his cousin Llywarch is represented as his constant ally, and his arms threatened Calchvynydd 'in the south'. These notices make Urien supreme in the west from Galloway to Shropshire; and his nephew Mouricus was installed as king in Glevissig, on the Severn Sea.

Urien was more than a king who overawed his fellows; he is celebrated as the one British king who organised his neighbours against the English and beat them soundly. He is well remembered because his bard was Taliesin; and Taliesin acclaims him

Urien of Echwyd	most liberal of Christianmen
Much do you give	to men in this world
As you gather,	so you dispense
Happy the Christian bards	so long as you live. . . .
Sovereign supreme	ruler all highest
The strangers' refuge	strong champion in battle.
This the English know	when they tell tales.
Death was theirs	rage and grief are theirs
Burnt are their homes	bare are their bodies.

The poem, like most that Taliesin addressed to Urien, ends with a signature:

> Till I am old and failing
> In the grim doom of death
> I shall have no delight
> If my lips praise not Urien.

These words were probably written while Urien was still alive, and are the oldest living European literature. The idiom is impressionistic, altogether alien to the imagery of English, or of Greek and Latin poetry. It appeals to the ear and the emotions rather than to the eye and the understanding. A line of two or three long words outiines a figure that a Latin or Germanic poet describes in a stanza;

and the resonance of the individual syllables observes a musical notation as strict as the harpist's. The structure of the English language admits no comparable use of words; and translation cannot therefore do more than hint at the force of the original.

Taliesin's poem was written late in Urien's life, when the English had become his main enemy. But in the early 570s, when Urien grew great, the British were still preoccupied with wars against each other, and Urien's rapid victories earned him enemies. The northern English were not yet seen as a greater menace, for they were still confined to their small settlements, tucked away on the north-east coast between Tyne and Tweed, remote from the main centres of British power. Their earlier history is obscured, because the southern editors of the Saxon Chronicle thoroughly misconceived northern history. They treated the two widely separated regions of Deira and Bernicia, the East Riding and the north-east coast, as though they were already the single united Northumbria of later times. They therefore tidied up the distinct records of the two peoples into a neatly dated scheme, that made Aelle of Deira the successor of Ida of Bernicia and the predecessor of Ida's sons. Its confusions persist because the Saxon Chronicle is easy reading, and tempts the uncritical historian to brush aside the evidence that contradicts it.

But the northern evidence is strong enough not only to show that the Chronicle is wrong, but to outline the history it distorted; for other records give the context in which the Welsh poems are set. The Cambrian Annals were better informed than the Saxon Chronicle; so were Bede and his contemporaries, and among them were the authors of the northern genealogies and king lists, who equipped their texts with brief notes and commentaries, some of them probably set down in the 7th century, just within living memory of the events they describe.

All records agree that the English conquest of the north was the work of the Bernicians, not of the stronger and more numerous Deirans. The revolt began when Ida fortified Bamburgh, and thereby proclaimed independence. The date and scope of his wars is uncertain, but it seems probable that he died shortly before the rise of Urien. He is said to have united the Bernicians under a single command, but their unity was not permanent; on his death, their tiny territories were split between several separate leaders. But they are not reported to have fought each other, and one of them, Adda, is said to have destroyed Gurci and Peredur, joint kings of York, at Caer Greu, in 580. The site is not known; but since it was the Bernicians who killed the York kings, not the Deirans, it is probable that the kings had marched north to destroy the growing power of Bernicia, and were killed in Bernicia. Their defeat was as decisive for the north as Cutha's victory had been for the south nine years before. The British kingdom ended with its last kings; and York was necessarily the most important of the British northern states. Peredur's son Gwgaun is remembered in British tradition among the 'passive' chiefs who failed to recover their inheritance, bracketed with Llywarch Hen. With his father's army dispersed, York was undefended.

Hitherto there had been no sign of rebellion by the English of Deira in the East Riding. But their king Aelle is described as an independent sovereign in the pleasant tale of Gregory the Great's encounter with Deiran boys in Rome, dated between 585 and 590, and also by Bede in 597. It is likely that he, or his father, occupied the city when Peredur's army was routed in 580.

The sudden and total destruction of the greatest of the northern British kingdoms compelled its neighbours to unite; and Taliesin's poems describe their response. Urien mastered Catterick, the northern bastion of the lost kingdom. Catterick is the strategic nerve-centre of northern warfare, for it commands Scots Corner, where the road from York branches north-west over Stainmore by the Bowes Pass to Urien's Carlisle, and northward to the Tyne and Bernicia. Its seizure kept the two English kingdoms apart, and defended Urien's Reged against invasion from Deira. English record lists the Bernician rulers of these years, apparently lords of small districts, contemporaries of Adda. Urien fought one of them, who was named Theodoric, after the kings of the Goths and Franks, and killed another, called 'Ulph' by the Welsh, who was perhaps either the Theodulf or the Freothulf of the English lists; but the battleground, 'at the Ford', is not identified. The Bernicians united in face of Urien's assault, and 'Fflamddwyn', the Firebrand, probably the Welsh name for Aethelric, invaded Reged in command of four Bernician armies combined under his sole command. He demanded hostages, but Urien and his son Owain beat him 'on a Saturday morning' in 'Argoed Llwyfein', Leven Forest. The year is not known, and neither is the site. Leven names survive near Bewcastle, near the Roman fort of Netherby, north-east of Carlisle, and also in Furness; Bewcastle is geographically more probable, but other northern rivers, that now have English or Scandinavian names, may have been called Leven in Urien's time.

Urien's elegy calls him the 'Pillar of Britain' and rejoices that he 'overcame Bernicia'. One of Nennius' documents brings him nearer to the stature of a national British leader than any other northern king; and gives detail of his effort to expel the English altogether, of his near success, and of the cause of his failure.

> Hussa reigned 7 years. Four kings fought against him, Urien and Riderch Hen, and Gaullauc and Morcant. Theodoric fought bravely against the famous Urien and his sons. During that time, sometimes the enemy, sometimes our countrymen were victorious, and Urien blockaded them for three days and three nights on the island of Metcaud (Lindisfarne).

The allies were Urien's northern neighbours. Riderch of the Clyde and Guallauc of the upper Forth had been his enemies before; Morcant, whose territory probably included Lindisfarne, was a hereditary enemy of Riderch. Necessity compelled the kings to forget former enmities; but it did not rally all the British north, for the list leaves out the princes of Edinburgh, Dunaut of the northern Pennines, Rhun map Neithon, probably of Selkirk and Peebles, and others. The list is limited to British kings, but other texts add other allies. One Irish story recalls that Aedan of the Dal Riada Scots and king Fiachna of Ulster, who reigned from 589 to 628, fought together against the English; and another Irish story relates that Fiachna took Bamburgh, received hostages, and apparently installed an Irish garrison. The stories cannot concern Aedan's later campaign against the English, when he had different Irish allies. They imply that Urien enlisted Irish as well as British armies, and that the allies took Bamburgh and drove the English from the mainland, to stand siege on Lindisfarne, the offshore island opposite Bamburgh. These stories also indicate the date; it was some time before 593, the year in which Bede begins the reign of Aethelric's successor, for Aethelric outlived Urien; but not earlier than 589, when Fiachna's reign began. The time is therefore very near to 590.

The Bernicians were on the verge of annihilation. They were saved by the discord of the British. The Nennius text continues

> But while he was on the expedition, Urien was assassinated, on the initiative of Morcant, from jealousy, because his military skill and generalship surpassed that of all the other kings.

Tradition names his murderer, Lovan; a variant blames the princes of Edinburgh, whose names the Nennius text markedly omits. But the tales suggest that Morcant's jealousy had an immediate occasion. Bamburgh lay within his territory; it was from him that the English rebels had seized the fort and to him it should return. But when the Irish took the fort and held it as the prize of victory, Urien's consent ceded Morcant's territory over his head.

These are the motives of discord that the surviving evidence implies. If there were more evidence, it would doubtless modify or amplify the causes of the quarrel. But whatever the causes, the murder was fatal to the alliance. The besieging British army disintegrated, the English were saved from extinction, and Taliesin lived to lament the fate of Urien's sons, who were now bound to avenge their father's murder in war against his former allies, and were therefore exposed to the assaults of British enemies as well as of the English. They fought alone, but not in vain. The English recovered from their near disaster, rallied behind Aethelric, and attacked Urien's son Owain. They were heavily defeated, and one of Taliesin's finest poems celebrates the last northern British victory

> When Owain slew Fflamddwyn
>> It was no more than sleeping.
> Sleeps now the wide host of England
>> With the light upon their eyes
> And those who fled not far
>> Were braver than was need. . . .
>
> Splendid he was, in his many coloured armour,
>> Horses he gave to all who asked

> Gathering wealth like a miser
>> Freely he shared it for his soul's sake
> The soul of Owain son of Urien
>> May the Lord look upon its need.

If Fflamddwyn was Aethelric, as is probable, the date is 593. But his death and defeat did not quell the English, for Owain's cavalry might win a battle, but could not on their own expel or exterminate the homes where their young men were born and trained to arms. After the defeat, Aethelric's son Aethelferth permanently united the separate portions of the Bernicians, and soon overwhelmed the north.

Owain died or was killed soon after, for Taliesin's poem is an elegy upon his death, and knows of no later wars or victories. The kingdom of Reged died with him. Its military glory was short-lived, for barely 20 years passed between Urien's early victories and the death of Owain. But Urien's wider vision of British unity and Taliesin's verses have made it the most famed of the British kingdoms. Its fame was earned in their day, and perpetuated by their immediate successors, for Urien's death is the central tragedy of many of the poems attributed to his cousin Llywarch, that were set down in their present form something over a century later. The elegy on Urien's death is vivid.

> The head I carry at my side,
> The head of Urien, the open-handed captain.
> On his pale breast black carrion. . . .

Urien's sister grieves that he was slain by the assassin Lovan at Aber Lleu, the estuary of the Low, that enters the sea opposite Lindisfarne. The Christian armies are now 'a swarm without hive'. Urien's enemies are listed; Dunaut the fierce rider bears down upon his sons, Owain and Pascent, and Guallauc upon his other son, Elphin; Morcant and Bran attack, and the speedy end of Reged is depicted.

> This hearth, wild flowers cover it.
> When Owain and Elphin lived
> Plunder boiled in its cauldron. . . .

> This hearth, tall brambles cover it.
> Easy were its ways.
> Reged was used to giving.

> This hearth, dockleaves cover it.
> More usual upon its floor
> Mead, and the claims of men who drank. . . .

> This pillar and that pillar there.
> More usual around it
> Shouts of victory, and giving of gifts.

The later poet laments a vanished age, the society of the warrior states of the north, that had perished in the relatively recent past. He mourns the death of a kingdom and a stronghold, not the death of an individual king. He does not say who killed Owain or destroyed Reged, but he blames its destruction upon the enmity of its British neighbours. He had no need to point the moral of their folly, for men knew that the fall of Reged had brought them all to ruin. When Owain died, the halls and hearths of Reged died with him, and so did its military force. Aethelferth's strongest enemy was gone, and the defence of the northern Pennines and of Catterick, the strong-point that severed the Bernicians from Deira, necessarily fell to Dunaut. But Dunaut was killed in 597, presumably by the Bernicians.

Catraeth

In the next year, 598, the Annals enter the battle of Catraeth. The powers of the far north made a last attempt to rescue the Pennines. Mynydawc and Cynan of Edinburgh led a northern army to confront the English near Catterick, perhaps within the earthworks of the ancient pre-Roman fortress of Stanwick, in the angle of the strategic road fork at Scots Corner. The gain that victory would have brought is obvious. The army of Edinburgh took the Bernicians in the rear, evidently approaching through Carlisle and down the Bowes pass. At that date Aethelferth had not yet annexed York; Aelle was still king in Deira. His attitude is not known, but he had as much cause as the British kings to fear the power of Bernicians. Victory would have made a British–Deiran alliance possible, with a reasonable hope that the British might prove the stronger partners, and that the allies might again drive the Bernicians into the sea, as Urien had done a few years before. It is possible that the alliance had already been agreed, and that the circuitous march of the Edinburgh armies was designed to make contact with the Deirans, for the British complained of Deiran treachery. But these prospects were not realised. The expeditionary force was annihilated. Its defeat is the theme of the longest and best-known of the early poems, the *Gododdin* of Aneirin, the 'sovereign bard'; the core of the poem was probably composed not long after the battle, and it quickly became a widely loved epic, recited in all surviving British courts, for verses were added during the seventh century that brought into the story the heroes of very many dynasties, some of whom died long before the battle, and some of whom lived many years later.

Aneirin's solemn lines contrast the confident enterprise of the Edinburgh British with the fearful emptiness that followed.

> Men went to Catraeth
> Shouting for battle,
> A squadron of horse.
>
> Blue their armour and their shields,
> Lances uplifted and sharp,
> Mail and sword glinting. . . .
>
> Though they were slain, they slew.
> None to his home returned. . . .

> Short their lives,
> Long the grief
> Among their kin.
>
> Seven times their number,
> The English they slew.
> Many the women they widowed
> Many the mothers who wept. . . .
>
> After the wine and after the mead
> They left us, armoured in mail.
> I know the sorrow of their death.
>
> They were slain, they never grew grey. . . .
> From the army of Mynydawc, grief unbounded,
> Of three hundred men, but one returned.

Aneirin describes a single small cavalry force from one kingdom. It may have been accompanied by allies from other states, but the wide popularity of the poems in other kingdoms, while the expedition was still remembered, guarantees that it formed the core of the expedition. The force was totally destroyed; the army of Edinburgh was eliminated, like the armies of the Pennines. Aethelferth's English were numbered by the thousand; their losses were heavy, but the survivors might march at will to the Forth, to face the kingdoms beyond. The prudent rulers of the Clyde are not reported to have challenged them, but Aedan of Dal Riada prepared to halt the English advance. He sought help from the Irish of the mainland, and Mael Uma, brother of the High-King, brought a task force of shock troops to aid him against the Northumbrians. In 603, at Degsastan, whose site has not been determined, Mael Uma's men overwhelmed and killed Aethelferth's brother, but Aedan was driven from the field, decisively and permanently beaten. Northern resistance was crushed. 'From that time forth', wrote Bede 'no king of the Scots dared face the English in the field.'

Chester

Aethelferth was free to turn south, and in 604 he occupied York and annexed Deira. The children of its royal house escaped; Aelle's son, Edwin, is said to have found refuge with the king of Gwynedd, his relative Heric among the British of Elmet, about Leeds. For ten years, no further wars are reported; but in or soon after 614 Aethelferth attacked north Wales, perhaps in fear that the British might endeavour to restore Edwin. The Northumbrian army marched to Chester and defeated the combined forces of Gwynedd, Powys and the lowland Cornovii. Over a thousand of the monks of Bangor-on-Dee accompanied the British army to battle, praying for its victory. The pagan Aethelferth protested

> if these men invoke their God against us, they fight against us, even
> if they have no arms,

and launched his first attack upon them.

The loss of Chester severed Wales from the Pennines, as the loss of Gloucester 25 years before had sundered it from Dumnonia. The Welsh were confined to Wales, and Cadfan, the new king of Gwynedd, is the first of its rulers who is known to have resided in Anglesey, as far removed as possible from the English border. He fought no wars, and his tombstone styles him the 'wisest of kings'. He was a realist, accepting defeat, and turned his wisdom to the consolidation of his kingdom. But, as on the lower Severn, though the British kingdoms were destroyed, the English were still too few to people the lands they had subdued. Aethelferth may have plundered captured territory and may have placed garrisons in Chester and nearby, but his limited manpower was needed for his army rather than for colonisation, for wars against the other English drew him south. While he had conquered the north, Aethelbert of Kent had mastered the southern English. All Britain south of the Clyde was overshadowed by two great English kings, and each might hope to win the sovereignty of the whole island. One strand in Kentish thinking seems to have contemplated the conquest of Northumbria, but Aethelbert died in 616. The southern English rejected the authority of his son, and southern supremacy passed to Redwald of East Anglia. He sheltered the exiled Edwin of Deira, and Aethelferth marched against him. He was defeated and killed. But the power of the Northumbrian armies was unbroken. Edwin was accepted as king by both the Bernicians and the Deirans, and Aethelferth's sons went into exile among the Picts and Scots. The last British Pennine king, Cerdic of Elmet, was speedily removed. Edwin overran north Wales, reduced the Isle of Man, and asserted a supremacy over the southern English that they did not challenge.

All that remained of the British north consolidated around the kingdom of the Clyde. When the line of Riderch failed, early in the 7th century, the throne passed to nearby lords, apparently the kings of the Lothians. But they moved to the old centre of government, the impregnable fortress of Dumbarton, downriver from Glasgow, a base as fit for a navy as for an army. The centre remained, and even when quieter times made the more comfortable situation of Glasgow a safe royal residence, the kingdom changed only its name, from 'Alclud', the Rock of Clyde, to 'Strathclyde', the Vale of Clyde. Its fortunes and its frontiers varied. On its southern borders the people of Urien's northern Reged kept, and still keep, the national name of the fifth-century British, the 'countrymen', *cives* or *Cumbrogi*, that the English called Cumber Land; and when Northumbria later weakened, the Clydesiders quietly regained control of what had been Reged, and in the 10th century extended their borders as far as Leeds, briefly regaining most of the Pennines. But the Clydesiders never seriously challenged English Northumbria; they were not a British power intent on evicting the English, but a northern kingdom on a par with its neighbours. Its kings were content to hold what they had, to acquire only what fell to them without risk. Their business was to keep their kingdom intact, free from English conquest. They succeeded, and were spared not only invasion, but also the dynastic warfare that emaciated medieval

Wales. Throughout their long history, there is no hint of division between heirs; son succeeded father as king of an undivided inheritance for five or six centuries. Too late the British heeded Gildas' warning that civil war would bring upon them the wrath of God, and deprive them of their patrimony.

Catwallaun

Elsewhere, the armies of the northern British were dispersed before the death of Aethelferth. But English rule was not yet secure. Speedy conquest risked re-conquest, and a still small English population ruled vastly greater numbers of subject British. On the south-west, the power of Gwynedd was still unbroken. For long, it offered no threat. King Cadfan ruled quietly, while his people recovered from the disaster of Chester. But his son Catwallaun revived the ancient military reputation of his forbears. His early history is obscure, for the vestiges of poems that honoured him can only be discerned in fragments em-bedded in a distorted 18th-century paraphrase. Bede reports that Edwin invaded Gwynedd, and subdued the 'Mevanian Islands', Anglesey and Man; but he gives no date. In the Welsh tradition, Catwallaun was at some time besieged on Puffin Island, Priestholm, off Anglesey, and spent seven years in exile in Ireland; in Gwynedd, Edwin's armies were opposed by the local king of Lleyn, opposite Anglesey.

But Edwin withdrew. Catwallaun returned, rallied his countrymen, enlisted the support of other north Welsh kings, and found an ally in Penda, king of the Mercians, who 'separated the kingdom of the Mercians from the kingdom of the Northerners'. The allies killed Edwin in 633, and Catwallaun marched his army to the north, repeating the exploit of his ancestor Rhun, ninety years before. For a year he ruled as a high king from the Thames to the Forth, supreme over British and English underkings. Had his rule endured, he might have recovered London and the south, and restored the empire of Arthur. But reconquest came too late. The northern British had accepted English rule for nearly half a century, and only the very old remembered the days of independence. Catwallaun's plunder-ing armies came as aliens, and Penda's pagan English were worse. Hungry armies far from home were a threat to farmsteads that Edwin's settled rule had protected. Catwallaun aroused no national movement, and found no welcome as a liberator. His empire quickly collapsed, destroyed in a single battle, when Oswald, the exiled son of Aethelferth, returned from Ireland and caught him off his guard, on Hadrian's Wall.

Oswald immediately succeeded to the overkingship of Catwallaun, and extended it to include the English south of the Thames. He permanently destroyed the fighting power of the British. The Irish Annals report the burning of Bangor in 634. The king of Merioneth was killed on the Severn in 635; Oswald was then in Wessex and was presumably his victorious enemy. The dynasty of Gwynedd was deposed, and so was the king of the Clyde, who had in that year perhaps supported Catwallaun. Both thrones passed to 'plebeian' kings; though it may be that the subjects of both kingdoms organised rebellion against kings and nobles who had suffered defeat, it is more probable that the words describe nominees intruded by Oswald, who had no royal ancestry, for both were removed when he died. But the restored dynasties ventured no more counter-attacks. The Clyde kings held their frontiers, and in Gwynedd Catwallaun's son earned a reputation like his grandfather's, honoured as a saint rather than as a warrior. Almost nothing is known of his successors save their names, until a new dynasty revived the power of Gwynedd in the 9th century.

Cynddylan

Oswald's supremacy lasted for eight years. He was killed in 642 at Maes Cogwy, or Maeserfelth, that was thereafter renamed Oswestry. His enemies were the old allies, Penda and the Welsh; but with the power of Gwynedd broken, Penda of Mercia, and not a Welsh ruler, was the supreme king. Oswald's wide supremacy passed to Penda, and the Mercian kings maintained it for a century and a half. It was interrupted for three years, when Oswald's brother Oswy rebelled in 655, killed Penda at 'Gaius Field' on the river 'Winwaed' near Leeds, and regained supremacy. Penda's son, Peada, ruled a reduced Mercia as Oswy's tributary, but in 658 the Mercians rebelled, killed Peada, and enthroned his brother Wulf here; he and his successors reasserted Mercian supremacy over all the English except the Northumbrians, and retained it until the coming of the Scandinavians and the rise of the West Saxon dynasty in the 9th century.

On the north-western borders of Mercia, in the modern counties of Shropshire and Staffordshire, the *civitas* of the Cornovii held the remnants of the Roman British lowland, and maintained its independence under its own kings throughout Penda's lifetime. They are known from poems preserved in Powys, in the collection that bears the name of Llywarch Hen. Their territory had been divided, probably by partition among heirs, and in the early 7th century the borders of king Constantine reached southward to the Wye near Hereford, while Cyndrwyn the Stubborn ruled Wroxeter, whose armies fought against Aethelferth at Chester. The poems immortalise his son Cynddylan,

> Whose heart was like the ice in winter . . .
> Whose heart is as the fire of spring. . . .

He ruled Pengwern, the Shrewsbury region, and Wroxeter, the

> White Town by the woods . . . twixt Tren and Trodwydd . . .
> twixt Tren and Traval,

that was his father's home. To survey his heritage, the poet looked down from the top of Dinlle Wrecon, the Wrekin, the pre-Roman fort that preserves the old name of Wroxeter, Vriconium. The army may have reconditioned the ancient fort, but recent excavation suggests that a significant urban population remained in the centre of Wroxeter, living in well-built timber houses, when

Roman building technology in masonry had been forgotten; no close date can be put upon them, but the royal hall of Cynddylan or his forbears may well lie among them.

The first dated notice of Cynddylan's wars concerns the year 642.

> I saw the Field of Maes Cogwy
> Armies, and the cry of men hard pressed.
> Cynddylan brought them aid.

The next verse names his ally, a prince of Powys. Cynddylan fought with Penda against Oswald at Oswestry. Two separate elegies upon his death survive. One, partially rewritten by a later poet, describes a different campaign. Each stanza ends with a signature, like Taliesin's.

> Till I am in my oaken coffin
> I shall grieve for the death
> Of Cynddylan in his glory . . .

> Glory in battle, great was the fortune
> Cynddylan won, who led the attack.
> Seven hundred was the army in his court.

> When the son of Pyd commanded
> For him there was no marrying, he was not wed.
> By God, whence came his tribute?

> Till I rest beneath the mound
> I shall grieve for the death
> Of Cynddylan, honest in his fame.

Pyd is the Welsh word for danger; but it also transliterates Peada, and the word-play fits the idiom of Welsh verse, that commonly gave Welsh epithets to English kings, as Flamddwyn for Aethelric. The statement that 'he was not wed' might refer to a proposal for dynastic marriage that was rejected; but similar usage elsewhere means the death of a very young man, not yet old enough to be married. The probable meaning of the verse is that some English king, probably Peada or his son, demanded tribute from Cynddylan, and was killed when he tried to exact it, or died before he was able to. The date is therefore probably 655 or soon after, the context that Cynddylan refused to pay tribute to an English overlord.

Other verses describe a victory won at much the same time. Detail is precise, but the context is enigmatic.

> My heart is aflame, like a firebrand. . . .
> Brothers I had, better it was when they were alive,
> Heirs of great Arthur, our strong fortress.

> Before Caer Luitcoet they triumphed;
> There was blood beneath the ravens, and fierce attack;
> They shattered shields, the sons of Cyndrwyn.

Till I am in my resting place
I shall grieve for the death
Of Cynddylan, the full famed lord.

Glory in battle, great plunder,
Before Caer Luitcoet, Morfael took it.

Fifteen hundred cattle, and five (stewards?)
Four score horses, and splendid armour.
Each bishop rushing to the four corners,
Hugging their books saved not the monks.

Caer Luitcoet is Wall-by-Lichfield. Only one other medieval text names a prince called Morfael; the genealogy of a local lord in south Wales claims descent from Morfael, who moved from Luitcoet to Glastonbury in the 7th century. Two contemporaries both with the same unique name, both from the same town, are clearly the same person. The exact list of booty suggests the enemy. They were settlers with many cattle, but their army had few horses; their eighty contrast with Cynddylan's seven hundred; and bishops and monks are numbered among the enemy.

These particulars hint at the context. Morfael of the Lichfield region reigned on Peada's borders, for pagan Saxon burials, that last into the early 7th century, stop short of Tamworth, the future Mercian capital, seven miles east of Lichfield, and also at Yoxall and Wichnor, the same distance to the north, where the Trent formed the frontier. Morfael and Cynddylan fought in alliance at Wall. Their infantry enemy was English; and the enemy were accompanied by clergy, who cannot have been present with the English earlier than 653, when Peada first received Christian priests from Oswy. The context argues that the battle was a consequence of the British refusal to continue tribute to the conquerors of Penda, and was fought about 655. The terse notice of the Cambrian Annals that Oswy 'came and raided' in or about 656 perhaps refers to the same campaign. It was the last lowland British victory, and was soon after avenged. Morfael fled to Dumnonia, and Cynddylan was killed by the English; his son withdrew to Powys, and Wroxeter was in Mercian hands a few years later, for its people are entered as the *Wrocensaetna* in the census of Mercian territories termed the 'Tribal Hidage', that was probably drawn up in or about 661; and a ford over the Severn, in the neighbourhood of Melverley, ten miles west of Shrewsbury, received the name of 'Wulfhere's Ford'. The Severn there remains today the border between England and Wales; and the ford may be the place where Wulfhere and the king of Powys met to demarcate their permanent frontier.

The English who killed Cynddylan might have been Wulfhere's Mercians, soon after 658; but were more probably the Northumbrians of Oswy, whose raid in 656 avenged the British victory at Wall. But whoever killed him, Cynddylan and his kingdom were brought down. The stateliest of all the old Welsh poems mourns their destruction, praising Cynddylan, who 'defended Tren as long as he lives', and turns to his fatal end.

> Cynddylan, hold thou the hillside
> Where the English come today. . . .
>
> Cynddylan, hold thou the ford
> Where the English come through Tren. . . .

The English came, and the poet looks upon the ruin that they left.

> Cynddylan's hall is dark to-night.
> There burns no fire, no bed is made.
> I weep awhile, and then am quiet.
>
> Cynddylan's hall is dark to-night.
> No fire is lit, no candle burns.
> God will keep me sane.
>
> Cynddylan's hall. It pierces me
> To see it roofless, fireless.
> Dead is my lord, and I am yet alive.
>
> Cynddylan's hall is desolate to-night
> Where once I sat in honour.
> Gone are the men who held it, gone the women.
>
> Cynddylan's hall. Dark is its roof
> Since the English destroyed
> Cynddylan, and Elvan of Powys.

In the empty hall, now there is 'no warband, no bright fire, no singing, no lord and no company'. Then the poet turns to the future of Cynddylan's heirs.

> High may the mountain be.
> I care not that I herd my cattle there.
> Thin, thin seems my cloak.
>
> Hard is my goatskin bed.
> Yet once I was drunk
> On the mead of Brynn.

He contrasts the vanished past.

> Gone are my brethren from the lands of the Severn
> Around the banks of Dwyryw.
> Sad am I, my God, that I am yet alive.
>
> No more the well trained horses, no more the scarlet cloaks,
> No more great golden plumes.
> Thin my legs, bare, uncovered. . . .

Brothers I had who never lost heart,
Brothers who grew like hazel saplings.
All are gone, one by one. . . .

The dykes endure. He who dug them
Is no more.

The Loss of Britain

The dignity of Cynddylan's requiem accepts final irrevocable defeat without self pity. The northern poets each mourned the loss of one leader or one kingdom; Cynddylan's poet wrote the epitaph of a nation. His sentiments are those of a later generation, but of one that was near enough to its heroes to know the full worth of all that was lost. The poet who looked from the top of the Wrekin across the wide and pleasant midland plain had lost more than mountain peoples could know or understand. When he contrasted past glories with the mountain cattle and the goatskin beds, he accepted perpetual exile to the bleak unlovely hills. His words are an explicit recognition that the British had lost the fairer part of Britain, and were to be Welshmen for the rest of time. His fellows accepted their lot, and made ready to shape the future of the Cymry.

The end had come with appalling speed, compressed within the compass of a single adult lifetime. It was a melancholy commentary upon the warnings of Gildas. Kings and people had not ceased from evil, and God had delivered their inheritance into the hands of the heathen. Gildas had looked to the reform of political society; but the young men whom his words inspired withdrew from it, to pattern a new and better way of life, in monasteries that were in time to matter more for Britain and for Europe than any patching of a dying society. They withdrew because their world was utterly rotted. It fell to pieces, for none could heal its manifold divisions. The English triumphed because the British could not unite. The immediate causes of disunity varied; in much of Wales and the south, close relatives slaughtered each other in dynastic dispute, but in the north wars between kinsmen are less in evidence. There, the Pennine kingdoms fought against neighbours in the farther north, and in Wales and the South.

The occasions of war, and their consequence, have deeper origins. The men of the fifth century had fought to defend and restore Roman Britain. Their arms were in the end victorious, but the tragedy of Arthurian Britain was that victory came too late. The Roman society it championed was already dead, and the forgotten forms of government that it sought to revive could not be rooted in a poisoned soil. The failure of Arthur denied any chance of success to those who came after; the military units that had won the war could not be demobilised, and since their business was warfare, they fought each other when there was no foreigner to fight. Though the personal prestige of the victor of Badon held his empire together while he lived, it could not be inherited. Its military forces dissolved into warbands, who bled each other and their country to death.

The warbands ceased to protect their people, and became a grievous burden, a more real and present threat to the working farmer than the unseen danger of distant Saxons. The poems praised the open-handed munificence of kings called *hael*, 'generous', who 'gathered wealth like misers' and freely gave horses and other gifts to their fighting men. But the poets say little of whence the wealth came; for the corn that the 'well-fed horses' ate, the barley for their riders' food and drink, and much else beside, had to be extorted from impoverished farmsteads. Though a successful raid might sometimes seize the cattle of a nearby kingdom, the arrogant soldiers whose honourable virtues were bloodshed and deep drinking were poorly equipped to protect the cattle of their own subjects; the monumental scale of the Wansdyke, and the numerous lesser ditches that line the borders of the successor states, proclaim the constant need for such protection, but their great length far exceeds their kings' capacity to garrison them, and the dreary routine of a frontier patrol does not rank among the glories that the poets honour. Cynddylan's poet proudly acclaims the warrior's ideal, longing for the excitement of byegone wars, when

> Commoner was the broken shield
> Come home from battle, than the returning ox. . . .
>
> Commoner was the blood upon the grass
> Than the plough in fallow land.

He sang of an adventurous world that might stir young heroes, but could only offer a hateful and fearful insecurity to their inferiors who ploughed the land.

Warbands so weakly rooted could endure reverses, but could not survive defeat. Once they were dispersed, their power of compulsion was gone. No survivor could requisition new horses, constrain peasants to deliver grain or meat, or raise fresh recruits, unless there was a will among the population to recreate the warband. There are no signs of such will. When each king lost his men and his horses, political government ceased. His subjects were eased of a burden, and waited passively until the English came, a week later or half a century later; and when the foreign English came, they imposed a less costly government that gave a surer defence against cattle robbers and armed strangers. But the English infantry were less vulnerable than the British warbands. Their national armies had infinite resources, for unless an entire population was literally exterminated, even the total destruction of an army could be made good in a few years, as children grew to manhood. The English won England because they were a nation in arms; the British lost their inheritance because their 'ill-starred generals' enfeebled and disgusted their own countrymen.

When the British lost the greater part of Britain, they ceased to be British, and became Welshmen, confined to the western extremities of the island. But though their kings failed them, the independent energy of the British people determined the future history of the British Isles. Their churchmen brought the Irish and the northern barbarians into a common polity with the former Roman province. In two centuries of resistance, the subjects of Arthur and of the successor states set abiding limits to English conquest, and delayed the hardening of English society until the English had forgotten much of their Germanic past, and were ready to accept the religion and the political conventions of their new homeland. In taming the English, the British pioneered a civil society that greatly differed from that of Europe. There, the quick and easy victory of the Germanic invaders led to speedy fusion. The rich barbarian became Roman, and the poor Roman was barbarised. Institutions useful to authority survived, to cripple early medieval Europe. The heavy hand of the Roman landlord was not removed, and it acquired the added strength of a barbarian sword, that long overawed submissive peasants. In Britain the institutions of authority were smashed, but much of the peasants' culture survived; for in Britain, alone among the former provinces of Rome, men still speak modernised versions of the indigenous languages that their ancestors spoke in Roman times. The country was divided between natives and newcomers, who interacted, but did not fuse. Yet from the empire of Arthur and from the church that his successors built, both inherited a conviction that Britain was or should be a unity. The long resistance of the British imposed upon the future a fruitful diversity within unity, greater local responsibility, and a stronger sense of the rights and freedom of the individual; it enabled concepts of national identity, rooted in popular beliefs of what was fitting, to mature sooner in Britain than in Europe.

In the sixth or seventh centuries no one intended or foresaw these remoter consequences. But it was the last generations of the independent British who created Wales, who brought a monastic church into being, and who inspired the universal legend of a just and powerful sovereign, enshrined in the name of their own emperor. The last age of the British was clear-sighted. More clearly than most others, it diagnosed its own disease, though it could not cure it; Gildas' analysis moved men's hearts because they knew it to be true. Though they could not act upon it, they bequeathed to their successors a passionate belief that sooner or later arbitrary authority must yield to the rule of law. They knew the past for what it was, but they recognised the present and the future. Cynddylan's poet knew that his people were the 'heirs of great Arthur', the last of the successor states of Roman Britain, and when he addressed 'Cynddylan, vested in purple', he echoed the last devolution of imperial Roman authority. But he also knew that the empire of Arthur was a fading memory, failed and finished, severed from the bleak future.

Sixth-century Britain died because its people no longer wished it to live. It was not destroyed by the rebellion of the English. Their blow fell upon a ruin already rotted. Yet it died in honour. The passing of the warlords redeemed their sordid history; though their triumphs were futile and petty, they turned disaster to a greater glory. Urien and Cynddylan were men who inspired the affection and enthusiasm of great poets. When the last battles were lost, leaders who were left alive without followers accepted their fate without pretence, leaving fevered prophecies of the ultimate reconquest of England to the fretful boasting of a meaner age. The calm dignity of Cynddylan's poet looked the future in the face, without hope, without fear, and without illusion.

CHAPTER FOURTEEN
BRITTANY

The Armorican British have no early annals and few pedigrees. But their Saints' Lives are earlier, fuller and better preserved than those of the British; for in Britain interest in the stories of the early monks was revived by the discords of the 11th and 12th centuries, when most of the original texts had perished, and much of what remained seemed rugged and offensive to elegant ecclesiastics. But in Brittany interest in the origins of the nation and its church was revived by the victories of kings Nominoe and Salomon in the 9th century, when many old texts still survived, and were held in high esteem.

One Life, Samson's, is preserved entire as it was written, about 600 AD or perhaps a few years before, thirty or forty years after its hero died. Ninth-century texts are numerous, and many of them drew upon manuscripts not yet decayed, for they reproduce names of people and places in old-fashioned spellings that hardly outlived the sixth century. In addition to the texts that survive, many disappeared in the French Revolution. Some were rescued by odd chance; one, brought to England by a refugee, and then lost, was tracked down in 1881 by the pertinacious enquiry of a French scholar, who ultimately recovered it from a pile of magazines in the drawing-room of a Yorkshire country house. But the industry of a 17th-century priest salvaged something of many that did not survive the Revolution. Father Albert Le Grand of Morlaix read and epitomised a vast number of texts and translated his own versions into French. His volatile imagination commonly rendered 'Britain' by 'Angleterre', and turned the British *duces* into Earls of Oxford or the like, leaving out the names of greater kings, but making them wear their crowns in London. Many of the places and people he so disguises cannot be recognised, and his text is sprinkled with Roman emperors and startling Roman dates, selected by himself from such printed histories of the late empire as he knew. But when this bizarre ornament is removed, what remains is a collection of medieval Lives, in varying stages of devolution, that share the normal difficulties of such texts, heightened by Le Grand's translation and imagination, but made easier because many of the sources that he used were early and well-informed. In addition, three collections of medieval charters include corrupted lists of kings and bishops, with a few doctored grants that adapt fifth-century names.

The main political events of 6th-century Brittany are well dated, for the Armorican peninsula formed part of the Roman province of *Lugdunensis III*, whose ecclesiastical head was the bishop of its metropolis, Tours. Gregory, the historian of 6th-century Gaul, was bishop of Tours from 573 to 594. He knew the recent history of his own territories; his statements about the Armorican British are not numerous, for their churchmen gave small respect to his nominal diocesan authority, but most of the people he names were his contemporaries, and many of them are prominent in the Lives of the Saints, and they include rulers whose careers also concerned mainland Britain. Gregory's stories are also an important illustration of how the sixth-century monks and kings behaved, and of the beliefs and assumptions that moved them. He himself received at Tours a penniless ill-kempt British ascetic, who had set off in a provocative goat-skin dress to walk to Jerusalem; though this pilgrim halted at Tours, he undertook a journey that many of the British saints are said by their later biographers to have completed. Gregory's plain tale of the dramatic adventures of Macliavus of Vannes, murderously pursued by his brother, tonsured, consecrated bishop, and then made lay ruler, recalls Gildas' account of Maelgwn and Constantine in Britain, and is also matched by the colourful stories of the murders of Melor and Meliau and others in the Saints' Lives. Their many tales of distant pilgrimage and lurid violence might easily be dismissed as pious fancy, if Gregory's sober record did not show that such things actually happened.

Insular British texts also have much to say of Brittany, and distinguish three main migrations from Britain to Gaul. Their belief is firm and clear that the armies which Maximus took to Gaul in 383 never returned 'to Britain to their wives and children and property', but were settled in

> many regions from the lake on the top of Mount Jove to the city called Cant Guic, and as far as the western mound, that is the West Ridge; and they are the Armorican British.

'Cant Guic' is Quentovic, a lost port near Etaples and Le Touquet, and the territory defined, covering the whole of modern Normandy and Brittany, includes nearly all of the fourth-century Roman coastal command known as the *Tractus Armoricanus*. The leader of these settlers is consistently called Cynan Meriadauc, whose residence was Nantes, and whose name is still preserved by several places in the Vannetais, the Roman *Civitas Venetorum*, in south-eastern Brittany. The story is unconfirmed, but is not silly, for the emperor Theodosius, who subdued Maximus, is praised by contemporaries for his clemency towards the rebel's followers. He had a use for troops in Gaul, as well as an incentive to deprive the turbulent army of Britain of recent rebels; for it had enthroned four usurpers in Gaul in the past hundred years. Some of the place names of northern Brittany are military. Leon is the *pagus Legionensis*, the legionary district, and Plou Dalmezeau, probably *plebs Dalmatarum*, bears one of the commonest of the names of fourth-century army units. Such place names suggest that some army units were settled in Armorica at some time in the 4th century.

The second migration, about 458–460, after the first Saxon revolt in Britain, is abundantly attested by Roman writers. It was located in the same wide region, for contemporaries place the British 'north of the Loire', in the territories of Aegidius of Soissons, and a scatter of place names, especially 'Bretteville', extend throughout Normandy. The emigrants also settled in Brittany, for the Roman writer Sidonius, bishop of Clermont-Ferrand, corresponded with their leader Riothamus, who is remembered in the legends of Brittany, along with Gradlon and other local leaders of the mid fifth century.

The British of Normandy were absorbed into the empire of the Franks and the diocesan structure of the Gallic church, but the Franks failed to conquer Brittany, and the Armorican sees disappear from the records of the church councils. Actual independence was secured by token submission; the tactful rulers of the British were content to relinquish the title of king and accept the status of counts, but they admitted no Frank armies, and continued to dispute possession of Rennes and Nantes with their nominal suzerains. When the Franks mastered western Gaul in 507, the British were still weak, and might in time have been absorbed, in Brittany as in Normandy. But within thirty years they received the powerful reinforcement of the third migration, sparked off by the movement of the monks, but strengthened by the participation of numerous armed laymen.

Riwal and Fracan

Emigration was on a considerable scale, organized, led and encouraged by governments. Contemporary notices locate Conomorus as a strong king who ruled in both Britain and Brittany, and later Lives say the same of Caradoc Vreichvras. Riwal, who in his own day was apparently known by the Roman name of Pompeius Regalis, was a 'chief of Dumnonia', and is therefore linked with its dynasty, and made a descendant of Arthur's Gerontius and Cato. He

> came from the overseas British with a multitude of ships, and took possession of Lesser Britain;

he was 'chief of the British on both sides of the sea', the 'first of the overseas British to come' to Brittany, in the sixth century. From Britain the central and eastern coasts of northern Brittany took the name Dumnonia, and retained it in French, as Domnonie. Riwal is said to have had his headquarters at St. Brieuc, in western Dumnonie. His followers included Fracan, who is also made a relative of Cato. Fracan

> discovered an estate of moderate size, just about right for a single *plebs*, surrounded by woodland and brambles, that is now known by its founder's name, and is enriched by the waters of the river Gouet.

Modern Plou-Fragan, *Plebs Fracani*, near St. Brieuc, retains his name and lies two miles south of the banks of the Gouet.

Very many miracles relate to the colonists' preoccupation with the clearance of new land, and with the care of corn and stock. A few concern new forms of recreation devised by the pioneers, and one of the most striking describes a novel sport conceived by Fracan. He challenged his powerful neighbour Riwal, who lived six or seven miles away, to a contest

> about the speed of their horses ... over a measured course. ...
> Highborn and lowborn attended the meeting in numbers; the
> lightest boys, specially trained for the race, were mounted ...
> Fracan's horse was leading, but his rider, Maglos son of Cunomaglos,
> ... could not hold him, and was thrown among sharp stones. ...
> His people took up his dead body. His parents were in tears, and so
> was Fracan, who was held responsible for the unhappy outcome.

It was decided to bury the body, but Fracan's son Winwaloe asked the crowd to draw back, insisting that the boy 'is not dead, but very ill'; and restored him to health.

The story is contemporary, for Cunomaglos and Maglos are spellings of the 6th century. Fracan was blamed for a dangerous innovation, for earlier race-horses had been harnessed to a car or chariot, controlled by a standing driver. Light jockeys galloping over a measured course were new. Winwaloe saved the reputation of his father's experiment, and ensured that flat-racing should spread beyond its birthplace, Plou-Fragan.

Paul Aurelian

Other settlers also took over abandoned Roman estates. Paul Aurelian, on the west, in Leon, landed with a dozen priests, and as many nobly born lay relatives, with 'sufficient slaves'. He too found an 'estate', known as the 'Villa Petri', equipped with an ample spring or fountain, and also protected by 'thick woodland and a great marsh', which constituted one of the 'tribus' in the 'Plebs Telmedoviae'. It also took his name, and is now Lampaul in Plou Dalmezeau. But at another estate of Paul's, the 'Villa Wormavi', there was no visible water supply; the saint, who evidently knew that Roman villas must have had water, dug his staff several times into the ground until he located the fountains. Many other immigrants must have found similar estates, not yet wholly reverted to nature; and Paul Aurelian's Life includes a vivid description of a ruined Roman town. Paul travelled

> along the public road ... to the town which now bears his name.
> He entered through the town gate, on the western side, that is now
> nobly constructed, and immediately found a bright spring of
> moderate size. ... The town was then surrounded by earthen walls

built in antiquity, wonderfully high, but much of it is nowadays
fortified with stone walls built higher still. The place is like an island
on all sides but the south . . . stretched . . . like a fully drawn bow on
the British sea . . . facing south and looking to every aspect of the
sun from east to west.

It will not be absurd to describe the inhabitants that saint Paul
found in this town, . . . a forest sow; . . . in the hollow of a tree, a
hive, full of bees and honey; . . . a bear . . . that fled in fear at the
sight of the saint; . . . and a wild bull, which he expelled. . . .

The biographer, Wrmonoc, is clearly describing a place that he knew in the
ninth century, a substantial Roman town with both an earth bank and a stone
wall, though he is probably mistaken in supposing that the stone wall was built
after the Roman period. The description, however, better fits Roscoff, a few
miles to the north, where pottery from an ancient site has been found in the
sandhills, than modern St. Pol-de-Leon.

These stories describe the settlement of immigrants in a land of ghosts, far
emptier than Britain. A deserted city, a countryside full of abandoned farms,
had decayed far enough for trees to grow within the ruins, and for beasts to make
their dens within. But the decay was relatively recent. Some town buildings
still stood, for Paul was able to restore the city when he chased the animals away;
and in the countryside the boundaries of the neglected estates were still clearly
recognisable, the cleared land still distinct from the surrounding woodland and
waste. It was a little less than a hundred years since the peasant republics of the
Bacaudae had overset the political economy of Roman Armorica. Estates and
towns had not recovered.

The second migration of the British, about 460, had left fewer traces in
northern than in southern Brittany, and was evidently not numerous enough to
revive the failing economy. When Paul came to the city, he was seeking the local
comes, named Victor, to obtain permission to settle. Victor is described as

a pious Christian who ruled by authority of the Lord emperor
Philibert.

'Philibert' is Childebert of Paris, who reigned from 511 to 558; and Victor
turned out to be Paul's cousin. He lived in the offshore island of Batz and his
dominion was evidently small. But permission to settle was needed. It was
eagerly sought and easily obtained. Very many are said to have crossed, with
clerical companions ranging from a dozen to a hundred, often with laymen and
servants in addition. The modern place names preserve ample traces of the
settlers; there are over 150 lay *plebes,* now spelt Pleu-, Plou-, with similar
variants, together with almost as many ecclesiastical centres, *Llan, Locus* and

others, and many more that bear the names of individual saints. Wherever the origin of these names can be checked, the great majority belong to the sixth century. The migration plainly involved some tens of thousands of persons; though some came from Ireland, a few from Dumnonia and a few from north Wales, the great majority of the monks whose origin is given are said to have been born or educated in Gwent or Glevissig, the southern Welsh lands where Roman manners lingered. But the tradition of the secular immigrants is different. The greater part of their leaders claimed descent from the Cornovian princes of Dumnonia, and their district names proclaim the same origin. In the north-east the name Dumnonia probably prevailed from the 6th century onward, since it is common in the Saints' Lives; the south-western kingdom of Quimper was known as Cornouailles, but the name did not come into use until the 8th century or later, at much the same time as Cornwall became the usual name of the south-western tip of Britain.

The Armorican peninsula is naturally divided into clear-cut regions. A hilly wooded upland runs eastwards from the bay of Brest, dividing the northern from the southern coastlands, fertile regions of nearly equal extent; and rivers running north and south from the hill subdivide both coastal territories. Achm and Léon in the north-west are separated from Dumnonia by the Morlaix river, and the Gouet separates eastern from western Dumnonia; south of the hills, the Blavet is the natural frontier between the territory of Quimper, or Cornouailles, and the Vannetais. The size and fertility of the eastern states made them stronger than their western neighbours, and the constant need to hold their frontiers against the Franks forced them to maintain powerful armies, so that Dumnonian rule easily extended over Léon and Achm, and Vannes might as easily subdue Quimper. But in the west, the hills interpose a compact region between the northern and southern powers; they fork like a claw to enclose the territory of Carhaix. Its surrounding hills make it a natural fortress, that might serve a strong ruler as a base whence he could strike in all directions to subdue the rest of Brittany; but when its natural defences were breached, it became a prize to be disputed between Léon and Cornouailles.

The whole peninsula became permanently British from the time of the third migration, in the 540s and 550s, and was already known to Gregory, about twenty years later, as 'Lesser Britain', *Britannia minor*. The speech and identity of the former population was altogether obliterated and forgotten, though on the ill-defined eastern border the bishops and civic authorities of Vannes, Nantes and Rennes regarded the townsmen as Latin and Roman, isolated among the dangerous and unwelcome British of the surrounding countryside.

Budic

The immigrants brought with them the political conventions of their homeland, and their counts fought each other as readily as the kings of Britain. Little is remembered of the men of the first migration save the name of their leader,

MAP 14 BRITTANY

For numbered places and reference grid see Notes to the Maps

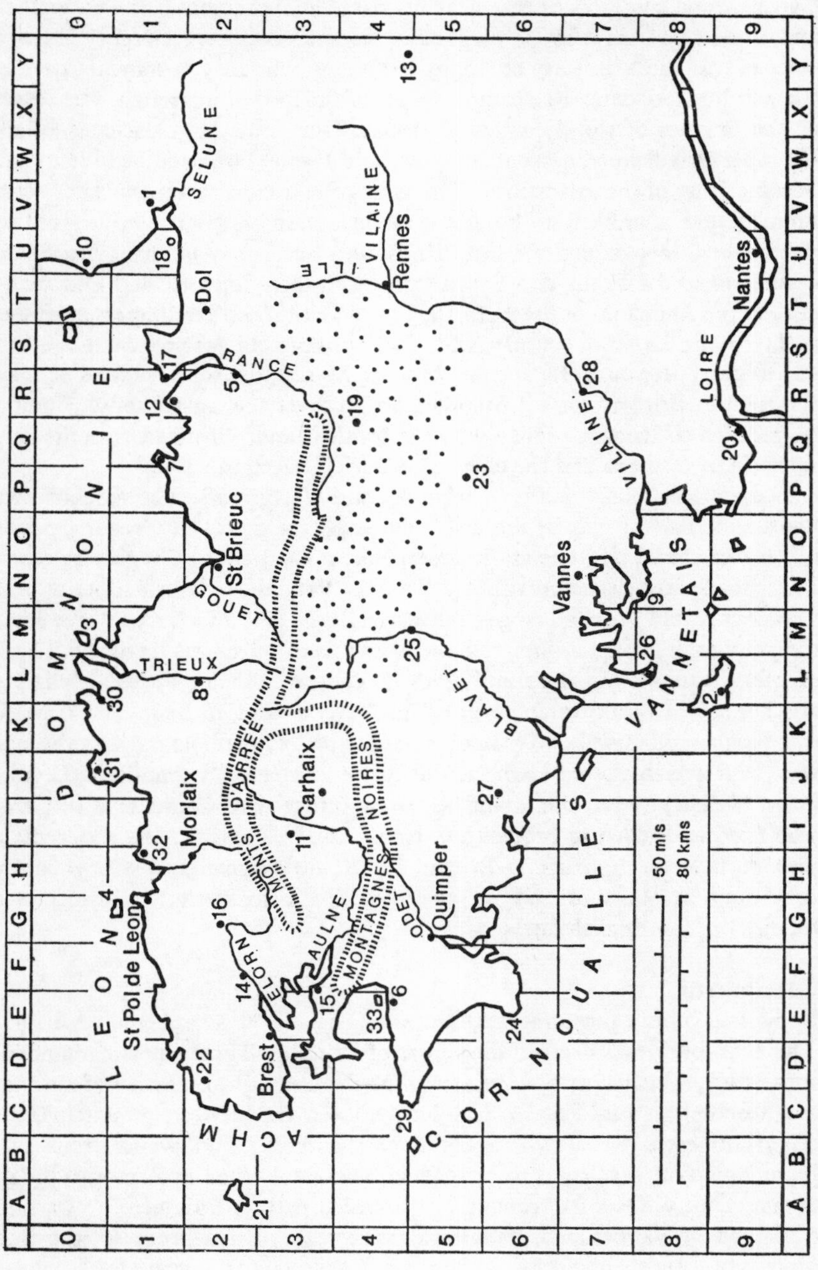

Cynan Meriadauc. Places that bear his name are commonest in the Vannetais, and Conan became a much-used name in later Brittany; Gregory knew of a ruler of this name, in early 6th-century Vannes, who may or may not have been the heir of Meriadauc. Riothamus, leader of the second migration, was regarded as the founder of the dynasties of eastern Domnonie, and the later rulers of Quimper also claimed descent from his 'son' Daniel Dremrud, who left Gaul to become 'king of the Alamanni'. The strange assertion served no later writer's interest, and is unlikely to be deliberate invention. It might derive from some unexplained misreading of a lost manuscript, but it may be that a British force accompanied the Frank and Saxon expedition that Childeric and Odovacer led against the Alamanni of northern Italy in the late 460s. Tradition is anchored to reality in the early 6th century, with Budic, whose old age and death are known to Gregory. In youth, he and his brother Maxentius, sons or heirs of Daniel, returned to Brittany to 'kill Marchell and recover their patrimony'. Budic was later exiled to Britain, probably by his brother, and reinstated with the help of Agricola of Demetia and the elder Theodoric, in Arthur's time.

Budic died about 556, after a reign of nearly forty years. The sequel is told in two unlike halves, part in the brief contemporary notice of Gregory, part in a much distorted Life. The stories complement each other. Gregory relates that Budic made an agreement with Macliavus of Vannes that when either was dead, the other would protect his son; but when Budic died Macliavus drove his son, the younger Theodoric, into exile in Britain, and seized his territory. The Life of Melor extends the story and gives its context. Melor's father, Meliau, was another son of Budic, established by his father as king in Léon, and married to the daughter of Riwal of Domnonie. Budic had evidently mastered the north-west, and overshadowed Carhaix. But Riwal invaded and conquered Léon, and killed Meliau; Melor, the infant heir, took refuge with Conomorus of Carhaix, who tried and failed to protect him from Riwal's assassins. His adherents also seem to have taken refuge in Britain, for the little-known boy saint is patron of Amesbury in Wiltshire, one of the very few British saints whose cult was localised in the English lowlands.

Conomorus

Budic had built a powerful western realm, that was dismembered on his death. The next four years decided the future of Brittany. Three rulers contended for supremacy, Macliavus, now master of the south, Riwal, master of the north, and Conomorus of Carhaix, enclosed between the western mountains. Their origins differed. Riwal was overlord of the recent immigrants from British Dumnonia, but Macliavus' subjects had been established in Armorica for more than a century. Gregory recounts his troubled past. A little before 550, Canao, or Conon of Vannes had made away with three of his brothers; the fourth, Macliavus, was sheltered by Conomorus. Canao was too strong for Conomorus to defy, and sought his brother; Conomorus hid him in a tomb, pretending that he was a corpse. Macliavus then had himself tonsured, and consecrated as bishop of his brother's kingdom; and when Canao died a few years later, he exchanged his crook for a sword, to become the new ruler. Conomorus was a Dumnonian king who still ruled in Britain, but in Brittany he was at first a lesser Lord. In Britain Paul Aurelian had visited his court at 'Villa Banhedos', Castle Dore by Fowey, and knew him as 'Conomorus, also called Marcus'. His name may still be read on the memorial stone of his son Drustanus, that stands on the cross-roads near Castle Dore, at Tywardreath. He quickly became the greatest of the three, in the accounts of Gregory as in the Lives, and he lives on in legend as King Mark of Cornwall; but until after Budic's death, he was still weak, unable to withstand either Riwal of Domnonie or Canao of Vannes.

Conomorus grew great by diplomacy and swift action. Monastic writers condemned his many marriages. He had been married to Budic's daughter. He had sheltered Macliavus in his adversity, and married his sister when he ruled Vannes, making him his enduring ally. Free from danger in the south, he annexed eastern Dumnonia, killing its ruler, whose son Iudual found refuge at the court of Childebert of Paris, in or before 557. When Riwal of western Dumnonia died, probably in 558, Conomorus occupied his kingdom, that included the recent conquests of Achm or Léon, and is said to have married his widow also. Conomorus was now more powerful than his ally Macliavus of Vannes, and controlled all the rest of Brittany. The northerners protested, and a deputation of clerics, headed by Samson, Paul Aurelian, and bishop Albinus of Angers, journeyed to Paris, to induce Childebert to restore Iudual. But Conomorus thwarted them by himself accepting the status of Prefect of the king of the Franks.

Conomorus overreached himself in a greater gamble that failed. He made a friend of Chramn, son of Childebert's brother Clothair, who had quarrelled with his father and found shelter with his uncle. But when Childebert died in 558, Clothair acquired his kingdom, and his rebel son fled. Conomorus received him in Brittany. The stakes were high. If Chramn had prevailed against his father and his brothers, he would have mastered the whole of the Frankish dominions from the Atlantic to the Elbe, with a fair hope of retaining them undivided; Conomorus might expect high influence at Paris, with his title to all Brittany secured, Rennes and Nantes added to his dominion.

The gamble failed. Clothair's army killed Chramn and Conomorus, in December 560. The hard fought campaign is told in dramatic detail by Gregory and in the Lives, which saw only the victory of Iudual, backed by Frank allies. Samson's biographer, writing 30 to 40 years after the event, describes his return from Paris with Iudual, by the way of the Channel Islands, where he distributed 'little gold coins', evidently Frankish *trientes*. The fullest story is told in Le Grand's version of a lost life of Samson. Iudual's landing inspired a general rising, that enabled his army to strike westward, pushing Conomorus back into his inland territory of Carhaix in two battles, and thereby winning control of the north coast. Conomorus brought over reinforcements from Britain, who included 'Danes, Northmen and Frisians'; though Danes and Northmen are words often used loosely of north German barbarians, Frisians have no such connotation. The word suggests a source written near to the time when Frisians were still a distinct entity among the Saxons of Britain, hardly later than the 6th century.

The German forces landed at Ile Tristan in the bay of Douarnenez, on the west coast. The name is arresting, for neither Le Grand nor his source knew that Conomorus was king Mark, or connected him or the island with the legend of Tristan; the name of the island implies an early association, perhaps a belief that Conomorus' son commanded the reinforcements landed there. Thus strengthened, Conomorus marched north to meet Iudual and Clothair at Ploueneur Menez, a dozen miles south of Morlaix. At first the Frisians overwhelmed the enemy infantry, but after two days they were broken by a charge of Iudual's formidable British horse. Conomorus was wounded in flight, fell from his horse, and was trampled to death in the press of the rout; his body was recovered and buried at Castle Dore. Chramn escaped to the ships, but returned to rescue his wife and children; he and they were caught, locked in a cottage, and burnt. The Germanic troops hastened to their vessels, but found them burnt by peasants, who wisely sided with the victors.

The battle was decisive for the future of the Franks as well as the British. Clothair died at Tours in December 561, a year and a day after the death of Chramn. As he died, the old king protested

> Wa! Wa! How great is the king of Heaven, who can kill kings as
> great as I am.

He was the last of the great Merovingian kings. His surviving sons divided his kingdom, but none of his descendants revived the united power of the vast empire that he had held, and that Chramn had sought to inherit. In Brittany, Iudual and the son of Riwal recovered their inheritance, and Macliavus retained or regained Vannes; one tradition asserts that Caradoc Vreichvras, a king in southern Britain, ruled Vannes for a time about the middle of the sixth century, and it may be that he ousted Macliavus in 560, either as the ally of Conomorus or of Clothair.

Waroc and Iudicael

Pre-eminence in Brittany soon passed to Vannes. Macliavus was himself killed in 577, by Theodoric the younger, who returned from Britain with an army that regained his father's kingdom of Quimper. Gregory gives the date and the event; the genealogists of Britain held that he married the sister of Urien of Reged, then all-powerful in the north, and the marriage suggests that at least a part of his army also came from Reged. But in Vannes itself Macliavus was succeeded by his son Waroc, who soon made himself the most powerful prince in Brittany.

The Vannetais was thenceforth known as Bro-Guerech, the land of Waroc; Gregory's last chapters report Waroc's stubborn campaigns, fought to win Rennes and Nantes. They were prolonged for more than 200 years, and seem to have succeeded soon after Gregory's death, when a British ruler is said to have been installed in Rennes.

Waroc evidently avenged his father's death, for the traditions of south Wales held that Theodoric returned to Britain to die on the Wye, where his son Mouric founded the dynasty of Glevissig. Thereafter Waroc united the Armorican British against the Franks; a second Budic ruled Quimper; a son of Conomorus campaigned as Waroc's ally; in the north, Iudual's son Iuthael was the ruler of Rennes, evidently also as Waroc's ally. His long reign shifted the centre of power to the north, for he married the heiress of western Dumnonia, and his son Haeloc ruled the united territory. His sole rule was maintained by a ruthless uncle and a forceful cleric. Haeloc's uncle ensured that his brothers were either murdered or tonsured, lest their claim divide the kingdom, and ecclesiastical pre-eminence passed not to the successors of Samson at Dol, but to the formidable and tempestuous Malo, whose biographer praised his aristocratic contempt for the rabble, and emphasised the widespread hostility that his vast monastic estates aroused. But in the end an 'impious generation arose', expelled Malo, overthrew Haeloc, and fetched his brother Iudicael from his monastery to replace him, early in the 7th century.

Iudicael was a man of religion. He reigned in the generation when Irish and English monks were spreading the ideal of ascetic simplicity through northern and eastern Gaul. His own monastic allegiance was to Samson's pupil Meven, wholly alien to the prelatical ambition of Malo. He concluded a lasting peace with king Dagobert of the Franks in 637, and his close personal friends included Dagobert's ministers Eligius and Dado, better known as St. Eloi and St. Ouen. In 640, all three abdicated secular authority; Eligius and Dado became bishops; and Iudicael returned to the monastery of his friend Meven. His faith was shared by his family, for his brother Iudoc, St. Josse, founded numerous monasteries in eastern Brittany, as well as in Picardy and Flanders, and his son Winnoc of Wormhoult became, and remains, the patron saint of the Belgian littoral.

Almost nothing is recorded of the history of Brittany for two hundred years after the abdication of Iudicael. Its ninth-century kings made large gains in Normandy, but though they were driven back, Rennes remained British. Its dynasty had an illustrious future. Count Alan of Brittany brought a large contingent to the army with which William of Normandy conquered England; many were rewarded with lordships and lands on the Welsh border, where they understood the speech of the natives; one of them was the ancestor of Geoffrey of Monmouth, whose alleged 'little book' from Brittany made him the most influential writer on British history for centuries to come, and another was ancestor of the Fitzalans of England and of the Stuart kings of Scotland.

Brittany was named and created by the British in the first generation of

Arthur's successors. Theirs was the largest migration. The descendants of the earlier immigrants were ultimately absorbed into the native population, leaving nothing behind them but a few place names. Without the reinforcement of the sixth-century migration, the earlier settlers in Armorica might also have been absorbed; and could not have withstood Frankish conquest and colonisation. The best-remembered immigrants were monks. But the laymen who named tens of thousands of farms and hamlets and towns far outnumbered them. They left Britain to escape the society of the tyrants whom Gildas denounced. Armorica became Lesser Britain because the tyrants seized power and gave men cause to emigrate. The existence of Brittany is to be reckoned among the consequences of Arthur's victory and Arthur's failure.

CHAPTER FIFTEEN

ENGLISH IMMIGRANTS

The Homeland

The homeland of the English was the sandy coast of north-western Germany, between the Zuyder Zee and the northern tip of Denmark. Very many of the pots and ornaments there buried are exactly matched in fifth-century graves in eastern England, and a number of identical names for peoples, regions and persons were and are in use on both sides of the sea. The grave goods of the coastal peoples distinguish them from their neighbours; from the Danes, who then lived in southern Sweden, and from the Frisians, the Franks and the Suebian Germans to the south. They also mark their internal differences.

Roman writers and Germanic legend mention a number of Ocean peoples, Jutes, Varni, Angles, Myrgingas, Langobards, Saxons and others. Many of their names are long forgotten, but some endure. Jutland is still the name of northern Denmark, Angel of a district in north-eastern Schleswig, and Lower Saxony still describes much of north-western Germany; other names survive where emigrants took them, for the English, called *Angli* in Latin, now live in Britain, and the Langobards have given their name to northern Italy, Lombardy.

Peoples were on the move, and took their fashions with them. In the 4th and 5th centuries, the ornament north of the Elbe differed from that used to the west of the estuary. There styles began to mingle from the early or middle 4th century, several generations before the migration to Britain. Peoples originally distinct were combining to form a single nation. Late Roman writers knew that nation as Saxon, and extended their name to all the northern Germans immediately beyond the Frisians and the Franks; they neither knew nor cared to remark its internal divisions. Germanic tradition knew the Saxons as one among the constituent peoples, but does not clearly indicate their territory; it is commonly assumed to have lain west of the Elbe.

The emigrants moved for specific purposes, that stem from the history of the Roman empire and of barbarian Europe. The central fact of that history in the fourth and fifth centuries is the Migration of the Peoples, known to modern German writers as the *Völkerwanderung*; the voyages of the Saxon peoples were one relatively late part of that general movement. Migration had two aims; those who moved wished to leave where they were; and they also wished to settle where they arrived. But these aims were not equally easy to realise; for men could leave home freely, but they could only settle where they conquered or found a welcome; so that many peoples wandered far, and often fast, in an unsuccessful search for secure lands. The evidence is often oversimplified, for most of it comes from Roman writers, who observed the arrival of barbarians upon their borders, but were rarely interested in their origins. Sometimes powerful peoples, like the Ostrogoths and the Huns, subdued many other barbarian nations, and grouped them into large empires. Sometimes an entire population moved, or was absorbed by greater neighbours. More often, sections of a population, large or small, left home, sometimes with their women and children, sometimes as groups of adventurous young men. Several different detachments might leave the same homeland in different generations; some might settle in their new homes for a few years, some for centuries, and sections might move further on. It was therefore quite normal for several distinct groups of the same nation, like the Heruli or the Rugii, to live at the same time on or near different Roman frontiers, while others of their kinsmen remained in their old homeland; and in the conquered lands groups drawn from numerous distinct origins might combine into a single people in their new homes.

These complexities make it difficult to relate the archaeology to the statements of Roman writers. Often there is no archaeology, for small peoples, or those who moved on after a few years, left little behind them. Peoples who stayed permanently in their new homes, like the Saxons in Britain, left ample trace, but bands of footloose warriors, or of groups too small to take with them skilled jewellers and potters, could at most carry to their graves the ornaments they brought with them; their children must use the ornament available in their new homes, or none at all, as in Britain the Bernicians have virtually no ornament in the 5th and earlier 6th centuries. Moreover, ornamental styles do not always correspond with political groupings. When a Roman writer called the Chamavi of the eastern Netherlands a 'part of the Saxons' he was politically right, for he meant that they were allies or subjects of the Saxons; but they did not use Saxon ornament. Conversely, many writers carefully distinguish the Angles from the Varni, and some characteristic place names also help to tell the one from the

---

Map 15

Modern national frontiers   ━ ━ ━ ━ ━

In GERMANY and the NETHERLANDS
o   5th century saucer brooches
✝   5th century cruciform brooches

In DENMARK
⊤   Inhumation burials, probably 4th century
∎   probably 5th century
▬   Cremation burials,   probably 5th or 6th century

MAP 15 THE HOMELAND OF THE ENGLISH

other; but they shared the same ornament, and cannot yet be distinguished archaeologically.

The Saxon peoples were buffeted by the same stresses as the rest of the Germanic migrants; but their history is somewhat better evidenced than most. They learnt to write their own language much earlier than any European German people, and were able to remember some traditions of a distant past that had been forgotten in Europe before men bothered to seek it out. Their archaeology is simpler, for in Europe the repeated fission and fusion of separate peoples encouraged them to borrow and adapt their neighbours' fashions, so that the interplay of different styles is hard to decipher, and tends to limit modern study to a few dominant groups, Frankish, Langobardic and the like. But in Britain the Saxons were alone in an alien land, cut off by the sea, and their main ornamental styles evolved relatively simply, so that the impact of particular foreign influences is more easily detected, in the districts and at the time when each developed. None the less, the impulses that brought the Saxons to Britain are part of a European movement. Emigrants left home because a large population was squeezed into a small area of poor soil, and left when they saw reasonable prospects of finding more comfortable homes elsewhere. At first, only a portion of the emigrants came to Britain, and Britain also received some Germanic immigrants from other regions. The reasons that caused the bulk of the population to move to Britain, and to outnumber other Germanic peoples there, are explained by the history of the Germanic migrations in Europe.

The main direction of the migrations was from north to south; to later chroniclers in Italy, Scandinavia was the 'womb of the nations', the original home of Goths, Langobards and others. Germanic nations were established south of the Baltic before the 1st century AD, evenly spread over the north European plain, but the mountains and woodlands of southern Germany, Bohemia and the Carpathians confined them to smaller regions, separated from each other by wide tracts of empty upland, thickly forested. In the north-west, the Saxon peoples were limited to a strip of sandy coastland, and to river banks, for the rough hinterland of bog, heath and moor forbade agriculture and pasture. Except in east Holstein, the habitable area was compact and narrow, rarely more than a few hours' walk from sea or river to moorland. Earlier Roman writers give occasional glimpses of the attempts of the Angles and Langobardi to expand into the open lands beyond the heaths; they were thwarted, principally because the barrier of the Roman Rhine prevented the peoples they wished to dislodge from moving further.

It was from the Elbe lands that the assault of interior peoples upon the Roman frontier began. About 165, a portion of the Langobardi crossed Bohemia to raid the Roman Danube. They were repulsed, but the emperor Marcus Aurelius replied with an invasion of what is now Czecho-Slovakia, that failed. The frontier broke, the northern Balkans were overrun, and fifteen years of bitter warfare left the frontier where it had been. The war brought to the surface latent social, political and regional conflicts within the empire, and also taught the barbarians that Rome was not invincible. Within a generation, the small peoples of the upper and lower Rhine grouped themselves into the large federations of the Alamanni, the 'All Men' and the Franci, the 'Free Men'; the Goths and Heruli moved south towards the Ukraine, while other peoples of central and northern Germany pressed upon the Danube. In the middle of the 3rd century the combined assaults of these peoples smashed the European frontiers of Rome, while Persians and African barbarians overwhelmed the eastern and southern mediterranean. The frontiers were restored, but remained under constant attack; and the barbarians, hitherto raiders in quest of plunder to take home, began to aim at conquest and settlement.

The fourth century was an age of consolidation upon the Roman frontiers, of turbulence in central Germany. Constant warfare encouraged the coherence of larger political units, and stimulated the growth of military monarchy. Eormenric the Goth established a vast empire from the Baltic to the Black Sea, that included Slavs and Ests as well as Germans and Sarmatians. Roman writers begin to notice warrior kings among the Franks and Alamanni, who were now also pressed in the rear by Burgundians and Vandals from the Baltic; and also to distinguish the Saxons from the Franks, and to deplore their frequent raids upon the coast of Gaul and Britain, though at first only the Jutes seem to have contributed to the southward migrations, leaving Jutland considerably depopulated.

Native tradition differentiates between the constituent peoples. It emphasises that the Saxons themselves did not create a national monarchy until the 9th century, but it believed that among the northerners, the Jutes, the Angles and the Varni, the institution of monarchy was already established by about the end of the third century. The triumphs of Offa of Angel were remembered in two old English poems, in legends that the medieval monks of St. Albans adapted without understanding, in two Danish chronicles, and in the dynastic tradition of the Mercian kings. Offa's grandfather Wiglaet is said to have defeated and killed the Jutish king Amlethus, the original of Shakespeare's Hamlet; Offa's father was hard-pressed, losing the stronghold of Schleswig to his northern enemies, but young Offa secured the southern border of the Angles upon the Eider, and went on to greater conquests in his mature years.

The tradition is matched by the archaeological evidence. In the time assigned to Offa, in the later 4th century, Anglian brooches and pots spread eastward through east Holstein to Mecklenberg, in large cemeteries, in lands not peopled by their ancestors; in the 5th century they extended through Pomerania to the borders of Poland, mainly in scattered burials in lands that were formerly Burgundian or Vandal or Rugian. In the south, Anglian cemeteries became numerous in Thuringia, and stretched eastward to the Elbe about Dresden, whence smaller groups crossed the mountains to join the Germanic peoples of Bohemia, about Prague, and to mingle with Quadi on the Danube, about

Bratislava. In the west, Saxon cremation burials invaded Frisian territory in the northern Netherlands, where previously an exceptionally dense concentration of Roman objects argue that the power of the empire had long prevailed; and after the late fourth century, Saxon inhumation burials with Jutish brooches suggest an additional northern migration, early in the 5th century.

The reign of Offa approximately coincided with the Gothic empire of Eormenric, that was overturned by the Huns in or about 375. Their terrifying invasion pushed the German barbarians against the Roman Danube and beyond it, and in 378 the Goths destroyed the armies of the eastern empire. Their children pressed upon Italy, opening the passes to other Germans behind them. The imperial government stripped its frontiers to defend Italy, but in vain. Vandals, Alans and Suebi swept across the Rhine, and the Goths took Rome in 410. The Goths soon settled permanently in Aquitaine, and were followed by Burgundians and others. The rivers that had dammed the expansion of the Germans for centuries ceased to be frontiers; and one of the consequences of the fall of western Rome was the creation of an independent Roman government in Britain, whose needs drove Vortigern to enlist the followers of Hengest to defend his coasts.

Hengest

The early fifth century is the time in which the saga of Hengest is set. Its outline is preserved by two documents. The old English epic poem *Beowulf*, written down in Christian England, probably in the eighth century, concerns wars between the Danes and their neighbours early in the sixth century. In the poem Beowulf's warriors are entertained by tales of still earlier heroes, in a past that was already remote to them, and one of these tales is the 'Saga of Hengest'. The poem gives a summary of the story, and a small fragment of the full saga also survived in another manuscript, termed the 'Fight at Finn's Burg', evidence that at one time the story was well known in literate Christian England.

Much is obscure, but the essence of the tale is clear. The Danish king Hnaef, with a small retinue, visited his brother-in-law, Finn Focwalding, king of the Frisians, whose forces included a body of Jutes, apparently independent, relatively recent settlers accepted into his service. Fighting broke out in Finn's hall, and many heroes fell, including Hnaef; but the hall remained in the possession of the Danes, whose leadership was taken over by Hengest, a 'royal thane'. The Danes eventually agreed to enter Finn's service and to evacuate the hall; they were given another in exchange, which they held on the same terms as the Jutes, who lived nearby. Hengest himself passed the winter with Finn, probably as a hostage; but he plotted revenge, and in the spring, with the help of reinforcements summoned from home, he surprised and killed Finn. The inhumation burials indicate that a small number of Jutes had settled in Frisian territory about the years 400 to 430; they date the incident, and locate it to the Leeuwarden area.

The texts and the burial-grounds of Britain tell the sequel. Hengest was a successful adventurer, whom chance brought to the Jutes of Frisia. Vortigern's need gave him greater opportunity. He brought a small force to Thanet in three ships, that can hardly have carried more than a couple of hundred men; but Vortigern's continuing troubles demanded ever more men and Hengest's initial success attracted willing recruits. When their number grew, he risked rebellion, in the early 440s; but the revolt misfired, and fifty years of warfare left the Saxons in possession only of limited and defined territories.

Their extent and the origins of their population are chiefly known from their burial-grounds. The evidence is full and consistent; though undiscovered sites may well be 20 or 30 times as many as those that are known, what is known is a fair sample of the whole. A map of the sites and objects known in 1920 would have far fewer symbols than one drawn in 1970, but the regional variants it shows would not greatly differ. Modern understanding of the evidence has greatly increased, and is likely to increase much more in the next half-century, but the character of the evidence is unlikely to alter significantly.

The main guides to regional difference are the manner of burial and the type of grave goods. Close study of burial rites will doubtless reveal important variation, but so far only the obvious differences between cremation and inhumation have been generally noticed. The ornamental styles of pots and brooches show more difference in detail; urns are the principal evidence for cremation burials, brooches and buckles for inhumations. Their differences and similarities help to distinguish local communities, for fashions spread easily when brides are free to meet and marry men of other districts, and when peddlars may move freely; but when adjacent areas use quite different styles, political and ethnic frontiers intervene.

Grave goods of the 5th century are easily recognised, for they are paralleled in Germany. They cannot often be as closely dated as modern studies sometimes claim, for fashions last a lifetime and overlap; but it is possible to distinguish many that were most popular early in the century, and others that came into favour later. Their evidence is consistent, for though graves often contain objects normal in different successive generations, very few contain any that are farther apart in time; it was not uncommon for a woman to take to her grave the brooches she wore as a bride and those she acquired as a grandmother, but antiques and heirlooms are rare. Inference does not however rest upon individual objects or particular graves; when several graves in the same cemetery contain similar ornament of the same date, and when the cemeteries of a region repeat common characteristics, they show whence and when the population came.

Map 3 sets down the sites where objects of the early fifth century have been recognized, and Map 6 gives those of the later fifth century. The first map indicates where the first English communities settled, within the approximate date limits of 420 and 460. Of all their many grave goods some three or four brooches and a few urns were already old-fashioned by the 420s, in vogue a generation earlier; but they are a small percentage of the total, and cannot argue that the cemeteries came into use earlier, for any immigrant population brings with it a small proportion of old-fashioned gear. The evidence cannot distinguish sites where burials began before the revolt of the early 440s from those that came into use soon after; but the revolt did not expand the territories occupied, for each region and each kind of cemetery has something of the earliest grave goods, and Gildas and the Kentish Chronicle report that after the first fury of the revolt, the Saxons returned to their previous homes in Britain, and were obliged to fight hard for the best part of twenty years to retain them. The population was still too small to fill and hold its lands, not yet able to acquire new territories; those who immediately followed the first contingents settled near their predecessors. The map therefore signals the regions of the earliest settlement, in the 420s and 430s.

The Saxons were stationed where Vortigern wanted them, from the Thames Valley to the Humber waters, to guard the east coast. If Vortigern and his Council had decided to use them against the Irish, they would have been distributed between the Dee and the Severn estuaries. Their location has nothing to do with mythical 'routes' of 'invaders' who 'penetrated' up valleys; it is the simple consequence of a decision taken by a British government at a particular time. In detail, many cemeteries are located, like Roman cemeteries, outside the walls of Roman towns, large and small, indicating that the Saxons were billeted within the walls. Others are placed on or beside Roman estates; some guard river crossings, and most of the open country sites are located by river banks, on alluvial soils easy to till. It is very possible that those which are strategically located are the earliest, billeted by government decision, and that some of the rural sites in the same regions were established by kinsmen who crossed five or ten years later; but archaeological evidence cannot deny or confirm dates so close.

The burial rite distinguishes three sharply differentiated regions. From Norfolk to York, all the dead were cremated, with the exception of a small pocket of inhumation cemeteries in and about Rutland. By the Thames estuary all the dead were inhumed unburnt. But from Cambridge to Oxford and Abingdon, down the Icknield Way and the Ouse, in the area conveniently termed the Icknield region, both rites were practised side by side in most cemeteries, from the earliest burials onwards; and in all three regions the original burial rites were maintained in the earliest cemeteries for nearly two hundred years, until pagan burial ceased, without admixture of other rites. Other customs were observed at sites that did not come into use until later, but the original cremation cemeteries admitted no pagan inhumations of any period, nor did the original inhumation cemeteries admit cremation, save that occasionally one or two cremations, usually of children, are found in large inhumation cemeteries.

These well-marked differences are linked with the origin of the settlers. Cremation prevailed through most of the Germanic homeland, except among the Jutes. But the early inhumations cannot be attributed to Jutes alone, for the burial custom of late Roman Britain was inhumation, and many of the Thames and Icknield burials are the graves of men who lived in the richest centres of Roman civilisation and most readily adopted Roman ways; moreover different rites do not always bespeak different peoples, for some simple societies develop different rites for different kinds of people, sometimes, for example, inhuming bachelors and cremating married persons.

The difference of rite is no more than a general indication. Its meaning is explained by the grave goods. The cremation cemeteries cannot be examined in detail until a comprehensive catalogue of urns is available for study; but preliminary work suggests some important conclusions. Vessels paralleled in Jutland are also found in Europe in Frisia, but not in the lands between. In Britain they are commonest in Kent and Surrey, but elsewhere they have been observed only in the cremating regions, nearly all of them in the earliest cemeteries. Frisian urns of continental Anglian or Saxon inspiration are very numerous in earlier 5th-century graves, also commonest in the cremating areas. Anglian and Saxon traditions were already mixed to the west of the Elbe before the migration began, and are as mixed in Britain, though Anglian influence is somewhat more evident in many of the cremating cemeteries, Saxon influence in the mixed cemeteries of the Icknield region.

The indications of the pottery will remain faint and tentative until the whole assemblage can be surveyed; they suggest that in the early 5th century many of the immigrants did not move in compact bodies from one Germanic to one British region. Jutes, Angles, Saxons, Frisians and others were not each confined to one region of Britain; but though each region drew some settlers from several German districts, each had its majority element. Jutes were most prominent in the Thames estuary, Angles and Frisians in the cremation areas, Saxons somewhat more noticeable in the Icknield region. These indications are matched by the evidence of brooches. The newcomers used many kinds of brooch, but only those called 'cruciform' and 'saucer' are numerous and datable, and evolve continuously throughout the pagan period. Both evolve from small, simple and delicate early 5th-century forms to large ornate later versions. The early cruciform is a slender graceful brooch, its foot suggesting a horse's eyes and nostrils, its head decorated with three small knobs at top and sides, which give it its name; the saucer brooch is so termed because it is a concave disc, its common 5th-century decoration five running scrolls neatly rendered in chip carving. The earliest cruciform brooches are few, found in Kent and Essex, in and near Cambridge, by Bedford and on the northern borders of Northamptonshire; the smallest and simplest saucer brooches are found in the Oxford region, at Luton and in Surrey. In Europe both are found in Frisia and on the west bank of the Elbe; but between the Elbe and the Baltic, in Holstein and Mecklenburg, where 4th-century Anglian colonists were numerous, cruciforms brooches are plentiful, saucer brooches unknown. The cruciform brooch is in principle Anglian and Jutish, the saucer brooch proper to the mixed Anglian and Saxon culture west of the Elbe. In Britain each had its zones, the cruciform brooch most popular where Jutish, Anglian and Frisian urns are most used, the saucer brooch predominant at the southern end of the Icknield region; but these zones are not exclusive, for one of the early saucers was buried at Norwich, and in the fifth century cruciform brooches were buried by the middle Thames as often as saucer brooches. In the earlier sixth century, partition was to restrict each area to its own fashion, confining the cruciform brooch to the Anglian north and midlands, but as yet no frontiers barred the free movement of ornamental styles, and free movement was regained after the English victories of the late sixth century.

The mixed settlement of the fifth century was not remembered, and later national names implied a simpler link between the regions of Britain and of the homeland, so that in the 8th century Bede inferred that

> The nation of the English, or Saxons . . . came from three of the mightier peoples of Germany, the Saxons, the Angles and the Jutes. The men of Kent and Wight descend from the Jutes. . . . From the Saxons . . . come the East, South and West Saxons. From the Angles, of the country called *Angulus*, between the districts of the Jutes and the Saxons, which is said to have remained empty thereafter until the present day, came the East and Middle Angles, the Mercians and all the stocks of the Northumbrians. Their first leaders are said to have been two brothers, Hengest and Horsa.

Bede made a natural deduction from the names in use in his own day, when the Jutish origin of Kent was still remembered, to the names he knew in Europe. His summary says nothing of Frisians, or other smaller peoples, and he knew no details of the fifth-century migrations. But he knew that many other nations participated in them; in his day, Egbert intended to evangelise pagan Germany, for

> he knew that there are many nations in Germany, from whom the English, or Saxons, who now live in Britain, are known to have originated. . . . There are Frisians and Rugii, Danes and Huns, Old Saxons and Boructuari, and many others, who still observe pagan religious practices.

Bede lists the pagans whom Egbert meant to visit, not the ancestors of the British, for the Jutes and Angles are missing; but the context shows that in Bede's view these pagan peoples were or might have been among those whose ancestors sent emigrants to Britain.

Burial rites, urns and brooches hint at the origins of future kingdoms. The core of Hengest's first followers were Jutes and Frisians, widely distributed from Thames to Humber. But the recruits who followed in the next few decades were more compactly grouped, and included larger numbers from the Elbe lands, as well as more Frisians and Jutes. Many Angles settled in the territories that later took their name, and many Saxons settled in the Icknield region. These are conclusions inferred from the limited studies that have yet been undertaken. They of course leave many unanswered questions. The Bernicians are said to have followed Hengest's lieutenant, Octha, regarded as his son. They inhumed their dead without grave goods, and therefore they can only be shown on a distribution map by a question-mark, based on the written report, not on their archaeology. Elsewhere several of the cremation cemeteries are not known to have contained urns of the earlier 5th century, and can therefore be shown only on a later map; yet many are poorly recorded sites, only a few of whose urns survive; and it is likely that some of them belong to the earliest settlement. Some individual objects also raise queries. One brooch 'found in a tunnel' at Hornton near Banbury cannot people an otherwise empty region. In Hampshire, a few fifth-century objects have been found at Portchester and Droxford; but these few objects are more than a generation earlier than any others south of the Thames valley, within a distance of scores of miles, and until they are confirmed by future discoveries they cannot by themselves demonstrate isolated settlement at so early a date. But these queries are marginal, and do not contradict the clear pattern set by the majority of sites.

Icel

The second map shows what changed in the later 5th century, to about the time of Badon. Added territories are few. The most important are east Sussex, whose earliest grave goods contain plenty of the mid fifth century, but nothing that seems earlier; and Worthy Park by Winchester, whose first settlers brought Kentish and Sussex grave goods, towards the end of the 5th century. Both have a context. Sussex and Essex are said to have been ceded by Vortigern in the late 450s, and the Saxon Chronicle reports the landing of Aelle at much the same date. In Hampshire, the English who served Cerdic are said to have arrived about 480. But in older areas there is noticeable change, especially in the Cambridge region. On the northern border of the Icknield region of mixed cemeteries, an inhuming people settled near the River Lark. A single outpost cremation cemetery of the early 5th century, at Lackford, south of the river, was ringed by eight or nine inhumation cemeteries, all of which have 5th-century objects, none of them of the earliest period; and a few similar sites extend southward. One or two inhuming settlements were also established on and beyond the frontiers of the earlier Norfolk territory, in the north-west by the Fens and the Wash, and in eastern Suffolk. Such sites are also numerous, but more widely spaced, among the Middle Angles, between Northampton and Lincoln, and on both sides of the Humber; and a few were established near Banbury, and on the borders of the original middle Thames territory.

Though they buried their dead unburnt, the principal ornament of these newcomers was the Anglian cruciform brooch. The population of the Anglian regions grew, for in addition to the newcomers, burials in the older cemeteries were more numerous. Many more men and women had crossed the sea. One early record preserved by Nennius explains their coming. The earlier settlers throughout

Britain had all accepted the overall command of Hengest, but when he died, about 470, his hopes of conquest had faded, and the armies of Ambrosius and Arthur were winning important victories. So the English,

> when they were defeated in all their campaigns, sought help from Germany . . . and brought over the kings from Germany to reign over them.

The kings came when many of their people had gone before; and when the kings abandoned their homeland, the remainder of their population followed. The east Roman historian Procopius reported that early in the next century, a large empty land lay between the Slavs and the nearest Germans, the Varni, who were the northern neighbours of the Angles, on the modern border between Denmark and Germany. It had been the home of the Angles; and Bede was told that Angel was still unpopulated in the 8th century.

The only kings whom the English could bring were the kings of Angel, the successors of Offa. The later kings of Mercia claimed to descend from them, and knew the dynasty as the *Iclingas*, named from Icel, whose date is placed in the mid or late 5th century; and the Scandinavian epic *Beowulf*, preserved in England, recited the names of the kings who ruled in continental Angel down to Icel's father, but no further. These traditions imply a belief that king Icel moved his royal centre and the remainder of his subjects from Angel to Britain in the later fifth century. He came when the superior authority of Hengest failed. He inherited sovereignty over all the Angles, but not over Jutes, Frisians or Saxons; and in Kent, Hengest was replaced by Oesc, son of Hengest's captain in Bernicia, who came south to found the Kentish royal house, thenceforth known as the Oescingas.

The Iclingas were a dynasty, a royal family, and not a people. In their name later Mercian kings claimed sovereignty; the heir of a cadet branch, father of St. Guthlac of Crowland, ruled a substantial territory among the Middle Angles in the 7th century; and a village named Hickling lies near to Nottingham. But the places that bear the name of Icel and his dynasty concentrate in East Anglia. Hickling near Norwich lies in the heart of the old cremation area, but Icklingham lies among the new settlements on the Lark, and was in later times a royal residence, where a king's daughter was born; and Ickleton lies half a mile from one of the largest of the new cemeteries, outside the Roman town of Great Chesterford in Essex, south of Cambridge. Its contents, excavated nearly 20 years ago, are not yet published and cannot be examined, but it is known that of 200 or so burials no more than about 30 were cremations, doubtless of immigrants from the nearby Cambridge settlements.

It is therefore probable that Icel reinforced the Angles and established a royal centre among the East Angles of Norfolk and the lower Ouse. The new cemeteries reached northward to Kesteven, south of Lincoln, and occupied the south bank of the Humber, but did not reach Lincoln itself or the greater part of Lindsey;

and it is there that British tradition remembered the greatest of Arthur's battles before Badon. Icel, like Hengest before him, failed to win Britain; and when the southern English kings, who were not his subjects, made their last effort at Badon, the dynasty of Icel is not reported to have joined them; it may well be that his power had already been broken and contained.

The tiny territory of the Eslingas suggests how the power of Icel was curbed. Their homes were shielded from nearby Cambridge by a steep escarpment that serves as a natural dyke, but they also straddled the roads that lead from Cambridge towards London and the west. Their grave goods begin in the later 5th century, and are at first altogether alien from those of Cambridge, but resemble those used by the Saxons of the middle Thames, opposite Oxford. These differences suggest that they are likely to have been the enemies rather than the friends of the English of Cambridge. They came at a time when the political control of the region changed. Earlier in the 5th century, Cambridge had been the furthest outpost of the mixed cemeteries of the Icknield region, its burial customs distinct from those of East Anglia and the Lark; but in the later 5th century Icel and the new inhuming peoples engulfed Cambridge on the south and east. The Eslingas, with their Thames-side ornament, were settled there when Arthur was defeating Anglian armies, probably some years before Badon. Earlier Roman emperors had often enough levied men and families from vanquished barbarians, known as *Gentiles*, *Laeti* or by other names, and used them to guard Roman frontiers. It may well be that the Eslingas originated as subjects of Arthur's British, employed to watch the borders of the independent East Angles of Icel's kingdom.

Elsewhere movements of peoples are less noticeable. The kingdom of Kent was contained behind the Medway, and the grave goods of what is now west Kent are also akin to those of Surrey and of the Thames people. The Kentish kingdom itself was open to foreigners. Frankish influence began to be noticeable; Anglian cruciform brooches were numerous in Kent in and after the middle of the 5th century, but they ended within the century; and before they disappeared, saucer brooches began to appear in numbers. A little cremation spread in Kent and Surrey, but there, as among the Middle Angles, the history of the mixed cemeteries differs. In the Icknield region cremation and inhumation began early in the 5th century at the same time, and continued side by side; but among the Middle Angles late 5th-century inhuming immigrants appear to have joined earlier cremating communities, while in Kent colonies of cremating peoples seem to have joined earlier inhuming settlers. More exact study of the grave goods may in the future give a clearer idea of what happened, but at present the evidence gives no hint of why these people moved or upon whose authority.

The English in Europe

Grave goods in Britain show something of when and where the English came, but nothing of why they came. The burial-grounds of Europe suggest reasons. In the earlier 5th century many young men followed Hengest and brought their families; but many stayed at home, and many others moved elsewhere, eastwards towards the Oder, and southwards to Thuringia and Bohemia. The manner and the motive of the movement of the several peoples differed; the Angles, and their northern neighbours, the Varni, were ruled by kings, and had little or no Atlantic seaboard. Their earliest movement was in disciplined contingents, and at first by land. But the Saxons and the Frisians moved by sea, and the Saxons obeyed no kings. A fifth-century Gaul remarked with surprise that among the Saxons

> every oarsman is a pirate chief, so that all of them both rule and obey.

They plundered on both sides of the Channel, attracting most notice in the thirty years or so after 460, when they controlled the Sussex and Hampshire havens, raiding the Atlantic coasts of Gaul and Ireland as well. They moved fast in small mobile groups under temporary leaders, leaving little archaeological trace. In the middle of the 5th century 'Corsoldus' savaged Armorica, and Odovacer's Saxons settled briefly on the lower Loire; they followed him to Italy, and are no more heard of. A few remained, for there were some Saxons near Nantes a century later, and many more lived in northern Gaul; but there is as yet no way of telling whether these men were descended from Odovacer's people, or from later immigrants. Other substantial bodies of Saxons, with or without their families, are recorded on particular occasions in different parts of Europe in the 5th and 6th centuries, but few stayed long enough to leave recognisable burial-grounds, and the texts do not often distinguish Atlantic Saxons from the Angles.

English Expansion
in the Earlier Fifth Century

In the middle of the century the Angles and the Saxons and their allies were the most extended and the most vigorous of the northern Germans, in arms from Pomerania and Bohemia to the Atlantic. But by the end of the century they had all but disappeared from Europe. The fundamental reason is plain; they were too dispersed to resist the pressures that bore upon them. Had the whole nation migrated together to Britain in Hengest's time, they might have won the island quickly, and held it as firmly as the Goths held Aquitaine, or as the Vandals held Africa; or if they had all moved south together, they rather than the Franks might have mastered central Europe north of the Alps. But they were not yet a compact nation; Angles and Varni under their kings, Saxons and Frisians in separate bands, each went their own way. Yet theirs was an age when other barbarians were forming into large nations, and they succumbed to stronger peoples who pressed upon them from the south, the north and the east.

MAP 16 THE ENGLISH IN EUROPE

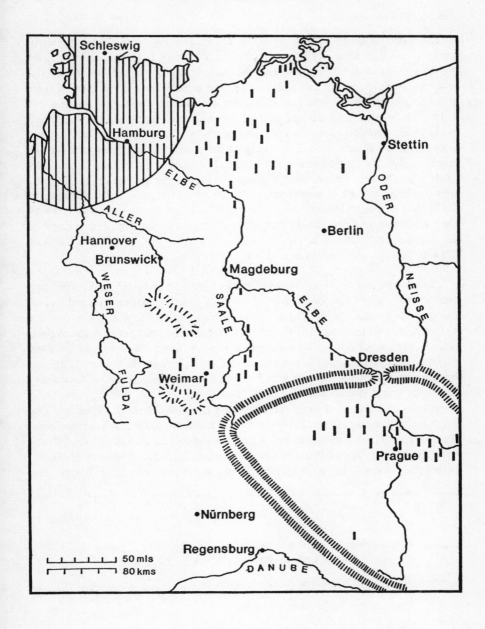

||| The Homeland (see Map 15) | English grave goods elsewhere

Pressures on the English

These pressures are not easy to assess, for peoples on the move are harder to study than those who stay in one region; and enquiry is further hampered by modern political divisions. Government budgets oblige scholars to survey the material available within particular states, and to seek the early history of their present populations. These limitations are not easy to avoid, but they do not help understanding, for the peoples of the migration age were not contained within these borders, and the ancestors of many modern nations had not yet occupied their future lands. The study of Britain is relatively easy, for the sea marks a frontier that time has not changed; but even in Britain it has until quite recently been fashionable to concentrate upon the origins of the English, disregarding the bulk of population as an irrelevant fringe of Celtic twilight, to be treated as though the natives were exterminated or driven into Wales, where their history should properly belong, without impact on the conquering English. In Europe, confusion is worse, for modern frontiers cut across the lands of ancient peoples, and remain sensitive and unstable.

The peoples nearest to the Roman frontiers are best recorded, and it was they who circumscribed the English on the south. Political power changed out of recognition during the later 5th century. In the middle of the century the Franks were still the people of the lower Rhine, and had not yet penetrated deep into the interior of Gaul. But in a reign of 30 years, from 481 to 511, king Clovis subdued all Gaul except the mediterranean south, and made it France. In 496 he also subjugated the Alamanni and mastered southern and central Germany; Frankish grave goods intruded into Thuringia, and in Bohemia Frankish cemeteries suddenly and completely replaced those of the north Germans. The break is sharp enough to mean that the former Langobard and Anglian population was driven out; the Angles merged with the Langobards, who established themselves on the frontiers of Pannonia, on the Roman Danube, in modern Hungary, before they crossed the Alps to occupy and name northern Italy in 568. The

---

Map 17

———	Western frontier of the Slavs, and of place names in *-itz*
—·—·—	Approximate limit of place names in *-in*
—	Place names in *-büttl* or variants
I	Place names in *-lev* or *-leben*
········	Western border of the Thuringians

MAP 17 PRESSURES ON THE CONTINENTAL ENGLISH

Franks also mastered the Frisians, and subsequently helped them to repel a Danish invasion, in about 525. The Frisians later spread westward to the Weser, into lands that had formerly been Saxon; but the wide dominion of the Franks already blocked southward movement from the English homeland.

Pressure from the north was gentler but nearer. During the later 5th century the Danes migrated from southern Sweden into the Baltic islands and the thinly peopled peninsula of Jutland; an occasional grave that contains both Jutish and Danish ornament suggests that they were accepted with little resistance, but their conquest was complete; they gave their new homes the permanent name of Denmark, and bore upon the territories of the Varni and the Angles.

Pressure from the east was stronger, but it is harder to define and to date. The archaeology of the northern Slavs is indifferently studied, for in countries that remain Slavonic to the east and south, interest concentrates upon their own territories, while in the lands that medieval immigrants conquered in the north, the study of early Germans is more popular than the study of Slavs. By the end of the 8th century ample evidence indicates a stable frontier. Slavonic territory reached near to Kiel and Hamburg, and the border ran southward on a line not greatly different from that which today divides eastern from western Germany. The Slavs expanded west of the middle Elbe, to include much of Hanover, which is now in west Germany; but Thuringia, now east German, centred upon Weimar and Erfurt, remained a German land.

The evidence is poorly studied, chiefly because of an easy modern view, which tends to assume without argument the Slavs 'filtered' late into lands that Germans had earlier abandoned voluntarily. But the place names and the archaeology are not easily reconciled with such romantic notions. The pottery of the Slavs is simple and conservative. The characteristic decoration of middle Slavonic vessels from the Baltic to the Balkans shared common designs, and the undecorated wares of earlier centuries were also similar in shape. They reached up the Danube and the Baltic coast; and on the Danube, where their approximate date can be determined by their association with the ornament of Romans and of other barbarians, they run on from the 5th century, but they are rarer in regions that the Slavs first occupied in and after the later 6th century. No evidence yet argues that they are significantly later in the north than in the south, and in the north their western limit is the town centre of Hamburg. The city is surrounded by earlier German burials, but none are reported from within its ancient walls. The accessible published illustrations of the Hamburg cemetery include Slavonic forms that on the Danube would hardly be later than the early or mid 6th century, together with vessels that recall late Roman provincial forms; though some German scholars admit them to be Slavonic products, others claim them as 'late Saxon', and most assert a later date.

The evidence that argues that Hamburg was founded by 6th-century Slavs naturally offends modern national sentiment. But though the frontier was later pushed back some 20 or 30 miles to the east of Hamburg similar evidence from other sites and from place names concurs. Slavonic place names have as yet received hardly any of the study that has been devoted to English, Scandinavian and Germanic names. The early spellings have rarely been studied, and only broad generalities can be extracted from a survey of their modern forms. Yet these forms show one outstanding contrast. The commonest terminations that are exclusively Slavonic end in *-itz* or *-in*, as in Chemnitz, or Berlin; but though the names in *-itz* extend to the furthest frontier of the Slavs, those in *-in* do not. They reach southward from the Baltic and northward from the Danube, but they are not found in a wide central territory between, that extends across the upper Elbe into Poland and Slovakia; and it is in this area, in the Elbe about Dresden, that Germanic burials last longer than elsewhere. Place names give no date; but the 6th-century Roman historian Procopius knew of Slavs by their final furthest Baltic frontier early in the 6th century.

So marked a frontier has a cause. Where place names are better studied, the immediate cause of such difference is regional dialect, but commonly a difference in date and stage of settlement underlies the frontier of dialect; so the varying forms of English names that end in *-ing*, *-worth* and the like differ in local and linguistic usage, but each usage was common at a particular time. The evidence can be no more than a pointer until Slavonic place names have been seriously studied. But the combined implication of the place names, the archaeology and the texts is that the Slavs pushed westward along the Danube and the Baltic at much the same time, during the 5th and earlier 6th centuries. In the north their advance is matched by the retreat of the English, whose Mecklenburg burial-grounds went out of use about the middle of the 5th century, a generation or more before those by the Elbe.

The pressure of the Slavs was subtler and more insidious than the assault of German armies. The centralised forces of the Germans were trained to war. Their excavated settlements show that successive peoples occupied the same cleared areas, separated by tracts of uncleared land; their history is clearest in the hillier south, especially in Bohemia, where hundreds of settlements were jammed together in a strip of fertile land in the north, no larger than an English county, where large rivers flow together below Prague, while in the upland that constitutes most of Bohemia scarcely more than half a dozen sites are known to have been cultivated before the coming of the Slavs. Throughout their history, the Germanic peoples had learnt to conquer districts already settled; and when they needed more land, they were readier to attack their neighbours than to clear wild woodland; for their historical experience equipped them to cut down people rather than trees. But the Slavs had as yet no centralised organisation, no armies, kings, or princes richly buried; they fought in armies only when they were themselves mastered and swept along by others, as by the alien Hunnic Avars in the Danubian lands. Otherwise, their pioneers advanced in large numbers of small groups, and held their lands because a different agricultural technology enabled them to clear scrub and woodland, and to till heavier soils that their predecessors had left wild. In the future, their technology was to revolutionise the economy and the warfare of Europe, for they and the Avars brought with them the stirrup, that enabled a mounted man to thrust with a heavy lance and to strike more strongly with his sword; and probably also the horse collar, that enabled medieval agriculture to plough the soil and transport loads four or five times more effectively than in the past. The Slavs did not conquer their predecessors; they surrounded and stifled thinly peopled regions, for they had no army to be destroyed in a single heroic engagement, leaving its lands defenceless; each settlement had to be attacked individually, and their settlements were very numerous, scattered in difficult terrain, well-placed to wear down and engulf any early German army that ventured among them.

In the mid fifth century, the homeland of the English was secure, and beyond it a choice of broad and open ways invited emigrants. But by the end of the century the expansion of the Franks, the Danes and the Slavs closed in upon the English. They were not expelled, but their possibilities of expansion on land were checked, and their territory was threatened. Icel led the remainder of the Angles to join the strongest of their colonies, who were in urgent need of reinforcement; and most of the Saxons followed their example. Together they formed the English nation in Britain; they left Europe because they could no longer maintain their ancient homes. The English came to Britain because they were squeezed out of Germany by the pressure of the Franks, the Danes and the Slavs.

After Badon

Britain was partitioned after the victory of Badon; and the main frontiers may well have been drawn before the last campaign. The English remained in a number of separate territories (see Map 8, p. 135). Their extent was reduced. In a wide stretch of country between Northamptonshire and the Thames, in the zone of the main fifth-century wars, where English settlement had been thin and scattered, few burials are known for three generations, except around Dunstable and Luton; and in Northamptonshire itself, the English were restricted. The normal brooches of the earlier 6th century are rare; the graves contained many of the little brooches termed 'small long' that are cheap imitations of Anglian cruciforms; but their dating has not yet been worked out, and it is uncertain whether any or many of them date early in the century. The meaning of the Northamptonshire burials cannot be learned until these brooches, and the urns, are more closely studied. At present it can only be remarked that the English who remained in the region did not have access to much of the ornament that their neighbours used. Elsewhere, harsh frontiers prevented the movement of fashions. Cruciform brooches were confined to the Anglian districts, saucer brooches to the Thames and the south, to the Dunstable area and to the Eslingas; and each district developed its own regional variations, that rarely passed beyond their own borders. Regional fashions in the naming of places also hardened, as

-ingham among the Angles, and others elsewhere. Gildas complained that the British did not visit the lands occupied by the barbarians; it is equally evident that the barbarians did not visit each other.

The cemeteries have little to say of the political government of those buried in them. Other texts do, and serve to explain something of the little that can be learned from the burials. English tradition is clear that only two kingdoms yet existed, that of the Oescingas in Kent, and of the Iclingas among the Angles. It is confirmed by the European contemporary notice of Procopius, who reported that in the 530s,

> three populous nations inhabit the island of Britain, each of them ruled by a king. These nations are named the *Angiloi*, the *Frissones*, and the *Brittones*, from whom the island is named.

Procopius was well-informed about the northern nations; he wrote of a time when Arthur, the last single king of the British, was recently dead. The heirs of Icel ruled the Angles and king Eormenric ruled the Jutes of Kent, who had not yet forgotten that their ancestors had come from Frisia. English tradition confirms Procopius, for it has preserved separate notices of the dates when other kingdoms came into being, all of them late in the 6th century; and it remembered that previously their peoples had been led by notables, not ruled by kings. The graves give some evidence of the notables. Burials of the 5th century show little social difference; the men were buried with spear and shield, the women with simple jewellery, few of them better adorned than others. But from the beginning of the 6th century, especially among the Middle Angles, datable swords become commoner in men's graves, and some women were buried with richer jewels and with emblems of authority, a spherical or faceted crystal slung between the thighs, a ceremonial iron blade by the arm. Differences of wealth and rank increased throughout the century, but the monumental barrows of kings and under-kings were not constructed before its last decades.

Most of the main territories contained a multitude of small peoples, each with their individual names, Wissa, Wixna and the like. None of these names are known to have been brought from Germany, and though some may have been, most are likely to have been adopted in Britain, as the men of each locality, often drawn from different continental origins, formed themselves into new political units. These were the communities that bred men of power and wealth, whose dignity the graves sometimes preserve. Some of the small English districts, about Abingdon or Luton, or the Sussex Ouse, may well have been grouped in a single community; but the larger Anglian regions each contained several peoples, many of whose names are known. Patient local study of variations in ornament and burial custom may in the future help to identify some of them, and determine their borders.

A few obvious inferences are yet possible. Since the lands of the Middle Angles in Leicestershire and Nottinghamshire were separated from the East

Angles of Norfolk and Cambridge, the same king could not effectively have ruled both; and since the Iclingas are reported in both territories, it may be that a cadet branch was established among the Middle Angles. Further north the settlements of Kesteven, south of the Lincolnshire Witham, formed a distinct unit; Lindsey, north of the river, accepted few of the later 5th-century inhuming immigrants, and may have remained a British territory less open to new settlement, except perhaps near to the Humber. Across the river the English of the East Riding had two main centres, about Market Weighton and Driffield, not yet joined into a single territory; in the Driffield area at least, British and English appear to have lived side by side, and the government may have been British. But the power of British York was still strong enough to be suzerain over both, and over the other scattered English communities south of the Tyne. Beyond the Tyne, the Bernicians still contained four separate small peoples in the later 6th century; these peoples may well have existed earlier, doubtless raiding their British neighbours when occasion served, but they were not yet able to assert effective independence.

Throughout Britain the English lived in very small communities each developing a class of notables. Only Kent and the East, and perhaps the Middle Angles, yet combined under a king; some of the small isolated communities may have accepted a local monarchical chief, for the Irish report of the pagan English at Abingdon at the end of the 5th century described their chief as a king. His people were no larger than an Irish *tuath*, whose ruler would not have been styled 'king' in later English usage. But English tradition gave them their own name, the *Gewissae*, and derived their dynasty from the Anglian element in their population, heirs of Wig, traditionally lord of Schleswig in Offa's time. Others may have been so ruled, for military insecurity and growing social differentiation encouraged a tendency towards individual authority, that is likely to have developed sooner in some regions than others. But whatever their internal structure, all the English were surrounded by stronger British neighbours; some of them were doubtless directly ruled by British kings, and all were confined within their borders.

In the earlier 6th century none of the English territories in Britain expanded significantly. But there was some new settlement. In the Thames estuary new immigrants arrived. Frankish fashions spread in Kent, numerous enough to suggest that Frank settlers as well as traders came, and the native English craftsmen developed Frankish ornament into the splendid jewellery of Kent, that became the greatest glory of all Teutonic art. Scandinavian influence is also noticeable in Kent, but its strongest impact was upon the opposite shore of the estuary. The Gippingas of Ipswich are the only English people whose well-furnished cemeteries contained neither the Anglian cruciform brooch nor the saucer brooch. Instead their women wore the earliest forms of the brooch described as 'great squareheaded'. It came into use in the earlier 6th century, and its wearers, who buried their dead unburnt, soon penetrated northward into the older East Anglian territories of Norfolk. But they did not join the old communities and share their cemeteries; some of their settlements were located immediately next to those of their predecessors, and may sometimes have superseded them, but others were placed between older communities. They were conquerors, for when the East Anglian kingdom achieved independence towards the end of the 6th century, its dynasty was not the Iclingas, but southerners, whose chief royal centre was at Rendlesham by Woodbridge, near Ipswich. Thenceforth the East Angles distinguished two distinct regions, of the North Folk and the South Folk, Norfolk and Suffolk; in defiance of natural geographical divisions, the South Folk annexed the lands by the Lark, between the homes of the original early 5th-century regions of Norfolk and of Cambridge, which had been peopled in Icel's time, in the later 5th century. The older North Folk were surrounded, contained and infiltrated. In Norfolk the conquerors brought with them their squareheaded brooches, but they also adapted and developed the native cruciform jewellery; and as the English expanded they carried their fashions westward into the lands of the Middle Angles and beyond.

One fragment, copied from a lost East-Anglian Chronicle, that was probably put together in or before the 8th century, remembers the newcomers.

> Pagans came from Germany and occupied East Anglia; and some of them invaded Mercia, and waged many campaigns against the British. But they were not yet organised under a single king. Many leaders occupied these regions by force, and fought many wars from there. But since the leaders were many, they have no name of their own.

Their first arrival is inserted into the narrative of medieval chroniclers at the year 527, but it is unlikely that the date meant anything more than early in the 6th century; and the advance of some of the raiders into the region that was later called Mercia is not likely to have been earlier than the mid or late 6th century. 'Germany' has no closer meaning than Germanic northern Europe, but the great squareheaded brooch gives a somewhat nearer indication. It is an English version of a popular Scandinavian brooch, that the Langobards and others spread widely in Europe; most of the Scandinavian and Langobard brooches are differently shaped from those of the English, but the nearest parallels to the English version, few in number, are found in the far north of Norway.

The Scandinavian invasion of East Anglia is dated to about the time of Arthur's death. It may have been a wholly independent movement, disregarding the British rulers; but the invasion was confined to lands already English, and did not touch British territory; and the interest of British rulers was served by the disruption of the most powerful English kingdom. It may be that they welcomed the invaders, or even invited them. Medraut perhaps opposed Arthur, and perhaps ruled in Suffolk; he might have introduced the *Gippingas* to fight at Camlann. But, however they came, they stayed in East Anglia, and did not subdue Colchester and Essex.

Other foreigners came to Deira in smaller numbers, at a date not yet determined.

A few English graves contained Alamannic grave goods and one place name locates a body of Alamanni, and suggests the manner of their coming. *Almanne Bire*, now corrupted to Almondbury, is the name of a prehistoric fort south-east of Huddersfield. It is very far from English territory, near to the natural frontiers that separated Reged from the eastern Pennine kingdoms, and its situation suggests that the kings of York stationed a Germanic force upon their borders, after Reged had asserted its independence, towards the end of the 5th century. That is also near to the time when the Alamanni were overwhelmed by Clovis the Frank, when some among them are likely to have sought new homes. They were not the only Germans to be deployed in British territory; for at half a dozen northern Roman forts, small cemeteries or burials with Deiran ornament of the late 5th or early 6th century have been observed.

It was not only in the north that English garrisons lined British frontiers. Map 18 shows their distribution. Some are of uncertain date. In Derbyshire south of the Trent, near to the probable border between the Cornovii and the Coritani, a few cemeteries have no known grave goods that seem earlier than the 6th century; they may mark new settlements, or it may be that they were earlier foundations, whose first burials chance has not yet detected. But the south-western borderlands of the Cornovii have plainer evidence; four large mixed cemeteries guarded the main crossings of the Avon on their side of the river, near Coventry and at Warwick, Stratford and Bidford. Their burials began very early in the 6th century, and their main ornament derived from the Middle Angles. Further south a larger number of smaller burial-grounds encircled the territory of Cirencester and Gloucester on the north, the west, and the south, approximately on the borders of the Roman Dobunni. The earliest of them, Fairford, may be as early as the Avonside cemeteries, but the ornament of most seems somewhat later, and was drawn from the Abingdon English; it passed on to Bidford, the nearest of the Avon garrisons, but only a little of it reached further north, though the Cotswold sites about Cirencester took little or nothing of the Anglian

---

Map 18

close shading areas shown on maps 3 and 6 (pp. 59 and 107)
  where early sixth century burials are numerous
wide shading areas shown on maps 3 and 6
  where early sixth century burials are few
  and uncertain.

  One dot beneath a symbol indicates period D 1 (510/540)
  Two dots indicate period D 2 (530/560)
  Symbols without dots indicate period C (490/530)

  Other symbols as on Map 3

MAP 18 PAGAN ENGLISH SETTLEMENT 3
THE EARLIER 6th CENTURY

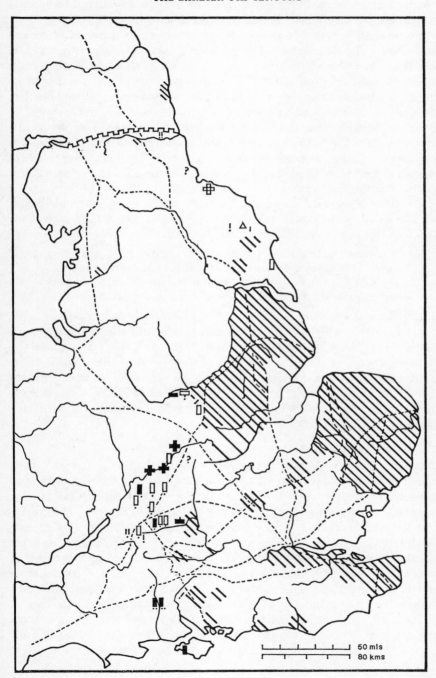

50 mls
80 kms

285

ornament of the Avon. Cornovian territory admitted brides and peddlars within its borders, but Cirencester allowed no traffic in the opposite direction.

No other such English detachments are known until a group of cemeteries immediately outside Salisbury, by Old Sarum, came simultaneously into use. The date is probably a little later than that of the Cirencester sites, but is perhaps earlier than the rebellion of Cynric in 550. The situation and the date of all three groups suggest that they moved to their new homes as the allies rather than the enemies of their British rulers, on similar terms and for similar reasons to those which had brought their ancestors to Britain in the service of Vortigern a century before. The British rulers needed dykes and rivers to deter the invasion of neighbours, who sought to drive cattle and other booty home; but they could not easily find native forces to hold their frontiers, and some found English infantry garrisons fit for their need.

Not every British king hired English defenders, for a strong current in British opinion feared the national enemy. Gildas reports and endorses the protest of one contemporary or earlier Briton, who complained that

> it is greatly to be desired that the enemies of the church should be regarded as the enemies of our people, without any kind of alliance; and that for the friends and defenders of our people we should have not only the federate allies, but also our own fathers and lords.

The writer is deliberately using words with a classical, archaic meaning; *amici*, friends, is used of the allies of the Roman people, and also of the emperor's advisers and officials; *patres*, fathers, is used of senators, and in the 4th century *foederati*, allies, is the technical term used of Germanic barbarians settled within Roman territory, like the Goths in Gaul. The rulers of Wroxeter and of Cirencester and Gloucester, perhaps of Lichfield and Salisbury, were evidently numbered among those whom Gildas and his fellows criticised for welcoming pagan English *foederati*.

Migration from Britain

Save for the few who found service with the British, the English did not expand in Britain for some 70 years after Badon. They stayed within the borders assigned to them and won no new territories; but their growing population had need of more land; for they emigrated in considerable numbers to Europe. The Frankish cemetery at Herpes in Aquitaine contained much early and mid 6th-century Kentish ornament; the small Kentish squareheaded brooch is found in numbers in Frankish graveyards from Flanders to Bohemia, and some other brooches in such burials may be Kentish. Scattered Saxon saucer brooches are found on several sites, especially in Belgium, and their adaptations and imitations reach down to the Danube and beyond, occasionally as far as the southern Balkans.

These are the traces of individuals and small groups of emigrants, whose children were absorbed into the nations among whom they settled. Several large well-organised expeditions also left Britain, and some of them long preserved their identity in Europe. Procopius describes and dates one English invasion of the Low Countries, and explains its root cause; in Britain

> there was such overpopulation that every year large numbers migrated with their wives and children to the Franks, who settled them in the emptier parts of their territory.

One major incident in this general movement was an English attack upon the Varni, whose ancestors had been their neighbours in Europe, located between Angel and Jutland, in what is now Denmark. In the 530s, all or part of the Varni were briefly settled on the northern bank of the Rhine mouth. Their widowed king married a sister of the Frank king Theudebert, who reigned from 533 to 548, and betrothed his son Radiger to the sister of the king of the *Angli* of Britain; but he died soon after, and advised his son to reject his English bride and marry his Frankish stepmother, since the Franks were more immediate neighbours. The outraged English virgin crossed the sea with a vast armament conveyed in 400 ships, commanded by another brother, defeated the Varni, and captured Radiger. The terrified prisoner expected torture and death, and was delighted to escape with no harsher sentence than a command to honour his broken promise and marry his captor.

This general movement, that Procopius observed in his own time, has left tangible traces in many English burials in northern Frankish lands, notably in the large cemetery of Anderlecht, near Brussels, and at Rhenen, by Arnhem on the Rhine; some among them may be the graves of those who fought the Varni, and settled among the Franks rather than return to their overpopulated homes. But the fleet that came to the Rhine brought warriors, and most of them went home, for no clear signs of large and permanent English settlement have yet been detected in the Low Countries.

Such signs are plentiful to the west, where the coasts of Gaul are nearer to Britain. There, over a hundred villages behind Boulogne, extending eastward as far as Lille, bear English names, like Ledinghem, slightly disguised in French spelling. More than three-quarters of them are of early types that are common among the East Angles of Norfolk, and are relatively rare elsewhere; their date appears to be indicated by the discovery of one or two Anglian cruciform brooches of the early 6th century in the same region. A migration so extensive and so concentrated is not easily explained as the casual spontaneous movement of landless individuals; it was plainly one part of the deliberate Frank policy that Procopius remarked in the decades before 550, of planting English colonists in lands that they could not themselves people; for the conquests of Clovis had recently annexed vast territories, far too large to be occupied and policed by men of Frankish birth alone. The dense settlement behind Boulogne suggests the enlistment of a particular English force at a particular moment; that force may have been the origin of the 'Saxons of Egwin', who formed one of the eleven divisions of the Frank army, and were prudently resettled on Montmartre,

MAP 19 THE ENGLISH

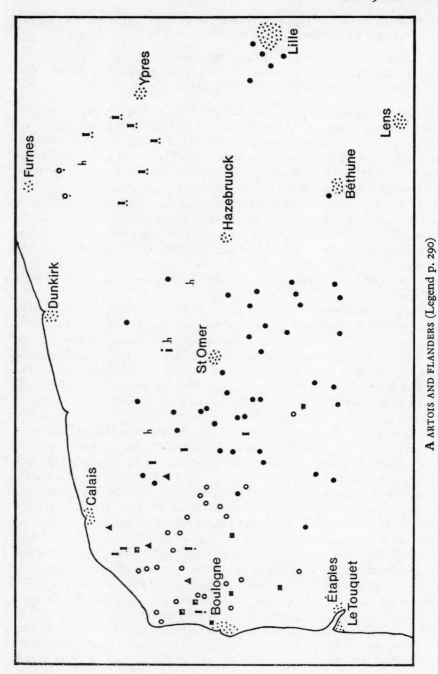

Lille

Ypres

Furnes

Lens

Béthune

Hazebruuck

Dunkirk

St Omer

Calais

Boulogne

Étaples
LeTouquet

A ARTOIS AND FLANDERS (Legend p. 290)

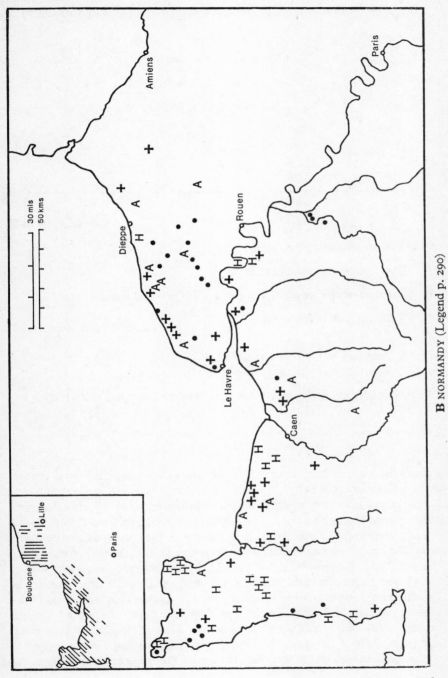

B NORMANDY (Legend p. 290)

Key to Map 19 A

Place names in

-ingues	I	*-inghen*	O	*-thun*	▲
-ingue	!	*-inghem*	●	*-incthun*	■
-inge	.!.	*-ingem*	♀	*-enthun*	◨
-inghe	i				
-inckhove	h				

Key to Map 19 B

A   Places named *Anglesqueville*

H   Place names in *-hou* and variants

+   Place names incorporating an Old English personal name

•   Other English place names

Inset

III   Summary of symbols on map 19 A

∥   Summary of symbols on map 19 B

No comparable study is available for several of the areas here shown blank.

---

outside the walls of Paris, under the immediate eye of the picked royal guards, by king Clothaire II in 627.

Not all colonies were so concentrated. Another hundred villages of English origin extend throughout the coastal regions of Normandy, from Picardy to the borders of Brittany. Their names differ markedly from those of the Boulogne area. The early East Anglian forms are altogether absent; the majority are those that are found all over the English parts of Britain, but are commonest south of the Thames, especially in the central and eastern south coast counties; and are in Britain more usual in areas of secondary colonisation than in the districts of the earliest settlers. In Normandy the discovery of a little 6th-century English ornament has also been uncertainly reported. Though the names are spread along the whole of the coast, their distribution suggests two distinct regions of thicker settlement, one between the estuaries of the Seine and the Somme, the other in and about the Cotentin peninsula, behind Cherbourg; and there Gregory of Tours knew of a substantial independent body of Saxons, established in the territory of Bayeux well before the end of the 6th century.

These considerable English colonies were installed by the western Franks in recently conquered Roman lands, that had previously adhered to the kingdom of Aegidius and Syagrius; and had accepted a large number of British refugees in the previous century, whose descendants inherited a profound hostility to Germanic invaders in general, and to the English in particular. There the colonists were in time absorbed, their earlier differences ultimately obliterated by the Scandinavian Northmen of the 9th and 10th centuries, who imposed upon the whole area its lasting name of Normandy. But other English expeditions were enlisted by the kings of the eastern Franks, and retained their identity. A later German chronicler transcribed an account of one of them, asserting that

> the Saxon people . . . leaving the *Angli* of Britain, urged on by the need and desire to find new homes, sailed to Hatheloe on the German coast, when king Theodoric of the Franks was at war with the Thuringian leader Hermenfred. . . . Theodoric sent envoys to these Saxons, whose leader was called Hadugat . . . and promised them homes for settlement in return for victory.

The date is probably 531. The place is Hadeln, the small district around Cuxhaven that had been the Saxon homeland, and includes Wester Wanna, Galgenberg and other early cemeteries.

Hadugat's men came back to the land of their ancestors. He sent some of them to help the Franks to victory, and they were settled in the Thuringian lands they subdued; they were perhaps the same Saxons who 'rebelled' against the Franks, with Thuringian support, a generation later, in 555. Others stayed by the Elbe, to become the nucleus of later Lower Saxon people, who halted the advance of the Slavs, recovered Hamburg, and held the frontier until their remote descendants overran and subdued the Slavs of the north European plain and made it a German land. They brought with them from Britain quantities of plain rough pottery, that is most closely matched among the Middle Angles, and continued to manufacture it for some generations; they also brought the characteristic Anglian place name *-botl*, a defended stronghold, that in Britain was most used by the Northumbrians and Mercians, and in Germany marks the concentrations of the Saxons, and is nowadays spelt *-büttl*. In Germany later chroniclers believed that the continental Saxons descended from the colonists who came from Britain in the 6th century. That tradition was unknown in Britain; in the 8th century Bede and others called their continental namesakes the 'Old Saxons' and assumed that the Saxons of Britain were the emigrants, a portion of a people who had remained continuously in their European homes. The archaeological evidence now available is not conclusive; but it suggests that both were largely right. In the ancient cemeteries by the estuary of the Elbe, burials all but ceased by the end of the 5th century, when the bulk of the population crossed to Britain; but a few later burials are known on some of the old sites, and it is probable that Hadeln was not as entirely deserted as Angel. Yet those who remained were few and weak. The strength and capacity of the continental Saxons was restored by large scale 6th-century immigration from Britain.

The identity of these various groups is not easily determined, for migration had already altered the meanings of national names before the middle of the 6th century. Procopius, writing about 550, already used *Angli*, English, as the general term for the Germanic settlers in Britain who were not Frisian, and the story of Hadugat observes the same usage, distinguishing the Saxons who made their homes in Europe from the *Angli* who stayed behind in Britain. Most European writers indiscriminately applied the word Saxon both to the Germanic inhabitants of Britain and to the people of the Lower Elbe; but in Thuringia the immigrants from the Elbe lands were called *Angli* and *Varni*, and there Anglian pottery and the widespread place names in *-leben*, confined to Thuringia and to Varnian and Danish territory, confirm their usage. Other historians report other peoples elsewhere who were known as Saxons; but the word does not contrast 'Saxon' with 'Angle'. Just before the Langobards invaded Italy in 568, they were joined by 20,000 of their 'old friends' the Saxons, with their wives and children. They could have come from Thuringia; or they might have been descendants of Hadugat's men or of other recent emigrants from Britain; perhaps of the Angles who had lived with the Langobards in fifth-century Bohemia; of those who had come to Italy with Odovacer; or of other unrecorded emigrants. Whoever they were, they quarrelled with their Langobard allies soon after the conquest of Italy and sought new homes in southern France, but without success; they were driven thence to their previous homes in Germany, to find that the Franks had installed Suevi in their place, and most of them perished in a vain effort to expel the intruders. Chance records name a few groups of Angles and Saxons, some of them from Britain; others are likely to have lived and moved without record.

These notices of English migration from Britain to Europe are confined to the earlier 6th century; and so is most of the archaeological evidence that matches them. The movement is most marked in the years between 520 and 560. The cause is plain. A very large population had come to Britain in the closing years of the fifth century, and had been confined within precise borders by the victory of Arthur. When their children grew to manhood they needed more land. Though the area of their reservations looks large upon a map, the extent of light alluvial soil was more restricted; and nothing suggests that the pagan English, before the coming of the monks, were any more accustomed to the clearance of wild woodland than other Germanic peoples. They could not find land at home, so they went abroad. Most of the few who were able to find new homes within Britain appear to have moved with the consent of the British authorities; it is evident that the English still considered the British states too strong to challenge or to defy. They accepted the consequences of their grandfathers' defeat at Badon, and continued to do so until after the great plague of the mid sixth century.

CHAPTER SIXTEEN

ENGLISH CONQUEST

Rebellion

The second Saxon revolt was no concerted national rising, like Hengest's rebellion in the 440s. It began as a trickle and became a flood. The memory of Badon had contained the English within their borders for three generations; though the military strength of Arthur's empire soon dissolved, fear of superior British power long outlived its reality. Its weakness was revealed when Cynric seized Salisbury in 550; though he made no further conquest, his little local victory demonstrated that British supremacy might be challenged with impunity.

The challenge was not taken up elsewhere until 568, and then at first it failed. Young Aethelbert of Kent broke out beyond his frontiers, evidently towards London, into the lands of the settled Saxons of the North Downs; the armies of Ceawlin and Cuthwulf came to the defence of the city, and 'drove him back into Kent'. The main military forces on both sides were English, and victory emboldened the victors. In 571 Cuthwulf destroyed the midland British at Bedford, and marched to Oxford; six years later his heir joined Ceawlin in the conquest of the lower Severn. In less than ten years British political authority in the south had been abolished. The crumbling dam crashed suddenly, and the English flooded over open lands.

Ceawlin commanded the English of Winchester and Salisbury. Various testimonies point to the homeland of Cuthwulf, called Cutha for short. The Eslingas of Haslingfield (Map 20, p. 295), south-west of Cambridge, had developed a new technique in the manufacture of saucer brooches; their jewellers punched the ornament on to a thin plate from the rear and soldered it to a base plate. In the later sixth century they evolved elaborate designs in this technique, most popular among them a Maltese Cross enclosing comic faces; these brooches are found beside the route of Cutha's army down the Icknield Way to the Thames and beyond, and so are some other related brooches; they also reach westward from the Eslingas towards the Middle Angles. Places named from Cutha also clustered along the Icknield Way, to Cutteslowe in north Oxford, probably his burial-mound, and mark the settlements that held the newly conquered military route. The genealogists give the same origin. A late gloss on the Saxon Chronicle explained Cuthwulf as the 'brother' of his ally Ceawlin, and the name of Ceawlin's predecessors, Cynric and Cerdic, are intruded into his pedigree. But the pedigree descends from Esla 'Gewising'; Gewissae was the earlier name of the middle Thames Saxons, whence the Eslingas had originated. Cuthwulf seems to have come from the Cambridge region, and to have died as the ruler of Oxford. His was the tiniest of all the earlier English territories, and Ceawlin's people were also small; yet it was they who seized the initiative and destroyed the British. They had much to gain and little to lose, for in their isolated territories their small forces lived more precariously than their greater neighbours, and also had less room for internal expansion. Ceawlin's people lived many scores of miles from the nearest English, and in the past a little local frontier had prevented the Eslingas from carrying their ornament to nearby Cambridge, and had exposed them to a double danger, from the British of the midlands and from strong unfriendly English neighbours.

Cuthwulf's victories liberated the rest of the southern English. The spread of late 6th century burial grounds, shown on map 21 (p. 297), describes the immediate consequence. A flood of immigrants colonised the lands between the districts in which the English had formerly been confined, and so joined the scattered English territories into a single block of territory. The most important further advance was the seizure of Ilchester. Half a dozen small sites surround the town, the furthest four miles to the north-west, at Pitney, by Somerton. They are known from chance finds, but from several of them chance has preserved grave goods fashionable well before the end of the century, earlier than any others known so far west of the old centres; and the unimportant little village of Somerton gave its name to a distinct people, the *Sumorsaete*, whose expanded territory is still known as Somerset. The seizure of Ilchester was clearly a deliber-

---

Map 20

⚒ 571	Approximate site and date of battles
C	Places named after *Cutha*
+	Saucer brooches with Maltese Cross design
ı	Saucer brooches with Six Face design
□	Great Squareheaded brooches with border of free standing faces *(Leeds type B6, 95-100)*
●	*-tuns* taken by Cutha in 571
○	Modern towns

See Notes to the Maps

MAP 20 THE ENGLISH CONQUEST OF THE SOUTH

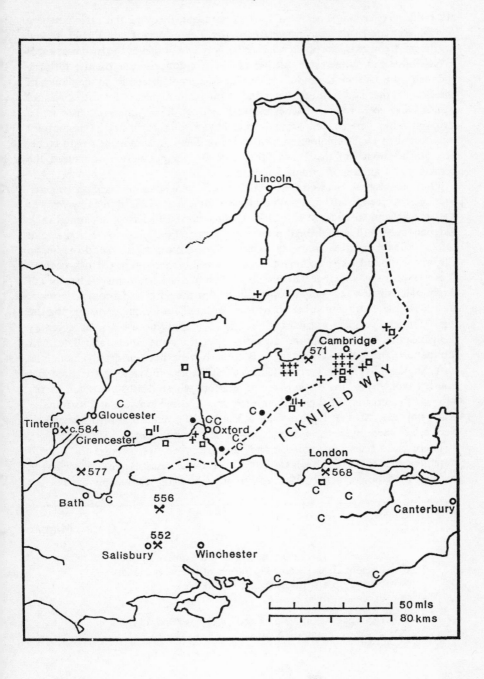

ate military decision. The town was the strategic focus of the region, where several Roman roads converged; there the Fosse Way from Exeter forked northwards, towards Cirencester, Leicester and Lincoln, from the road eastwards to Salisbury and Winchester, Silchester and London; right across the fork ran the road from Dorchester and from Portland and Poole harbours to the mouth of the Parrett, that had formerly been one of the main highways from Ireland and South Wales to Europe. At Ilchester, the first English of Somerset constituted a garrison. They were needed, for in the marshes ten miles to the north Glastonbury is reported to have remained in British hands for several generations to come, and at the mouth of the Parrett the large British population who used the cemetery of Cannington endured as long.

The colonies that followed Cuthwulf's victory were not haphazard settlements, founded by carefree adventurers on their private initiative. Within a few years of 571, the several districts of the English are reported to have proclaimed their independence and established permanent monarchies. Records are few and brief, for Bede reported almost nothing of sixth-century history, and the Saxon Chronicle limited its selection of events to those that interested 9th-century West Saxon kings, together with a scanty botch of northern history. The story of the midlands is lost, for only a few fragments of the Anglian Chronicle survive. But these fragments remembered the foundation of future kingdoms, noting the 'first king who reigned' in each region; and their tradition was also accepted by the genealogists, who name the dynasties after the same rulers, and date their foundation. Independent monarchy is said to have been asserted among the East Angles in 571, the year of Cuthwulf's victory, and among the East and South Saxons by a king of the same generation, whose deaths are noted in 587 and 590; the creation of the Mercian monarchy is placed in 584, and its founder is also named as the first English ruler of Lindsey. The late sixth-century colonies were established under the authority of the new monarchies.

There is no record of midland and East Anglian wars, beyond the general statement that some of the pagans who had occupied East Anglia earlier in the century went on to 'invade Mercia' and to fight many campaigns against the

---

Map 21

   o   sites with 5th century and later 6th century burials, without clear evidence of earlier 6th century burial
   ⌂   primary barrow burials
   ▲   excavated royal centre

Other symbols as on Maps 3 and 18 (pp. 59 and 285)
  \\\\ Areas shown on Map 18

MAP 21 PAGAN ENGLISH SETTLEMENT 4
THE LATER 6th CENTURY

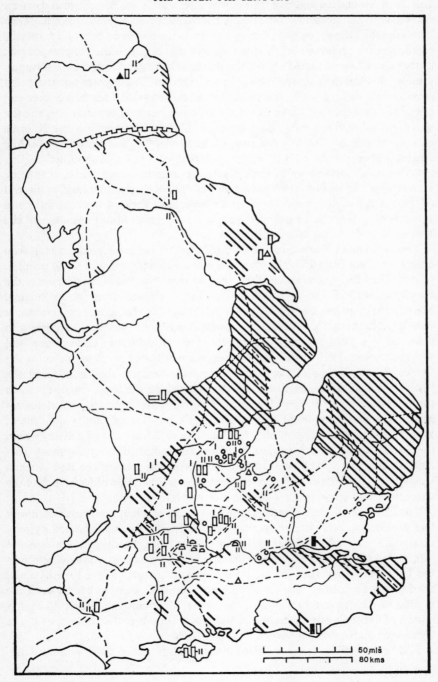

50 mls
80 kms

British. A few notices suggest a little of what happened. The East Anglian dynasty, named Uffingas from its first king, Uffa, were the dynasty of Suffolk. They displaced the Iclingas in Norfolk, perhaps in 571, perhaps earlier; and it may be that it was the pressure of their new kingdom that impelled the Eslingas, or part of them, to move westward against the British. Grave goods attest their advance, erasing the frontiers of the earlier sixth century. Their great squareheaded brooches are difficult to date; it may be that one or two had reached Sussex and the northern Angles in the middle of the century, but later versions swept in the wake of Cuthwulf's armies; they are especially numerous among the Eslingas and on the middle Thames, like the punched brooches, and among the Middle Angles and on the Avon. Those who took them did not give the East Anglian kings political sovereignty in these regions, but their spread argues that some East Angles had moved into these territories. There they settled; and at the end of the century their jewellers evolved a monstrous hybrid of the cruciform and squareheaded brooches, particularly popular among the Middle Angles and the Deirans.

The augmented English of the midlands united behind Creoda, a king who claimed descent from Icel. His kingdom was a federation of very small peoples, who assumed the general name of the 'frontier men', the Mercians, the men of the march, or border. The text termed the 'Tribal Hidage' knew of an 'original Mercia' that was half the size of 7th-century Mercia; the figures suggest that it comprised numerous peoples of the Middle Angles and the Avon, together with those of the Banbury area on the borders of northern Oxfordshire and Worcestershire. Their main territory approximately coincided with that of the former Roman *civitas* of the Coritani, and the frontier they held faced the Pennine British across the Trent and the Cornovii on the west. One list records the early rulers of Lindsey. It regards Creoda as its first king and notes his origin. The first name listed after Woden is 'Cretta Vinting'; and Vinta, 'son of Woden', is the name of no person, in English or in British, but of a place, Venta, the Roman name of Caistor-next-Norwich, the centre of the 5th-century East Anglian kingdom of Icel. It may be that Creoda was himself the East Anglian king whom Uffa of Ipswich expelled; or that he was heir of a cadet branch of the dynasty, whose origin in the Norwich area was remembered.

The creation of Mercia entailed the overthrow of whatever British authority had previously been asserted in the north midlands. But the Mercian dynasty emerged in the course of wars between different English dynasties, and is not reported to have fought against the British for many centuries. Campaigns across the Trent are not recorded so long as the further shore remained in British hands; the Mercians remained allies of the Cornovii on their western border until the middle of the 7th century, and of the Welsh kingdoms thereafter; all that is known of Creoda's own campaigns is that his death is linked with the wars of the Gewissae on his southern border.

The Saxon Chronicle briefly noted events that its editors did not understand.

They recorded the victories or deaths of kings, for these were the notices that they found in their sources; but they knew little of the kings' subjects. Their archaeological remains proclaim the important consequences of the wars. Map 21 outlines the expansion of the English in the years of Ceawlin's supremacy, and immediately thereafter. Most of the new sites are small poorly furnished cemeteries, or else the isolated graves of individuals, often wealthy, in sharp contrast with the large undifferentiated cemeteries of the fifth century. The majority of the new sites were in the midlands, around and between the borders of earlier English reservations. There the subjects of Ceawlin and Creoda lived secure, in small groups and family units, often settled immediately beside a Roman British farmstead, that was either still inhabited, or not yet reverted to the wild, or else beside a small town that was now under English political control.

Ceawlin's capture of the Cotswolds and Cirencester had made him great, and tradition honoured him as the first supreme commander of the southern English since Badon. He inherited small forces in Winchester and Salisbury; his rule was accepted by the Gewissae, and he is said to have annexed the South Saxons. But his power did not endure. The English were badly beaten by the British on the Wye, and in 584 Ceawlin returned home 'in anger'. In 591 a new king is said to have ruled in his place, evidently over the Gewissae, and in 592 Ceawlin was 'expelled' after a great battle at Woden's Barrow, near Alton Priors, east of Devizes, just south of the Wansdyke. Wars between the English had driven him back into his original territory. The Mercians were involved, for in the next year, 593, the Chronicle entry reads 'Ceawlin and Cwichelm and Crida died'. The name Cwichelm is rare, used otherwise only by a later Wessex king and perhaps a Kentish bishop; but it names one of the earliest Wessex royal burial-mounds, of the late 6th century, by East Hendred, near Wantage, evidently the district that Cwichelm ruled. The name of Crida, Creoda or Cretta is rarer still, otherwise known only through a few place names, near Cirencester and elsewhere.

The Chronicle entry does not say who fought whom, or whether the deaths were connected; one tradition says that the enemy at Woden's Barrow were British, and it may be that Creoda fought with Welsh allies; one West Saxon tradition included him among their kings, and it may be that he annexed part of their territory. But whatever the combinations, the strength of the Gewissae and the Mercians was reduced, and southern hegemony passed to Aethelbert of Kent. Little is known of how he acquired or held it; his sister married the king of the East Saxons, whose pedigree is attached to Saxon gods. But the pedigree abounds in Anglian names, that recall those of the dynasty of Deira; and some grave goods of his time are common to Deira and to the Thames estuary. It may be that Aethelbert allied with Aelle of Deira to establish the new East Saxon dynasty, for its next king, his nephew, accepted his suzerainty. Elsewhere, Kentish ornament spread widely in the south, and a few specifically Kentish burial-grounds in the south midlands suggest the posting of Kentish garrisons and perhaps of Kentish royal officials in subject territory. But the reality of Aethelbert's supremacy is known only from Bede's emphatic statement.

Consolidation:
Aethelferth and Aethelbert

A few years later Aethelferth of Bernicia won a like supremacy in the north, first destroying the British kingdoms and then annexing English Deira and York. At the beginning of the 7th century, the English were grouped into two large and powerful realms, both recent, but very different from each other. In the north, two small kingdoms had suddenly overwhelmed a large British territory, thinly peopled. The more numerous English of the south were divided into many kingdoms, a few of them large, many very small. Greater kings overawed the smaller, and the king of Kent asserted suzerainty over all of them; the accidents of their history had prepared them for a hierarchy of kingship, whose future was uncertain. The power of the sovereign dynasty might prove permanent, rooting in England a wide authority like that which king Diarmait had briefly held in Ireland; or it might dissolve into a loose and nominal superiority over numerous kingdoms that were in practice independent, as had already happened in Ireland, and was in the future to happen in Europe, under the revived Roman empire of the west.

Men knew that their present kingdoms were insecure, for power quickly won may as soon be lost; and the strength and structure of the several kingdoms greatly varied. In the north the Bernicians and the Deirans had little in common but their language. The ancestors of the Deirans had settled in a prosperous sophisticated countryside, where well-educated gentlemen were masters of obedient tenants, near to a great city; but the Bernicians had always lived among barbarians beyond the border. The Deirans controlled infinitely richer resources, but the Bernicians were a simple and hardier folk, greatly more experienced in warfare. The southerners were even more diversified. In the older kingdoms men lived on lands that their forbears had tilled for nearly two hundred years; between these kingdoms, pioneers established new homes quietly, in safe lands far removed from the surviving British states; but on the western borders colonists had to contend with a still obstinate Welsh resistance.

The political and social structure of the English was not uniform. After five or six generations the population of the old kingdoms was already divided into great men and small. But the pioneers and the colonists were of mixed origins. Some were coherent bodies detached from a single parent kingdom; others were small groups or individuals drawn from different kingdoms, not yet fused into political entities in their new homes. Their allegiance lay open to whichever ruler might offer greater security at any given moment, whether he were king of the West Saxons, of the Mercians, or of Kent, king of a small people or of a restricted region, or simply a capable leader of their own. In the early seventh century there were as yet no accepted institutions valid for all the English.

Their society and their political government was infinitely varied, its outline still to be formed.

In the time of Aethelbert and Aethelferth, the issue of a single battle might enable one of the two great kingdoms to subdue the other, and establish speedily a united England. Men weighed such possibilities, for when the men of Kent accepted Christianity from a Roman missionary the pope instructed him, in the summer of 601, to carry the faith to the north and to establish a bishop in York, with equal metropolitan authority. The pope's ruling plainly answered a query first raised by the Kentish church; and the proposal could not have been put forward without the approval of the king, for it concerned politics as deeply as religion. In 601 Deira was still independent. Aethelferth had destroyed the British of the Pennines, but had not yet turned south. But the writing was large upon the wall; his future invasion was already a danger to be dreaded. If the Deirans accepted a bishop in York, sent from Kent, they thereby riveted a political alliance with the king of Kent, admitting his stronger power in the north as well as the south. If Aethelbert took Deira under his protection and alliance, he automatically confronted Aethelferth of Bernicia; if he prevailed against him, his victory would make him sovereign of all the English in Britain.

The alliance did not mature. Aethelferth's victories overwhelmed Deira, bringing him to the Humber, and perhaps beyond, within three years of pope Gregory's letter. Later in the century, the pope's ruling became the legal foundation for the permanent division of the English church into two metropolitan provinces, but it had no immediate effect. After 604 Aethelbert led no crusade against the pagan north. When he died, in 616, the kings of the south refused allegiance to his son, and ended Kentish hegemony for ever; they also rejected Christianity. It was Aethelferth who marched south, against king Redwald of the East Angles, who for a short while asserted primacy over the southern kingdoms, and sheltered Aethelferth's exiled rival, Edwin of Deira. Victory might have made Aethelferth acknowledged sovereign of all the English. But he failed, and Edwin took his place in the north. The Bernicians accepted Edwin, and Aethelferth's sons went into exile.

Edwin and Oswy

Edwin overshadowed the south; when he married a Kentish princess he accepted her Christian religion and made friends and allies among those numerous southerners who adhered to the new faith or returned to it. He made war upon the Welsh, and the patriotic pride of Bede asserts his power at home. To later generations his strong rule seemed a golden age, for

> such was the peace of Britain at the time . . . that it is even today a
> proverb that if a woman with a new-born babe then wished to walk
> across the land from sea to sea, she would come to no harm. . . .
> King Edwin so considered his subjects' comfort that when he saw
> clear springs by the highway, he had posts set up with bronze cups

attached for the refreshment of travellers, and no man dared . . . or wished . . . to touch them beyond his need.

He left a different reputation in the south. There the West Saxons were again united under strong kings. Ceolwulf campaigned against the South Saxons, and repeatedly fought the 'Angles and the Welsh'. His Anglian neighbours were Mercian, and nothing is remembered of the then Mercian king save that he had at one time befriended the exiled Edwin. Cynegils, who succeeded Ceolwulf in 611, crippled British Dumnonia, destroying its army near Axminster, and planting colonies in Dorset and north Somerset just before pagan burial rites passed from use. He reigned for more than 30 years, and was the only over-king of the West Saxons before the 9th century to bequeath his sovereignty intact to his son. He came nearer than any other early king to establishing a powerful West Saxon monarchy, and from Cirencester he looked north against the Angles.

Edwin broke the power of the West Saxons in 626. One of their under-kings attempted to assassinate him, and he replied with a full-scale invasion, killing five West Saxon regional kings and a 'great number of people'. The Mercian kingdom was reorganised; Creoda's grandson Penda began to rule in 626, and until 642 divided the kingdom with his brother Eowa. The new kings were enthroned when Edwin's armies overthrew the West Saxons, clearly with his approval; and they pushed back the West Saxon borders. In 628 Penda fought their kings at Cirencester and 'reached agreement'. Thenceforth the northern Cotswolds were Mercian, and the West Saxons were permanently cut off from the lower Severn crossings; their energies were thenceforth directed against Dumnonia, no longer against Wales.

Edwin's empire was as fragile as his predecessors'. He overran north Wales, but his invasion ended in defeat. Catwallaun of Gwynedd recovered his own kingdom, defeated Penda, and then enlisted him as his own subject ally. His Welsh and Mercian army defeated and killed Edwin in 633, and for a year British hegemony was restored. But the Northumbrians rallied. Oswald, the son of Aethelferth of Bernicia, returned from exile among the Scots and Picts, killed Catwallaun, and was accepted by both Northumbrian kingdoms. He immediately recovered Edwin's wide authority, constraining Cynegils of Wessex to accept Christian baptism and chastising the Welsh upon the Severn. But he too failed to hold his power. The 'English rose against Oswald' in 636, without success; but Penda soon after revived the grand alliance of the Welsh and the southern English, and killed him in 642. Penda plundered the north, and a contemporary Welsh record remarks his splendid distribution of the spoils by the Forth, the *Atbret Iudeu*. Penda's victory made him master of his allies as of his defeated enemies, and a few quick campaigns enforced the obedience of the West Saxons and the East Angles. Thenceforth, Mercian sovereignty lasted for 150 years. It was interrupted only for three years, when Oswald's brother Oswy killed

Penda in 655 and briefly reasserted the dominion that his brother and Edwin had held before; but in 658 the Mercians recovered their independence, under Penda's son Wulfhere; they quickly regained control of the south, conquered the West Saxons, re-established a separate kingdom of the South Saxons, to whom they gave control of Wight, and subdued Kent.

Northumbria was not conquered and did not at once accept defeat. Oswy looked north, making 'the greater part of the Picts and Scots tributary'. The Pictish king was killed, and an English under-king established over part of his kingdom; the king of the Clydeside British was also killed, and replaced with Oswy's brother-in-law. But Oswy's son Egferth tried to recover his father's southern authority, until he was compelled to accept the Trent as a permanent frontier in 679. Checked on the south, he turned his arms against foreigners, invading Ireland in 684, against the strong protest of his churchmen. But when he was killed by the Picts in 685, the lay and clerical leaders of Northumbria deliberately rejected their military past, and chose as their new king the elderly and pacific scholar Aldfrith, who had spent most of his life among Irishmen and monks. He ruled for 20 years and was patron of the monasteries where Bede grew to manhood, whence came the glories of Northumbrian art and learning; but on his death, the political fabric of eighth-century Northumbria dissolved amid the personal and dynastic discord of weak kings, brutal or feeble, whose authority commanded little respect at home and none abroad.

The Mercians

South of the Trent the kings who followed Penda built a powerful monarchy, which retained its supremacy into the 9th century. The dynasty, the Mercian peoples, and the lesser southern kingdoms clung to their unity. Wulfhere left a young son, not old enough to rule; his younger brother Aethelred therefore succeeded him, but no factions raised civil war in his nephew's name, or impelled him to make away with his nephew. When he abdicated and retired to a monastery, in 704, the nephew succeeded him, in preference to his own son; and when the nephew also retired to a monastery, Aethelred's son succeeded, for a brief and vicious reign. He was replaced by Aethelbald, descended from Penda's brother Eowa, and after forty years of sovereignty a distant cousin, Offa, also heir of Eowa, reigned as long and as secure, sovereign of an undivided realm now long-established. The five great kings of Mercia consolidated the English into a nation and a kingdom, whose identity proved strong enough to survive the fearful strains of Scandinavian invasions, that followed hard upon the death of Offa, in 796. When Egbert of Wessex destroyed the Mercian power he did not found a new united kingdom. He imposed a new dynasty upon a nation that had been formed long before.

Expansion

The Mercian dynasty enabled England to grow from origins immensely diverse.

The conquering English acquired vast territories and numerous foreign British subjects; and their own English past varied greatly. The second Saxon revolt was the work of three of the smallest peoples, the Bernicians, the Eslingas, and the Hampshire Jutes. The older and larger states profited from their success, but played no recorded part in its leadership. They had small cause. When the revolt began their inhabitants farmed the lands where they were born; they had lived at peace since their grandfathers' time, sending their adventurous youth and surplus population to Europe. They gave no sign that they felt able to attack their British neighbours, or wished to do so; and the princes of the British were still free to make war upon their relatives and rivals without fear of English attack. To outward appearance a Celtic Britain seemed able to absorb the English in course of time. Yet in a generation the tiny forces of three enterprising local captains were able to blow away the British power and to make the fairer parts of Britain permanently English.

The British collapsed because their states were rotted and hollow. The English prevailed because each initial success recruited larger and bolder armies, which had no need to guard against counter-attack. The circumstances of their victory bequeathed to their successors a remarkable and unforeseen consequence, the predominance of the north and the midlands, of Northumbria and Mercia. In all previous and subsequent history, Britain has been dominated by the fertile lowlands of the south and south-east, rich in easy soils, easily co-ordinated, strategically placed to rule the rest of the country. Now, war had wasted the fertile lowlands, and strengthened the hardier north.

The North and the East

At the beginning of the 7th century, each English kingdom inherited a different past, and fronted different present needs. In Northumbria, a very few English ruled a large British population. In the last generation of pagan burial their ornament spread through the East Riding from its original centres in Deira, and extended to the Bernicians and the lands between; but hardly any of it penetrated or crossed the Pennines. A few place names suggest the strongholds of English lords in the dales and in strategic west-coast regions, but the bulk of the English lived east of the road from York to Corbridge and Edinburgh, and were for centuries too few to colonise the west. The west offered no threat; and such

Map 22

 Areas shown on map 18, p. 285

 Areas shown on map 21, p. 297

Other symbols as for Maps 3 and 18 (pp. 59 and 285)

MAP 22 PAGAN ENGLISH SETTLEMENT 5
THE 7th CENTURY

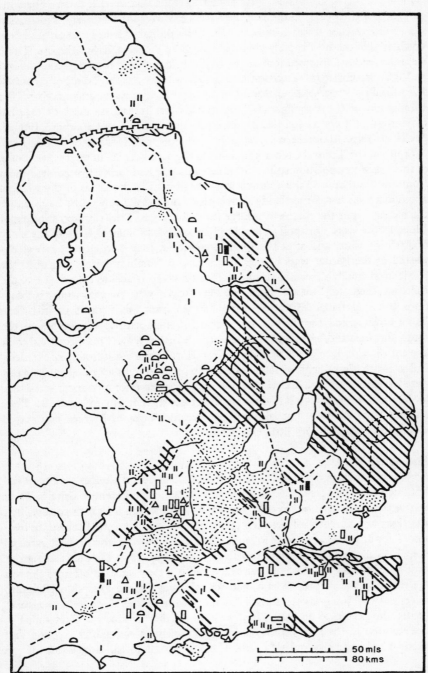

50 mls
80 kms

colonies as the English could afford went to lands that needed them. The wide ambition of their early kings asserted suzerainty over the southern English, and were content when it was acknowledged. Their military victory also carried them northward to the Forth and beyond into southern Pictland, in Strathmore. These were the lands of untamed foreigners, who would not yield to absent conquerors; and it is there that the English place names witness the migration of colonists. Northumbria expanded northward near to the east coast, and accepted the submission of the Pennines and the north-west. It had no need of external expansion, and ended southern wars when the midland and southern English decisively rejected northern suzerainty.

South of the Trent the older kingdoms of the east were set in their ways. Some of their excess population spilled into the lands that had formerly separated them from one another, and others doubtless contributed to the needs of the western kingdoms who had larger lands to colonise. But the old kingdoms had neither the incentive nor the means to enlarge their dominion. The scattered Lindissi of Lincolnshire were unhappily placed. Their lands had loomed large in the story of Arthur's wars, and after the English conquest, they were at first repeatedly wasted in the border wars of the Mercians and Northumbrians: not until the border was finally determined, in 679, did they win peace, as a province of the Mercian kingdom. Further south, the East Angles were isolated from the Mercians by their fenland frontier, and separated from the Thames basin by the Essex forests; and formidable dykes guarded their natural approaches to the south and west through Cambridge and the Icknield Way. They preserved their ancient division into a North Folk, descendants of the earliest Anglian settlers, and a South Folk, heirs of later immigrants, whose dynasty ruled both. They were numerous enough and well enough protected to offer a stronger resistance to Mercian supremacy; but they were not strong enough to reject it. They retained their dynasty, but admitted the greater power of Mercia, and stayed within their borders with little expansion.

The South East

Across the Thames the English of Kent had taken over a Roman society in full working order, by agreement with the then Roman government of Britain. Their first settlers were planted in their formative years within a Roman society, that was sharply differentiated between great landowners and servile tenant cultivators. They acquired their Roman lands half a century before the Franks mastered Roman Gaul, and the dazzling wealth of their jewellery is the outward sign of lords as aristocratic as those of Frankish Gaul. But they were cut off from the rest of Britain by the sea, the Weald, and the Medway, whose exceptional breadth prevented the integration of their colonies west of the river with the main Kentish homeland to its east. They made no further conquests. They failed to take London in the fifth-century wars, failed again in Aethelbert's youth, and failed to hold the city on his death. London passed to the direct rule of the weaker kings of the East Saxons. They, and the small peoples of the regions that later ages knew as Middlesex, the Middle Saxon land, and the Southern District, Surrey, were easily subjected to Mercian rule; when the Mercians went on to invade Kent in 676 and sack Rochester, the port of London passed permanently into the control of the Mercian kings, whose supremacy was challenged only on the rare occasions when West Saxon kings were strong enough to threaten Kent and the East Saxons.

The early settlers of Surrey and Sussex were confined to the easy Downs and coastland. From the early seventh century onward, they and the men of Kent spread into the Wealden country between, and tamed it by an arduous agricultural technology unknown to their ancestors. Their kinsmen north of the Thames also spread more thinly over the uninviting London clays. Throughout the south-east, expansion was slow, and empty lands sufficed to absorb the offshoots of the small early kingdoms. But in the west the frontier kingdoms of the West Saxons and the Mercians had other opportunities and other needs. In the early 7th century the men of Wessex were few, and the lands they mastered large. Their two small peoples had overrun huge parts of the most fertile soils in Britain, and in many of them no English had settled before the conquest. But their borderlands made stronger demands upon their manpower, for their ill-defined frontier faced the still unconquered power of British Dumnonia and was defended by no natural obstacles of hill or river.

The West

The West Saxons were obliged to fight continuously on two fronts, against the Mercians on the north and the Dumnonians on the west, and had also to contain the Welsh within their borders. The latest pagan burials, early in the 7th century, shown on Map 22, mark the first stage of their expansion. Most sites lie in secure lands, on the edges of earlier settlement; as yet there was little penetration beyond Cirencester, below the Chiltern escarpment into Gloucestershire. A few colonists lined the Bristol Avon, and the Dorset coast, but none are yet known to have penetrated into Devon.

The recorded western wars of Wessex are confined to the years when Wessex was least harassed by other English kingdoms. In 614, just before the death of Aethelbert of Kent, the kings

> Cynegils and Cwichelm fought at *Beandun*, and slew 2,065 of the Welsh.

The only known place so named is Bindon, by Axmouth, just on the Devon side of the Dorset border, just west of the furthest known pagan burial-ground on the south coast; and is near to the Roman road that runs from Ilchester to the mouth of the Axe. The precise figure of enemy casualties is exceptional among the Chronicle entries; it may be that the battle was celebrated in a poem that the Chronicle cited; the size of the figure proclaims that the victory was regarded as unusually important. The location suggests that the garrison of Ilchester, 25 miles away, may have marched south to intercept an invading Dumnonian army, that used the quickest road eastward from Exeter.

The date implies that the Dumnonians co-ordinated their effort with the kings of south Wales, for the traditions of Glevissig held that the peace on their borders also was broken in 614, 30 years after the campaign of 584, and another report remembers a victory in Gwent early in the 7th century. If it were so, the English won the campaign, for fighting in Gwent meant that they had advanced beyond Gloucester; and the Welsh claim no gains in English lands. Thereafter, the West Saxons were concerned with Northumbrian and Mercian enemies, and the Welsh remained the allies of the Mercians. No further western wars are reported for nearly 40 years, until king Cenwalh, son and successor of Cynegils, fought at Bradford-on-Avon, east of Bath, evidently against the Welsh or the Mercians or both. Mercian pressure was eased with the fall of Penda in 655, but was renewed after Wulfhere's accession in 658. The Welsh of Glastonbury are said, however, to have been reinforced by the arrival of the Cornovian Morfael, the last British lord of Lichfield, probably expelled by Oswy in 655, and in the next few years the last efforts of the British to recover the fertile lowlands are recorded. In 658

> Cenwalh fought at *Peonna* against the Welsh, and drove them in flight as far as the Parrett.

The place is probably Penselwood, deep in English Wessex, almost halfway from Ilchester to Salisbury. The pursuit to the Parrett implies that the river then became the boundary; the new frontier entailed the English occupation of Glastonbury and secured the region that the garrison of Ilchester had hitherto controlled. Easy contact between the Dumnonians and the South Welsh across the narrows of the Severn estuary was ended.

Cenwalh is then said to have recovered territory from the Mercians, and to have invaded southern Dumnonia thereafter. In 661, he fought at *Posentesburh*, probably Posbury by Crediton, beyond Exeter. Then, or soon after, Exeter was opened to the English. English place names attest heavy colonisation that spread inland from Exeter; and the city itself was long partitioned between the English and British. The date was not long after Cenwalh's campaign, for Boniface, the future apostle of Germany, was educated from childhood in an English monastery in Exeter, and is said to have been a native of Crediton. He was born in the 680s, and was presumably a son of one of the first colonists.

The English conquest of south Devon outflanked the northern Dumnonians, but they long resisted; in 682 Cenwalh's grandson 'drove the British as far as the sea', probably in a campaign that swept from the Parrett through north Somerset; but the region was not secured, for the fortress of Taunton, only eight miles west of the Parrett, was not constructed until the time of king Ine, perhaps when he 'fought Geraint, king of the British', in 710. Ine tried and failed to reduce

Dumnonia, for the Cambrian Annals claim the heavy defeat of an English invasion in Cornwall in 722, and in the same year the English acknowledged that Ine's queen dismantled his own fortress of Taunton, perhaps again withdrawing behind the Parrett. The West Saxons were also pressed from the north, for eleven years later the Mercians annexed Somerton. The ultimate conquest of Dumnonia was postponed. Egbert of Wessex invaded Cornwall in 815, but ten years later the Dumnonian kings fought back in Devon, and Egbert failed to take Launceston. A dozen years thereafter the Cornishmen found new allies in the Danes, and the fate of Cornwall was henceforth merged in the struggle against the pirate host. Independence ended in the later 9th century; the Cornish bishop at Bodmin acknowledged the authority of Canterbury in 870, and five years later the last known Cornish king, Dungarth, died by drowning, perhaps in battle. Final conquest was delayed for another half-century, but from about 950 the Cornish permanently acknowledged English kings, and accepted bishops with English names.

The conquest of Dumnonia was delayed because the West Saxon kings were continually harassed by the Mercians. In 661, the year when Cenwalh fought at *Posentesburh*, Wulfhere overran Wessex, and detached the South Saxons and the Isle of Wight, to form a separate kingdom. The South Welsh seized their opportunity, and the Cambrian Annals noted that in 665

> Easter was celebrated among the Saxons for the first time. The second battle of Badon. Morcant died.

The Easter entry confirms the date, the year after the Synod of Whitby, in 664. The entry probably means that Morcant of Glevissig was killed at Badon; but even if the statements are not linked, the British had crossed the Severn in arms. No victory is claimed, and it was their last recorded attempt to recover western Wessex. They failed, but Wessex was not free to counter-attack. Cenwalh had moved his capital from Dorchester-on-Thames to a safer centre at Winchester, but after his death the under-kings ruled on their own, and the central government of the West Saxons lapsed. It was restored by a king with a British name, Ceadwalla, who revived West Saxon supremacy in the south-east, recovered Wight, enlisted the South Saxons as subordinate allies and went on to conquer Kent. The West Saxon grip on Kent was soon loosened, but West Saxons remained united under the long rule of Ine, though at times he admitted Mercian supremacy, perhaps after an unsuccessful attempt to challenge it in 692. But Ine founded no dynasty and for 80 years his successors fought their own under-kings and the Mercians, until Egbert established a stable dynasty and broke the Mercian power, in the 9th century, in an age when the Norsemen were already savaging the old political structure of England.

The West Saxons expanded westward in two centuries of warfare, repeatedly planting colonies in newly conquered lands that still needed defence against the British. The expansion of the Mercians was peaceful. The neighbouring Welsh were their allies, with little sign of war until the middle of the eighth century. Then king Eliseg of Powys

> seized the inheritance of Powys, and recovered it from the power of the English for 9 years with sword and fire.

The years may lie between 743, when Cuthred of Wessex combined with his life-long enemy Aethelbald of Mercia to fight against the Welsh, and the events of 752, when Cuthred fought Aethelbald at *Beorgford*, perhaps Burford by Tenbury, near Ludlow, and of 753 when Cuthred 'fought the Welsh'; the causes and combinations of the conflicts are obscure, but these are the only wars involving the Mercians and the Welsh that the Saxon Chronicle records anywhere near the time of Eliseg. The threat persisted, until Offa marked the permanent frontier with a formidable dyke some decades later.

The Midlands

The Mercians had need of military colonies on their northern border, and some scores of earlier 7th-century warrior chiefs were buried in barrows in the Derbyshire and Staffordshire upland; several places in Cheshire are also named from English burial-mounds, though none have yet been excavated; and a few names that end in *-bold* derive from Mercian strongholds placed on the Northumbrian border. Similar names lie near the borders between Mercia and other English kingdoms, and Mercian names extend into the West Riding about Halifax; but there is no sign of defence against the Welsh until Eliseg's time. The latest pagan burials stop short of the allied British borders, and suggest that significant English settlement had not begun when the burials ended, early in the 7th century. But before the middle of the century an incidental story reports English settlers on the upper Severn, in lands not conquered by the Mercians, while the place names of Cheshire and the north-west suggest that the British states admitted the peaceful immigration of their Mercian allies well before the middle of the century. Further south the names of the constituent peoples of Mercia, the Hwicce, the Magonsaete and others, penetrated into the border regions and beyond without sign of wars and conquest; by the 670s the English were well established in Bath and Gloucester, Hereford and Leominster, where many of the names of people and of places suggest an untroubled mixture of English and Welsh.

Integration: the English

In the time of Bede, in the early 8th century, there was not yet a country called England. He lived in the island of Britain, in one of the regions that he called 'districts of the English'. He meant the districts where the English ruled. Their population was mixed, and included many British, whom the English commonly described as Welsh. Geography and recent history were none the less beginning to shape national and regional identities and loyalties. Permanent boundaries took shape in the age of conquest, and were thereafter adjusted, but not radically altered. The independent *Cymry* still called themselves *Britones* when they wrote in Latin, and remembered that they were a single nation who had lost their inheritance; but their segregation into the three separate highland zones ended cultural and political contact between them, and the Welsh who lived under English rule in time forgot their kinship with their unconquered fellow-countrymen.

Bede's countrymen called themselves English from the 7th century onward, *Angli* when they wrote in Latin. *Saxones* and *Saxonia* were literary affectations, as common in Northumbria as in Wessex, and were never used to distinguish Saxons from Angles; the East Saxons felt no closer kin to the West Saxons than to the East Angles, and no individual Englishman is ever termed a Saxon in his own language. Only in the 9th century, when supremacy passed to a West Saxon dynasty that lacked the description Anglian, was it necessary to invent the words *Angligena* and *Angelcyn*, to adapt the continental usage of *Angli Saxones*, English Saxons, in contrast to the Saxons of Germany, or to rename the West and South Saxons the West and South *Angli*. But these terms were short-lived Latin political devices, and no form of *Engle-Sexe* or the like ever took root in English language. The whole nation was English, though the territorial name *Engle Land* did not come into general use until the 11th century and was then first used to distinguish the English districts from the Danish.

These words are more than curiosities of language. They show what the early English felt about themselves. They sensed their national identity sooner and more keenly than the peoples of Europe because foreigners of different speech lived in the same island, beyond their borders and within their borders. But the English states were a compact group, geographically contiguous, while the Cymry were split between the three highland zones and Brittany, and many lived among the several English kingdoms. The bonds that united the Cymry looked to a fading past; those that united the English belonged to the present and the future.

The English were one people in the face of strangers, but their internal differences were many. Each Englishman belonged to his own small people, the Hwicce, the Wigesta or the like, and was also a subject of the kingdom that incorporated them into larger units, as the East Angles or the Mercians, the Northumbrians or the West Saxons. The ties that bound one man to another varied. The customs of the older kingdoms were already hardened, and were little changed by conquest. All were conservative, but each had its own conventions. The North Folk, the men of Kent, and some of the Middle Angles had settled in a world that was still Roman, and their first generations had learnt much from it; but many of the Middle and East Angles had come to England in large coherent communities, bringing with them ancestral custom, whereas Kent was a kingdom formed in Britain from diverse origins, and its situation readily exposed it to continuing European influence. The colonial lands differed from each other and from the old kingdoms; the Northumbrian English lived together in the east, in one part of their huge kingdom, but the Mercians and West Saxons were more evenly scattered throughout their territories. Their ways were not yet set; men whose adventurous ancestors had moved from Germany to Sussex, from Sussex to Hampshire, from Hampshire to Berkshire, and thence to Devon or Dorset, were readier for innovation than those whose ancestors had moved once, in a community, two centuries before, into Norfolk or Leicestershire.

The grave goods of the early western settlers indicate that men drawn from diverse English origins were often thrown together in their new homes; and the burial grounds show something of their formation. In the 5th century and much of the 6th most of the English lived in close packed villages and buried their dead in large communal cemeteries; many of these cemeteries remained in use until after the English conquest, and in some parts of the old kingdoms, especially in Kent and Cambridgeshire, the habit of burying the dead fully clothed, with brooches, belts and other articles of dress, continued after pagan burial had ceased. But in regions where there are no English burials before the later 6th century, large cemeteries are few; one or two bodies, or very small cemeteries are commonly found in isolation. The English no longer needed to concentrate for defence. They were the superior ruling element in the population, and their pioneers could afford to live in separate farmsteads without fear of effective native British assault. The new communities that grouped these pioneers were necessarily looser than those that united older villages; their population was also more open to the influence of their British neighbours; but the native population from whom they learnt were the heirs of the 6th-century warlord kingdoms, wholly different in outlook from the Roman British who had influenced the formative years of the old kingdoms.

The Subject Welsh

Most of the 7th-century English kingdoms included a large number of native British, whom the English sometimes knew by their native national name of *Cumbrogi*, or *Cymry*, but more commonly described in English as foreigners, *Wealh* or *Wylisc*. They are most prominent in Wessex, where the late 7th-century laws of king Ine contain many clauses that legislate for Welshmen. As in Wales, the Welshmen of Wessex might belong to a free or unfree kin, and the free landowners are divided into three classes, like the Welsh of Wales. Some were men of substance, for a Welshman who owned five hides rated with the middle grade of English nobility, and five hides was a great deal of land. The Welsh also held royal office, and the Welshman who rode on the kings' service ranked with the lower English nobles.

The laws do not show how many the Welsh were, or where they lived. Bede's language suggests that they were numerous, for he comments that Aldhelm's open letter to the king of Dumnonia in 705

led many of the British subjects of the West Saxons to the celebra-
tion of the Catholic Easter.

They doubtless included the inhabitants of the newly conquered border regions;
but place names in central Wessex like Andover, Candover, Micheldever
indicate a substantial Welsh population, in a region that is a more probable home
for noble Welshmen entrusted with royal missions than the borderlands of
dubious loyalty. The limits and extent of these names cannot be determined
until the survey of the place names of Hampshire is published, but the personal
names of king Ceadwalla, his brother Mul and his grandfather Cadda, of the
8th-century *ealdorman* Conbran, abbot Catwal, and others, suggest that at least
one among the small kingdoms of the West Saxons retained a strong Welsh
element for a long time.

Kings and nobles so named must have been at least bilingual, their English as
fluent as their Welsh; and perhaps they spoke little or no Welsh. But since their
parents gave them such names, Welsh origins remained respectable, and
imply intermarriage among the well-to-do. It is probable that most children were
soon given names common among the dominant English; and Welsh names went
out of fashion among the nobility after the middle of the 8th century, though they
lasted longer, with the language, among the poorer cultivators. The inferior
status of the Wessex Welsh persisted in Norman England, for when Henry I
reissued the laws of Ine, he dropped the obsolete provisions for noble Welshmen,
a class long extinct, but retained those that concerned Welsh bondmen; and since
he revised the compensation due, to bring it into line with 12th-century values,
he was not mechanically copying an ancient ruling, but was dealing with a law
and a class of persons who were still a reality.

In Wessex, where English colonists were dispersed through extensive fertile
lands that had recently been British, a class of wealthy Welshmen is more
prominent than elsewhere. But for that reason it was more quickly assimilated
among the ruling English. Yet equivalents existed in other kingdoms. The laws
of Kent provided for an inferior class of cultivators, known by the Germanic
term *laet*, who were divided into three classes, like the Welsh, and rated at the
same inferiority as the Welsh of Wessex. Some Kentish notables also used Welsh
names; Dunwald was an 8th-century royal officer who owned substantial
property in Canterbury, and the extensive rural territory of *Dunwalinglond*.
Dunwallaun, perhaps a relative, also witnessed charters, as did the priests Welhisc
and Maban. Malvinus, Kentish ambassador to Mercia in 787, also bore a Welsh
name.

The numbers and the status of these Welshmen cannot be clearly assessed
until the early English charters are adequately published, the names of peoples
and places indexed and studied. Comparable evidence is not available for the
East and Middle Angles and East Saxons, whose laws and charters are not
preserved; but in Sussex, whence a few charters survive, the names of king

Nunna and others may be Welsh. In western Mercia, however, where charters are numerous, British magnates are few, for most of the midlands lay beyond the region of rich Roman villas, and wealthy British landlords did not survive the long interval between the collapse of British authority in the lower Severn and the imposition of settled English rule.

In Northumbria, evidence is stronger. Chad, Caedmon and others had Welsh names. Earlier 7th-century pagan English burials are plentiful in the East Riding, but they barely extend into the North and West Riding. When the Pennine British kings disappeared, their subjects remained; and they were still Welsh enough in the 10th century to fall naturally and without struggle under the control of the Strathclyde British. Until then, their lords were English. When bishop Wilfred was granted lands in the regions of Ribble, Yeadon, Dent and Catlow, in the late 7th century, he received the estates of British monasteries whose monks had fled. The grant that he troubled to secure did not entitle him to unpeopled waste, but to cultivated farmland, whose British cultivators remained; and from the Mersey to the Tyne, British administration and land tenure lasted till the 12th century. Even east of the Pennines, near Harrogate, about 670, Wilfred had difficulty with an independent British village, whose obedience he could not command without a posse of armed men. York itself retained a class of *Wallerwenta* at least until the 10th century, and some of them were men of substance, for the laws provide for Welshmen who prosper, and own a hide of land.

Men of inferior Welsh status persisted as late and later in the south. The laws of 10th-century London sentenced a runaway bondman to be stoned 'like a Welsh thief', implying a different status from an English thief. In Cambridge, an 11th-century guild insured its members against the contingency that they might slay a Welshman, and so be liable for a compensation payment set at half the value of a free Englishman; there the nearby village of Comberton suggests the home of some of the Welsh whom the guildsmen might encounter. These laws imply that a class of persons with inferior Welsh status existed in some numbers in much of England from the English conquest until after the Norman conquest and later. Laws tend to illuminate the unusual, and do not show its size and extent; nor do they imply that men of Welsh status still spoke the Welsh language, for established interest may perpetuate the inferior status of a minority long after the circumstances that brought it into being have disappeared. Spoken Welsh was common in the 7th century. The river Beane in Hertfordshire was known to the later English by a Welsh name. British monks probably preached in Norfolk, and also in Hertfordshire, about the 590s; their activity implies a considerable population who understood their language. Near Peterborough, Guthlac was troubled about 705 by the still independent British of the Fenland, who were to retain their speech and untamed hostility into the 11th century. In Northumbria the poet Caedmon, Welsh by name, was an elderly layman of substance before he received the gift of song, and entered the monastery of

Whitby. But when he sang, he sang in English. He had been born and named not long after the English conquest, perhaps before, and English was an acquired language.

Men born British and reared in an English environment are likely to have become bilingual early. Some are also likely to have abandoned their ancestral language early, so that their grandchildren forgot that their grandfathers had been born Welsh. Among others, two languages are likely to have stayed longer in use; and in closed communities, Welsh may well have persisted for many generations. The old language is likely to have been dropped at different times in different regions, often influenced by purely local circumstances. But among most bilingual peoples, the minority language may linger for centuries, like Cornish, or Wendish in modern Saxony. It may recede gradually, or may disappear in a generation, like Irish, when some considerable upheaval suddenly extinguishes it. In Britain, both the Norse invasions and the Norman conquest were upheavals severe enough to kill what remained of peasant Welsh in many parts of Britain.

Something of the extent of the 7th-century Welsh in the English kingdoms may in time be learnt from the study of place names. Places whose Roman British names are preserved are few; apart from large towns, they are naturally most numerous in the West Riding, in the Welsh marches and in other border regions. Those that the English called villages of the Welsh or British are considerably more numerous. Some names carry dates, for forms like Comberton, Camberwell, Cumberlow were taken from British speech, before Welsh had transmuted *Cumber* into *Cymry*, hardly later than the 6th century, and are more plentiful in the areas of early settlement. Much more numerous are those described as *Wealh Tun*, Welshman's village, Walton and the like. Their study has been hindered by a curious modern myth, that

> the old English word *wealh* also meant 'a serf, a slave' in general,

which led to the speculation that such places

> might conceivably have been named from non-British serfs,

and thereafter grew to an assumption that many or most were so named.

The myth is quite untrue. *Wealh* never meant a 'slave or serf' in general. It carries that meaning only in West Saxon texts of the 10th century and later, written when in Wessex the only Welshmen left were servile. The usage did not extend to Mercians and Northumbrians, where free Welshmen remained unassimilated to a later date; it had not arisen in Wessex in the 7th and 8th centuries, when places were named in large numbers. The laws of Ine are explicit; when he provided for a *Wealh gafolgelda*, a Welsh taxpayer, valued at 120 shillings, he did not mean a servile person; when he referred to a servile Welshman or Englishman, he called him a *Wealh theow* or an *Englisc theow*, bondman. Some modern places called Walton and the like may take their names from a wall or a wood; but, when they derive from *Wealh*, they indicate the homes of Welshmen who lived among the early English, as do names that incorporate Cumber-, Britte-, and similar terms. Their study has been inhibited by a naïve and somewhat nationalistic reluctance to admit the existence of a considerable Welsh element among the ancestors of the modern English. The extent of these names cannot be assessed until they have been properly mapped and critically examined. Yet the evidence of the names of places and people, of laws and other texts, is ample. The population of the English kingdoms in the seventh century consisted of an uneven mixture of men of mixed Germanic origins and of descendants of the Roman British, called Welshmen, who are likely to have constituted the larger number in many regions. The history of the early English kingdoms is the story of the integration of this mixed population into a single nation.

CHAPTER SEVENTEEN

ENGLISH MONARCHY

Early Tradition

Englishmen, and the Welshmen within their borders, were integrated under the government of kings. The early history of the English monarchy is disguised by the sources which describe it. Bede emphasised the past power of his own Northumbria, and the editors of the Saxon Chronicle looked back from the standpoint of ninth-century Wessex. Both relate the main events of Mercian history, and silently ignore their meaning. No Mercian view survives. Later ages therefore easily absorb the viewpoint and accept the bias of the Northumbrians and the West Saxons. Bias there was. Bede listed the succession of English kings who 'held empire' over the southern English, and ended with the king who died a year or two before his own birth, Oswy of Northumbria. He did not remark that Oswy's supremacy lasted for no more than three years in a reign of nearly thirty years, although the evidence that he reports elsewhere told him so; and he ignored the southern supremacy of the three Mercian kings who reigned after Oswy's defeat, though he reports their victories in other chapters. Bede might legitimately close his list in his father's day; but when the Saxon Chronicle took his list, and added the 9th-century Egbert of Wessex immediately after Oswy, leaving out the great Offa as well as his Mercian predecessors, it deliberately falsified history; for the hegemony of Offa and the earlier Mercian kings was a great deal more substantial than that of Aethelbert of Kent and of others in the list.

The bias extends beyond a list and a viewpoint; it governs the selection of events and the context to which they are related. It is redressed by the evidence of charters, supplemented by the genealogies and other texts; but the Northumbrian and Wessex view of early England still predominates, for the charters have not yet been seriously studied, while the texts of Bede and the Chronicle have been repeatedly examined in detail. The evolution of the English monarchy is wholly misconceived if the empire of the Mercian kings is overlooked.

These misconceptions chiefly concern the matured monarchy; but they also cloud its first years. Its origins were many, for the early English learnt from different exemplars, from their own Germanic past, from the Roman and Frankish traditions of Europe, from the British of the 5th and 6th centuries, and from their Irish clerics. The institution of monarchy had developed among the

European Germans during the Roman centuries, but unevenly. The most glaring contrast was that between the Angles and the Saxons, whose traditions altogether differed, though they were near neighbours, closely connected. The Angles were believed to have obeyed a long-established monarchy in Europe since at least the late third century AD; and their monarchical convention differed from that of most other Germans, in that the undivided succession passed to the late king's nearest adult male relative, usually to his eldest son, unless he were a child or otherwise unfitted to rule. Their northern neighbours, the Jutes and the Varni, and some of the Scandinavian peoples, had similar traditions; but on their south

> in the old days, the Saxons had no king, but appointed rulers over each township. They regularly held a general meeting once a year ... where the leaders met with twelve nobles and as many freedmen and bondmen from each township. There they confirmed the laws, judged important legal cases, and agreed upon the plans that would guide them in peace or war during the coming year.

The European Saxons did not establish a permanent monarchy until the 9th century, and the practices of the 'old days' continued to annoy 8th-century Franks, who were exasperated at the difficulty of pinning down a multitude of local rulers and assemblies to a binding agreement.

Kent

From their first arrival, the English of Britain inherited something of both traditions. Hengest the Dane was their first leader, and he established a monarchy among his own immediate followers in Kent. They were Jutes, accustomed to monarchy, and on his death they fetched Oesc, the heir of his lieutenant in Bernicia, to found a hereditary dynasty; the later royal house was known as the Oescingas, not as the 'Hengstingas'. Oesc had high ambitions, for he named his son after Eormenric, the founder of the great Gothic empire of the fourth century. The aspirations symbolised by a great name were not realised, for Oesc fell at Badon, and Arthur's victory compelled Eormenric to keep within his narrow borders for the whole of his long reign. Yet ambition remained, for just before his death Eormenric married his son Aethelbert to a daughter of the Frank king of Paris, and Aethelbert twice attempted to assert wide empire; but his power died with him, and later Kentish kings stayed within their frontier. Though they were the earliest English kingdom, settled in a Roman world whose economy and social structure heavily influenced them, their monarchy leant more heavily on German experience than most; the king's notables were known by a Frankish

MAP 23 THE 7th CENTURY ENGLISH KINGDOMS

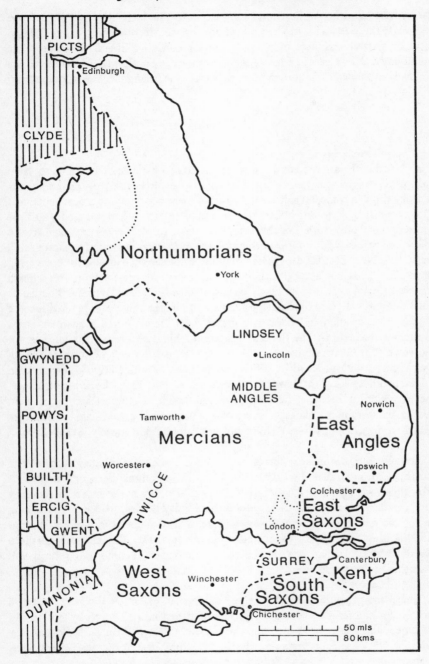

British and Pictish territory shaded.

name, *leode*, and his earliest ministers used the Frankish titles of *referendarius* and *graf*; there is less sign than elsewhere that the Kentish king ruled through local or central meetings of his subjects, or consulted them. The autocratic monarchy of Kent, cast in a European mould, proved unfitted to the needs of the English, and failed to hold their allegiance after the brief authority of Aethelbert.

The Northumbrians

The Northumbrian monarchy was differently constituted. It grew in hard fighting, its main root among the Bernicians. Revolt began with Ida, and 8th-century English tradition tidied the record of his successors into a neat scheme of dated orderly succession; but its dates contradict each other and Bede, and the contemporary observation of the British argues a form of government nearer to the Saxon model, with four leaders simultaneously in command of separate small territories. Near disaster drove them to unite under Aethelric, and the staggering successes of his son Aethelferth made the monarchy permanent. Aethelferth annexed Deira, expelling its newly constituted independent dynasty. Thereafter both kingdoms showed that they preferred unity under a single king, of whichever dynasty, rather than independence under local kings. When Edwin of Deira overthrew Aethelferth, the Bernicians accepted him, with no sign of support for their own exiled princes; and when Edwin fell and the Bernician Oswald returned, Deira accepted him as readily. When Penda of Mercia killed Oswald, he installed a Deiran under-king in Deira, but when the Deiran king clashed with Oswy, the new king of Bernicia, he could not find sufficient support among his own people to sustain his separate rule; and when sons of Bernician kings were detached to rule Deira, the Deirans did not rally behind those who rebelled.

Aethelferth's Bernicians were a nation united behind a military captain who led them to unparalleled success; his subordinate commanders, and their sons after them, were rewarded with territorial lordships, but in the earlier 7th century they developed no intermediate class of hereditary nobles, placed between king and subject, as in Kent and Wessex. Something of the way in which the kings ruled is illustrated by the excavated royal centre at Old Yeavering in northern Northumberland, that was established in Aethelferth's time and rebuilt and enlarged by his successors.

The principal buildings are a large oblong hall, evidently the king's, several smaller halls, a temple, which was probably turned into a church by Edwin and Paulinus, and an open-air meeting-place, plainly designed for periodical assemblies of the Bernician notables. Its architecture describes those assemblies. Planned like a slice from a Roman theatre, its several hundred seats rose row behind row, tapering downward to focus the attention of the audience upon a small dais, barely large enough to accommodate the king's throne, with a couple of attendants. This auditorium was not designed for the debate and discussion of contentious issues. It permitted the king to declare the policies resolved in council, and allowed the audience to shout approval, or to sit in silence. In such a structure, no district leader could rise from the rear or middle benches to question the policy propounded from the royal platform, nor be heard against the wind if he tried. The king's hall might permit the deliberation of a council, but the assembly place was designed for the king to communicate decisions to men who were expected to approve.

The kings had reason to expect approval. The men who met at Yeavering were the leaders of the most powerful kingdom in Britain. They had won their stature by their own effort, for men who were children when Urien and his allies shut the English up in Lindisfarne lived on into the reign of Oswy. They and their followers were proud of their achievement, and the kings who had led them from the edge of disaster to splendid strength deserved and earned their confidence. The architecture of Yeavering proclaims a popular monarchy, a trusted king respected by an equal people.

The purposes of the royal hall and open-air auditorium of Yeavering are explained by Bede's account of the debate in the Deiran royal centre of Goodmanham in 625, when the Northumbrians decided to accept Christianity. In Kent, the king had been converted, and sent priests endowed with ample estates and royal authority to recruit his subjects to the king's religion; there is no hint of consultation, and on his death his successors and their people rejected Christianity, and were won back with difficulty. But in Northumbria, Edwin first assembled his council of notables in the royal hall to hear the Christian priest; when a majority welcomed the new faith, he left them to urge it upon the people, by a dramatic demonstration of the impotence of the old religion.

The old Northumbria, and with it the buildings of Yeavering, survived into Oswy's time. The veterans preferred the austere piety of the Irish monks to the ostentation of the Roman church of Wilfred and of Kent. They were succeeded by a landed nobility in Deira and by unruly lords in Bernicia, whose licence Bede deplored. Their violence was checked in Oswy's time, but it brought military disaster under his son. The old austerity, fortified by the monastic church, regained control with the accession of Aldfrith, but on his death in 705 the disruptive ferocity of the new nobility ensured the quick decline of the monarchy, under a succession of child kings and weak kings. At the end of the century, their rivalries installed upon the throne a son-in-law of Offa of Mercia; though he was murdered when Offa died, his successors had no time even to attempt the restoration of the kingdom before the Norsemen swept upon their coasts.

Authority concentrated upon a trusted leader was based upon continuing Northumbrian victory; but it failed in adversity, when kings lost respect at home; and even the greatest kings came to the south as enemy tyrants, arousing a fierce resistance too resolute for them to quell. Aethelferth was destroyed when he ventured south of the Trent; Edwin conquered Wessex, and his victory inspired a grand alliance of the south that soon destroyed him; Oswald killed its British leaders, but the English Penda revived the southern alliance and overthrew him; Oswy in time broke the allied army, but the south threw him out within three years; his son tried and failed to regain control, and in 679 he was forced to accept the Trent as his permanent boundary. Northumbria began the long war with immense military superiority, sending a well-tempered and apparently invincible army of veterans against southerners who were in disarray after the dissolution of Kentish hegemony, and who had as yet no comparable military experience. But the south altogether rejected Northumbrian supremacy, doggedly renewing their resistance after each defeat. Devotion to a hero king was alien to their past and their present, and could not serve as a focus for the union and integration of the English nation.

The East Angles

Before they conquered the British, the southern English were grouped into a multitude of very small independent peoples and two considerable kingdoms. They briefly submitted to the empire of Kent, but they demolished it on its founder's death. Bede reports that Redwald of East Anglia then asserted a southern primacy similar to Aethelbert's. His was the only other kingdom with a large army capable of claiming the inheritance of sovereignty. Nothing is said of the nature of his monarchy, for East Anglia has left no written record. But the excavated royal tombs of the early 7th century bespeak its splendour. The great mound of Sutton Hoo, by the East Anglian royal centre near Ipswich, contained the funeral furniture of Redwald, or of one of his immediate successors. It is the most magnificent royal burial in Germanic Europe, the witness of a sovereignty no less exalted than the Northumbrian. It is not paralleled by any tomb of earlier or later generations yet known in Britain, but in its own day it did not stand alone. A burial at Broomfield, near Chelmsford, is similar in concept, though less splendid; and is probably the tomb of one of the early seventh-century East Saxon kings. A third burial, on the Buckinghamshire bank of the Thames opposite Maidenhead, approaches the wealth of Sutton Hoo. It is a tomb on a royal scale, and the place, Taplow, the burial-mound of Taeppa, preserves the name of the king there buried. Neither he nor his kingdom is otherwise known. The grave furniture resembles Sutton Hoo, and it may be that Taeppa was a regional king installed to hold the frontier against the West Saxons during Redwald's brief dominion, perhaps a son or a relative. The name and nature of the kingdom is suggested by its neighbour. Surrey, south of the Thames, is *Suder Ge* to Bede, the southern district; the usage implies that it was at one time paired with a 'Norrey' north of the Thames. Neither endured as independent kingdoms, and the origin of these districts is unknown; it may be that they were creations of

Redwald, for Taeppa's kingdom did not survive into the better documented generations of the mid and late 7th century; but the wealth of his tomb fits the ruler of a kingdom larger than the little territory in which he was buried.

Nothing is known of the later constitution of the East Anglian and East Saxon monarchies, save that their kings stayed within their borders, and won no authority over other English peoples. Political primacy passed to the frontier kingdoms, composed of small independent units, whose numbers greatly increased as colonists consolidated new lands to the west. They could not be bound together by a centralised absolute Germanic monarchy, on the model of Northumbria, East Anglia and Kent, or of the Goths, Franks and Burgundians in Europe. The form of government that they evolved was the starting point of one essential difference in the future history of the English and the peoples of Europe; in Europe Germanic monarchy was imposed upon a peasantry cowed into submission by late Roman institutions, but the circumstances of the early English forced them to adopt a looser authority, which was obliged to rest upon a stronger regional and local autonomy.

The frontier peoples of the 6th and early 7th centuries were heirs of the settlers whom the Anglian Chronicle described; they were grouped 'under many leaders', not yet 'organised under a single king'; their constitution resembled that of the continental Saxons, whose local leaders drew their authority from regular annual meetings of their people. The larger frontier monarchies were formed after the late 6th-century conquest, in the course of wars against the Welsh, against the Northumbrians, and between the Mercians and the West Saxons.

The West Saxons

The early history of the West Saxons is disguised by the ingenuity of the authors of the Saxon Chronicle. They needed to pretend that their own royal house was as ancient, as venerable, and as coherent as the dynasty of the Mercian Angles whom they had replaced. Their scholars did their best, but the evidence before them was stubborn and plentiful, and could not be compressed into the doctrine they proclaimed. Their own mutual contradictions, the numerous statements of Bede, and the evidence of the charters and many other texts disprove their thesis.

The central core of that thesis was that all West Saxon kings were sovereigns descended from Cerdic and formed a single dynasty. The genealogists tried to trace the descent of each king from Cerdic. They failed. They were unable even to contrive such ancestry for the more recent 8th-century kings, for living memory knew their immediate ancestors, and the genealogists had to be content with a generalised assertion that each king 'descended from Cerdic', without naming their fathers and grandfathers and with no attempt to link them with their 7th-century predecessors. Men still lived who knew that there were no such links. But the genealogies of the seventh century were more easily doctored; each sequence of two or three names was attached to either Cuthwulf or Cuthwine, who were turned into the brother and son of Ceawlin; and he became son of Cynric and grandson of Cerdic.

These authors did not fabricate. They adapted the conventions of British genealogists, who made no clear distinction between a pedigree and a king list. The British had attempted to show the succession of political power, and did so with rough and ready accuracy; but they agreed to assume that, as in their own day, son succeeded father, so that each Roman emperor was described as the son of his predecessor, and the last emperor in each table was treated as the father of the British ruler who inherited his authority. So the English transcribed the list of 6th-century West Saxon rulers, from Cerdic to Ceolric, as a succession from fathers to sons and brothers, confused by the intrusion of Creoda of Mercia into some texts. But their difficulties were greater in the 7th century, when texts and tradition remembered the fathers and grandfathers of some kings who were known not to have been kings themselves. Versions of the pedigrees therefore contradict each other; Cynegils, the contemporary of Edwin and Redwald, is given three fathers in different texts, and other kings have two fathers. Other reigning families, not connected with his, are traced to one or other Cutha by unlikely links.

The reality behind the fiction is discoverable, because some of the evidence that the genealogists manipulated is known independently of them. Bede knew that in Edwin's time Wessex comprised at least five distinct kingdoms, each ruled by an underking, who at times acknowledged varying degrees of sovereignty to a West Saxon overking. The still unstudied evidence of the charters names many of the people named in the pedigrees, and many more besides, as distinct regional kings; and the entries of the Chronicle itself name three contemporary kings in 661, two of whom died at the time of Wulfhere's invasion, doubtless in battle against him. Bede describes the failure of the early overkings. Cynegils was an effective sovereign, and was succeeded by his son Cenwalh. Between them they reigned for more than 60 years, from 611 to 672, but no other king is said to have been succeeded by his son, or any near relative, for more than 200 years thereafter, in the Chronicle or in any other text. Bede says that on Cenwalh's death the overkingship was discontinued, and the West Saxons were ruled by underkings for ten years. The overkingship was revived and maintained for 40 years by Ceadwalla and Ine; they came from different dynasties, and in the next hundred years half a dozen sovereigns are reported, whom no record links with one another or with previous dynasties, until an unconvincing list traces the descent of Egbert from Ine's brother. The Chronicle reports their frequent wars against underkings who refused to admit their authority, and reveals that some were forced to tolerate the independent defiance of local kings for decades.

The titles and the status of the regional kings varied with the power of the overking; sometimes in different contemporary texts, the same ruler is termed *rex*, *regulus* and *patricius*, king, underking and patrician, and sometimes some of the western regional kingdoms were altogether detached from Wessex, and were directly ruled by the Mercian kings. Exact study of the texts is likely to explain a good deal of the detail of the early history of Wessex; but the evidence that has already been collected is sufficient to show that no stable and lasting West Saxon monarchy was erected until the 9th century; then it was consolidated in the course of wars against the Scandinavians, out of the inheritance of the Mercian monarchy.

The Mercians

Early 7th-century Mercia also consisted of small independent peoples, some settled since the 5th century, others first established during the colonisation of the west. But its constituent peoples were much more numerous, and were quickly able to coalesce behind a powerful overking without internal wars. Their stability was grounded upon early success, and upon shrewd policies evolved by early kings that hardened into lasting principles of government. The Mercian kings won supremacy because they organised and headed southern resistance against the Northumbrians, and took the brunt of their attack. Thenceforth their northern border was secure, firmly marked by the lower and middle Trent. The Northumbrian danger had impelled them to make allies of the Welsh; and the long-standing alliance saved them from western wars, until the lowland was thoroughly settled by English speaking colonists, its border defined by the foothills of the mountains; a couple of sharp campaigns tamed the East Angles and permanently prevented further threats from their distinct and self-sufficient territory. The only open frontier of the Mercians faced the West Saxons on the south, and the Mercians retained superiority, periodically invading but never invaded, for they had one enemy only, while the West Saxons were distracted by wars against Dumnonia, by campaigns in Sussex and Kent, and by their own internal conflicts.

The first Mercian kings presided over the several peoples of the Middle Angles and the Avon. Some, perhaps all of these peoples retained their own local rulers, heirs of those who had led them before the English conquest, and before the central monarchy was established. The monarchy itself was at first small and weak, unable to withstand the Northumbrians; when Edwin subdued the West Saxons, his route took his armies through Mercia, with or without opposition. The Mercian kingdom was divided. Penda's rule began when Edwin was supreme, and included the western territories; his brother Eowa also reigned until 642, perhaps as king among the Middle Angles.

The Mercian Empire

The dynasty of Penda was acceptable because it claimed descent from the ancient kings who were held to have ruled all the Angles in Europe, the Iclingas, descendants of Icel, the king who transferred the monarchy to Britain. The claim may have been true, for one cadet branch of the Iclingas were already respected local rulers among the Middle Angles in the time of Penda's sons. But whether the claim was true or false is relatively unimportant; what matters is that it was believed and accepted. The local kings among the West Saxons and the British could brook no overlord, for each of them could claim ancestry as eminent as any potential sovereign; but the venerable antiquity asserted by the Anglian royal house gave it a stronger title to universal obedience than any rulers in Britain had been able to command since the last legitimate Roman emperors in Italy.

Penda's monarchy could claim ancestral right, but it could not rule by the simple direct authority that Offa of Angel or the Northumbrian kings had exercised over an equal people. The mechanics of government had yet to be worked out, to fit the conditions of the present. Penda learnt from his British allies, and from the experience of Ireland, the nearest established monarchical government. Like an Irish king, he exacted hostages and enforced tribute; he impressed British tradition by a distribution of gifts to his subordinate rulers, made in the manner of an Irish king or an 'open-handed' British king. He did not dethrone conquered kings and annex their kingdoms, as Aethelferth had annexed Deira, and as Oswy annexed most of Mercia in 655. He expelled Cenwalh from Wessex, but he left the regional kings alone; he restored the dynasty of Deira, but he left Oswy in Bernicia; and though he twice killed rebellious kings of the East Angles, he permitted their heirs to succeed them as his subordinate allies.

The clumsy Irish practice of levying tribute by forcing the tributaries to give hostages is not reported under Penda's successors; the relics of Roman administration showed more efficient ways of collecting taxes. Irish influence was strong at first, for the kings were Christian, and many of their decisions were guided by the advice of Irish priests, who drew upon the experience of their homeland; these decisions became formative precedents, that hardened into conventions of government. The Mercians adapted the principles of Irish monarchy, but did not imitate its detail. The high king ruled over many lesser kings, with an authority as strong as that which Diarmait had asserted in Ireland a century before. But the schematism of the Irish provincial kings, grouping smaller kingdoms behind a sovereignty intermediate between the high king's and the local king's, found no echo among the Mercians. Though Lindsey, the Middle Angles and the western territories were distinct geographical regions, each with its own individual history, the Mercians did not place regional kings over them, although the Northumbrian conquerors had in their time installed dependent rulers. The Mercian overking reigned over many separate kingdoms of different size. The far western lands between the upper Severn and the Wye were ruled by a dynasty that claimed descent from a son of Penda; on their east, the large kingdom of the Hwicce obeyed for centuries a dynasty of Northumbrian origin, that had perhaps been installed by Oswy.

Throughout their long history, there is no record of dynastic wars within these kingdoms, of wars between them, or of rebellions against Mercian supremacy. The titles of their kings vary; as among the West Saxons, the same ruler is sometimes described as king, sometimes as underking, sometimes as minister of the king of the Mercians; and in the rest of Mercia, lesser rulers, termed patrician or prince, ruled smaller peoples, equally without rebellion or internal discord. Within the Mercian dynasty itself, the succession was at times disputed. But the disputes were quickly settled; as in Ireland, men were chosen whose remote ancestors had once been king, and when they were chosen, they reigned for a generation or more without serious challenge. Loyalty to a stable dynasty built a monarchy stronger than the precarious sovereignty of Northumbrian, Kentish or continental kings. The Mercian monarchs retained their subjects' loyalty and increased their majesty because they continued the forms of government they inherited from the past, tolerating and encouraging the autonomy of dependent rulers, and leaving large areas of administrative, judicial and political decision in the hands of periodical local representative assemblies. They were content if their subjects accepted their supremacy, and kept peace with one another. Their sovereignty contrasts with the autocracy of Oswy, who, in 655, 'ruled almost all the English directly, or held empire over their rulers.'

Penda and his predecessors learnt from the British and Irish. His sons and their successors had other teachers. Their first priests and monks were Irish, but in the reign of Wulfhere the English church was reorganised by the flexible genius of Theodore of Tarsus, who brought to Britain the experience of the eastern Roman empire as well as of the church of Rome. The rapid spread of monasteries, bound together by common notions of what was right and wrong in the world of the living, profoundly influenced the practice of English government. Theodore found an apt pupil in Aldhelm, who had been taught by the Irish, but devoted his life to training English clerks and administrators as learned and as capable as the Irish. Aldhelm absorbed Theodore's experience, became the friend and counsellor both of the Mercians and of the West Saxons, and educated the next great Mercian king, Aethelbald, whose reign continued to 757, when Offa succeeded him. More than any other individual, Aldhelm gathered together the varied examples that could teach the English the practices of government, and sorted them into principles that their successors could observe. He and his royal pupils were the architects of the English monarchy.

The restrained might of the Mercian monarchs preserved their authority over all the English. They acquired sovereignty by conquest, but they retained it because their rule did not provoke the same lasting resentment that Northumbrian conquest had aroused. Penda twice invaded East Anglia, but no third invasion was needed. Wulfhere overran Wessex, and made Wight and Sussex a separate dependent kingdom. Aethelred annexed western Wessex, and in 676 invaded Kent. Thereafter the Mercians retained control of London, and from London controlled the south-west. Only the West Saxons renewed and maintained resistance; but the resistance of their fragmented kingdom failed to break Mercian supremacy. Mercian arms prevailed, and reinforced submission after each repeated victory.

The substance and the titles of Mercian supremacy are set down in the charters. Wherever charters survive, many of them are confirmed by the Mercian king. Some are preserved in their original manuscript, others are close copies of their originals, but many are much doctored by later copyists, who add particulars that enlarge or strengthen the claims that monasteries later founded upon the grants. The texts have not yet been assessed, for their interpretation has been obscured by an oversimple attempt to classify them as either wholly 'genuine' or wholly 'forged'; yet hardly any of them can be squeezed into these rigid categories. Most are in varying stages of corruption and manipulation; those that are closer to their originals commonly include a large number of witnesses, who were not contemporary with each other, but were near in time; for the original grants were commonly confirmed two or three times, not long after they were made, by subsequent kings, bishops and lords, and the earlier transcripts ran the successive witnesses together; but later copyists often left out large numbers of names that had lost their meaning, and sometimes put in their place the names of a few well-known potentates who lived at other times.

Normally the confirmatory signature of a Mercian king to a grant of land outside Mercia admits Mercian suzerainty, even if it is inserted by a copyist; for texts were not manipulated at random, but for the specific purpose of strengthening the title that the grant claimed. In and after the 9th century, when the Mercian power was broken, no monastic interest was served by adding Mercian authority in a kingdom that Mercia no longer mastered; even when the name of a Mercian king is wrongly intruded, the copyist who first inserted it did so when Mercian supremacy still prevailed, and thereby acknowledged that supremacy.

Many recipients did not require the sovereign's confirmation, or did not bother to obtain it. But many others did, and a close study of the wording of the texts is likely to explain changes in political power that often endured for only a few years; in some extreme cases, as when the West Saxons for a short time mastered Kent, a grant may be made by a Kentish underking or lord, witnessed by the overking of Kent, by the West Saxon king as overlord of Kent, and by the Mercian king as suzerain over the West Saxons. Such instances are rare; usually the king of each kingdom signs alone, and when another king signs, it is the Mercian monarch alone; and when the Mercian king grants Wessex lands without the West Saxon king, or grants exemption from the London customs dues without the king of Kent, he is commonly exercising direct authority.

The ideas that underlay Mercian sovereignty are expressed in the kings' titles. In most signatures, the king is content to be called simply 'king of the Mercians', for secure sovereignty did not need to be flaunted. No ruler is called 'king of England', for England did not yet exist, but 'king of Britain' is often used. 'King of all the southern English' is more frequent, with variants like 'king not only of the Mercians, but also of all the provinces commonly called southern

English'. Some drafting clerks used the grander style of the 'empire of the Mercians', and in 798, Coenwulf, the last of the Mercian kings to exercise effective supremacy, called himself *Imperator*, 'emperor', in a grant whose original manuscript survives.

The arresting title illuminates another of the main influences that gave the Mercians supremacy. Their monarchy had borrowed something from Germanic experience, something from Irish, and something from Europe. The concept of an island emperor was British. Nowhere in Europe is the title emperor used of any ruler but an emperor of Rome before the time of Napoleon; it is confined to the emperors in Constantinople, and to the successors of Charlemagne in the west. But from the time of Arthur, it remained in the political vocabulary of the British Isles, used only occasionally, but used by all peoples on occasions. One seventh-century Irish writer called an earlier high king of Ireland *imperator*, and another used the same title of Oswald of Northumbria, calling him 'emperor of Britain', not of the English; and in the 11th century, Brian Boru, the last great Irish king, himself asserted the same title. An Armorican British writer of the 9th century called the Frank king an emperor, and British poets celebrated the emperor Arthur.

The title was used rarely, for all men knew that emperors should be emperors of Rome. It was only in Britain that legitimate emperors had ruled who did not claim to rule the rest of the Roman empire. Men were chary of the high-sounding word, and archbishop Boniface sneered at its upstart use in the time of Aethelbald. But both the British and English perpetuated its substance in language more circumspect. The Welsh coined the title *Gwledic*, ruler of the country, and bestowed it upon Maelgwn, Urien and a few others, who came nearer than most to reviving the wide dominion of Arthur. The English early made the concept their own, and before Bede's time contrived a list of those who were sovereigns of the southern English. Bede put it into Latin, avoiding the personal title; he lists the men who were held to have 'held empire', *imperium*; the English language gave them the title *Bretwalda*, ruler of Britain; it came near to the imperial title, for a similar word, *Brytwalda*, 'wide ruler', was occasionally used of Roman emperors.

The list was artificially constructed. It began with Aelle of Sussex, who was no conqueror, but probably earned the title as commander of the force that was beaten at Badon. The next name is Ceawlin, whose conquest sealed the defeat of the southern British. Then came Aethelbert of Kent, who first reduced the southern English, and after him Redwald and the Northumbrian monarchs. Mercian historians may or may not have adapted and extended the same list in their own texts. Their texts have not survived, and it is possible that they ignored Bede's list, for if they had accepted it they would have been compelled to acknowledge past Kentish, East Anglian and Northumbrian overlords as legitimate sovereigns of all the southern English, in preference to their own royal house. But the West Saxon historians made much of Bede's list, exploiting it to justify the claims of their kings to inherit an authority over all Britain that was older than the empire of the Mercians.

The Northumbrian and West Saxon lists each make their own selection of English overkings. But the imperial sovereignty from which they made their partial selection was real and continuous; and its usages outlived its reality. *Imperator* became a favoured title of some later West Saxon kings. Official 10th-century documents style Edred 'king of the English' and 'emperor' of the Northumbrians, or of the 'pagans', or 'Caesar of all Britain'; and in the 11th century Aethelred's formal phrases define the meaning of the titles. He is king of the English, sometimes of 'Anglo-Saxony', and 'ruler of the Northumbrian monarchy'; he is also 'emperor of the British and of the other provinces'. Other documents bestow upon him and other kings Greek titles proper to the Roman emperor in Constantinople, 'emperor of the whole world of Britain' or of 'all Albion'. Sonorous titles are commonly proclaimed by the feeblest kings; just as the shrill and silly adjective *invictissimus*, 'most unconquered', was used by those later Roman emperors whose armies suffered heaviest defeat, so the pretentious assertions of later English kings increased, until the melancholy ruin of Aethelred made them wholly absurd. But his empty title, 'king of the English and Emperor of Britain', justly described the authority of his Mercian predecessors.

Aethelred's phrases none the less defined a solid reality of the recent past. His father Edgar had enforced acknowledgement of the supremacy he boasted, and Edgar had reasserted an ancient right. From the 7th century onwards the over-kings of the English claimed to inherit empire over the whole of Britain. The inheritance came to them from the dispossessed British, for the British kings who earned the title *Gwledic*, like the early English *Bretwaldas*, had tried and failed to unite the whole island under a single imperial dynasty; the Mercian monarchy was more successful, and bequeathed the name of emperor to later kings. But whatever their title and whatever the substance of their power, the kings who claimed superior authority, from Maelgwn to Aethelred, all revived the ghost of an ancient reality, the short-lived empire of Britain, whose last and most famous emperor was Arthur.

Ghosts work powerfully when men believe in them. Arthur's empire left a consciousness that all Britain had once obeyed a single emperor, and could and should in the future unite under a single paramount sovereign. The high title was dropped, but the claim persisted throughout the middle ages. Its repeated assertions had long prepared Welshmen and Scots to accept it in practice, and to acquiesce in formal genealogical claims, when the accidents of royal marriage and royal mortality bequeathed the throne of England to the real or alleged descendants of Welsh and Scottish kings, the Tudors and Stuarts. But no tradition incorporated Ireland within the empire of Arthur; English rule in Ireland was based on force alone, and no latent beliefs encouraged English kings to marry their daughters to Irish princes, or served to persuade Irishmen that the kings of England were the legitimate heirs of Irish dynasties.

The concept of a single government of Britain lingered feebly until the middle of the 7th century. It gained strength and permanence during the long quiet rule of the Mercian kings; they were effective overkings of the English and paramount allies of the Welsh, from Penda's time on. Mercian supremacy endured unchallenged until the last years of their greatest king, Offa, who died in 796. Its long continuance placed him among the mightiest western rulers of his day, second only to his greater contemporary, Charlemagne. But Mercian power died of its own greatness. Offa's overpowering majesty induced him to cut away the props on which it rested. He abolished the underkings, executing the last king of the East Angles, ending the Kentish monarchy, reducing the rulers of Sussex to the status of *dux*, introducing his dependants upon the thrones of Wessex and Northumbria; and called himself 'king of the English', no longer, like his predecessor, of the southern English alone.

Offa observed the immensely powerful centralised monarchy of Charlemagne, and endeavoured to transform his English empire into a Germanic and Roman absolutism. His innovations drove his subjects to rebellion; Kent rallied round a local rebel who claimed no royal ancestry, and though the rebel was crushed, the peoples of the other kingdoms, formerly obedient to native kings who admitted Mercian supremacy, now viewed direct Mercian rule with abhorrence. In the next generation, they transferred their support to Egbert of Wessex, enabling him to unite his own people, and to challenge and end Mercian domination. Mercian power briefly revived, but Egbert's descendants inherited Offa's centralised monarchy; the old regional dynasties were gone, and the Scandinavian invaders had come, at the moment when the English most needed self-reliant regional leadership. The evil was immediately apparent to contemporaries; a few months after Offa's death, when the first few pirate ships had recently landed upon unguarded coasts, the greatest scholar and statesman of the day, Alcuin of York and Tours, warned of coming disaster and explained its cause.

> An immense threat hangs over this island and its people. It is a novelty without precedent that the pirate raids of a heathen people can regularly waste our shores. Yet the English people are divided, and king fights against king. Saddest of all, scarcely any heir of the ancient royal houses survives, and the origin of kings is as dubious as their courage. . . . Study Gildas, the wisest of the British, and examine the reasons why the ancestors of the British lost their kingdom and their fatherland; then look upon yourselves, and you will find amongst you almost identical causes.

The great age of the united English had died with Offa, and the nation was left leaderless in the face of peril. It had grown great because it had learned from the past of the British as well as from its own traditions. The long governance of Mercia had formed a nation tough enough to survive. Though the arrogance of Offa had destroyed the bonds that held it together, his successors salvaged their fragmented people. The cost was fearful. The noble prose of the Saxon Chronicle describes the wars of Wessex kings, who rescued half the country from gentile conquest. But they could not restore the stable government of the Mercian past; the resolute energy of the Scandinavians destroyed strong kings and exploited the vacillation of feeble monarchs, until in 1066 the English succumbed to a section of the Norsemen whose barbarism had been tamed by long residence in France. In the end the English recovered their national strength, in the course of prolonged passive and local resistance to the ignorant brutality of Norman rule. They did so because the inherited traditions of English monarchy enabled the kings to curb their magnates as no European sovereign could. To maintain their own power the alien kings were forced to submit to the ancient usages of the conquered English and to reject the language and the crude political notions that their ancestors had brought from Europe.

Charlemagne's Empire

The example of the Mercian monarchy stirred the imagination of Europe in its own day. It was a novel concept of kingship, that had learnt to comprehend immense diversity within one organic whole. It combined the tradition of Roman imperial authority with a loose hierarchical kingship adapted from the Irish, and with a secure law of succession inherited from the continental English; and thereby offered a security unknown to the emperors of Rome. It provided a model that Europe welcomed; for in the same generation in which Offa infected and corroded the English monarchy with the brittle centralisation of Europe, Charlemagne endeavoured to strengthen Europe by adapting the experience of the English.

During Offa's reign, Charles the Great won a wider dominion than any western European ruler since the fall of the Roman empire. To organise his dominions, he looked to the English, and in 782 acquired the services of Alcuin of York, under whose guidance the clerks of the Frankish lands were trained, with the help of some English and many Irish teachers. Alcuin became the close friend and counsellor of Charlemagne, and began to talk to him of empire, in the same years in which the Mercian kings are first known to have displayed the imperial title in Britain. His letters address him by the affectionate but challenging pen name of 'king David', and in 799 he hailed 'David' as ruler and defender of the 'Christian empire'. In the same year he formalised his political advice.

> Hitherto, three persons have been highest in the world. The Apostolic Sublimity (the Pope); the imperial dignity of the second Rome (Constantinople), though now the ruler of that empire has been wickedly deposed. . . . The third is the royal dignity wherein the dispensation of Our Lord Jesus Christ has made you the ruler of the Christian people.

Alcuin's 'hitherto' advised that the future should be different; and that the moment was now, when the surviving Roman empire in the east lacked an emperor.

Charles determined to go to Rome next year, and urged Alcuin to accompany him. Alcuin excused himself on grounds of health and age, and Charles asked for a deputy to 'undertake his responsibilities' in his stead. Alcuin sent the English monk Witto, called *Candidus* (White), but emphasised that the 'responsibilities' now fell on Charles alone, and he clearly defined them in biblical imagery.

> David adorned the temple . . . when his general Joab had con-
> quered Syria. But David himself placed the crown upon his own
> head, though Joab had borne the labour of the fighting.

Alcuin, like Joab, had borne the labour of the political and diplomatic fighting that prepared the way; but Charles must crown himself without the aid of an English deputy. Charles hesitated, but was crowned Roman emperor in Rome on Christmas Day, 800. Many pressures and many circumstances determined his decision. But the strongest advice had come from the English Alcuin; it was the English who had developed the concept, alien to the Roman past, of an emperor who reigned over subordinate kings; it was an English sovereign who had first used the title emperor in an official document, two years before Charlemagne was crowned. The English usage was half-hearted, for the English did not rule Rome; Charlemagne had conquered Rome, and could exploit the English precedent to the full.

The substance of Charlemagne's imperial authority died with him, leaving an honorary title that persisted into the 19th century. But the substance of the Mercian empire lived on, without the title. Nations of half a dozen different languages grew accustomed to a single monarchy, supreme among the English, dominant throughout Britain, and accepted the guidance of a national monarchy more strongly rooted in the hearts of men than the kingdoms of Europe.

The English emerged as the permanent heirs to the ruins of Arthur's empire; the multiple origin of their population obliged their kings to admit infinite local and social difference, that hindered attempts to impose uniformity or to merge small units into unwieldy amalgamation. The flexibility of English administration was from the beginning able to avoid much of the arrogant ineptitude that centralised European governments inherited from Rome and the Germanic kings. Rulers were taught to respect the limits that each generation set upon the legitimate authority of king or lord; though the limits were repeatedly overridden, they were repeatedly reasserted. Kings who earned their subjects' respect found themselves more powerful than those who sought to command obedience by force alone. Their tempered leadership tolerated a greater local independence and a larger personal liberty than was possible in most of Europe.

English political society was formed in the age of Arthur and consolidated by the Mercian monarchy. From the beginning it was an unusual blend of local responsibility and strong central government. Though local potentates frequently overawed popular assemblies, each local and occupational community customarily decided its own affairs; central governments that guided and coordinated their mutual interests earned their respect, but those that overstepped their proper bounds were ignored or resisted. Excessive concentrations of property and power, in the hands of noblemen or the church, of foreigners or other interests, were repeatedly broken up when their size became a threat.

Direct rule by the central government provoked resentment, in the time of Oswy, of Offa, and of many later rulers. It was tolerated only in emergencies, and rarely for more than a few generations at a time, when severe disturbance crippled or destroyed existing forms, as in the age of conquest and conversion, after the destructive victories of the Northmen from the 9th century to the 11th, and in modern times; but after each emergency, established custom curbed the temporary extension of central authority, and devised new forms of local and occupational control. English society tamed the Scandinavian and the Norman, and outlived the tyrannical corruption of Angevin royal officers. Effective local power persisted for five centuries more, until its organs were corroded and destroyed by the violent impact of the industrial revolution.

Most of the familiar centralised institutions of modern society are at present little more than a hundred years old, and are already beginning to face criticism. They seem older than they are, for men cannot help reading the present into the past. Medieval writers equipped king Arthur and the Romans with the weapons, the clothing and the political morality of their own day; and in the last few generations many historians have dwelt at length upon the ancestry of modern institutions and ideas. Those aspects of parliament and other bodies that most nearly concern their present form have been emphasised, and the workings of earlier England have been explained in terms of modern notions of economics, government and morality; but until quite recently the important realities of local history have been ignored and even derided.

Nineteenth century forms of centralised government may or may not prove more durable than their predecessors. Critics who withstand ministries and national executives may be condemned or commended. But they cannot justly be represented as innovators, for they appeal, usually unconsciously, to the oldest traditions of English administration. Political prophecy is not the business of the historian, but he is obliged to stress the powerful influence of the past. Present tendencies in any society are easily misjudged if its origin and formative years are disregarded. The fundamental assumptions of English society were hardened under the Mercian kings, and were first fashioned in the age of Arthur. From the outset they have rested upon an equal balance of local or sectional autonomy and of national coordination. In the past these inbred assumptions have repeatedly curtailed the dominance of centralised authority, whenever it has exceeded the bounds deemed proper by public opinion, rarely more than a century or so after the central government has overstepped its traditional limits.

TABLE OF DATES

Capital letters denote Emperors, Popes and major rulers. (W . . West; E . . East).
Italics denote battles. Italic capitals denote Irish Kings.
The span of years shown indicates either the reign or the effective adult life of the
individual concerned; birth dates are not given.

THE EMPIRE

350
CONSTANS (W) 337–350
CONSTANTIUS (E) 337–361
MAGNENTIUS (W) 350–353
JULIAN (W) Caesar 355–361

360
JULIAN 361–363
JOVIAN 363–364
VALENTINIAN I (W) 364–375
VALENS (E) 364–378

370
GRATIAN ((W) 375–383
Adrianople 378
VALENTINIAN II (W) 375–393
THEODOSIUS I (E) 379–395

380
MAGNUS MAXIMUS (W) 383–388

390
Offa of Angel c. 390/420?
ARCADIUS (E) 395–408
HONORIUS (W) 395–421

400
THEODOSIUS II (E) 408–450
CONSTANTINE III (W) 407–411

410
Goths take Rome 410

Visigoth federates in Gaul
418

420
Eomer of Angel c. 420/460?
VALENTINIAN III (W) 423–455
Vandals take Africa c. 429

THE CHURCH

Hilary of Poitiers
353–368

Synod of Rimini 359

DAMASUS 366–384
Ambrose of Milan
371–397
Martin of Tours
372–c. 397

Augustine of Hippo
386–430

Victricius in Britain
c. 396
St. Albans, Whithorn ?
founded

Pelagius c. 400–418

Sicilian Briton 411
Fastidius 411
Amator, Auxerre -418
Germanus of Auxerre
418–448

Jerome died 420
CELESTINE 422–432
Germanus, Britain 429

BRITISH ISLES

MUIREDACH 325–355

Paul the Notary 353
EOCHAID 356–365

Barbarian raids 360, 364, 367

CRIMTHANN 365–378
Border dynasties founded c. 368

NIALL 379–405

First Migration to
Brittany ?388

Saxon raid c. 397

NATH – I 405–428

Britain independent
COEL HEN dux ? c. 410/420
AMBROSIUS the Elder
? c. 412/425
Drust (Picts) 414–458

VORTIGERN c. 425–c. 459
LOEGAIRE 428–463
HENGEST and Horsa land c. 428

ABROAD	THE CHURCH	BRITISH ISLES
430		
Aëtius supreme in the west c. 433–454	Patrick in Ireland 432–c. 459	Cunedda, and Cornovii, migrations c. 430?
	SIXTUS III 432–440	*Wallop* c. 437
440		
Aëtius consul III 446	LEO I 440–461	First Saxon revolt c. 441/2
CHILDERIC I (Franks) c. 440?–481	Patrick's *Declaration* c. 440/443	*Aylesford, Crayford* c. 445/449
	Germanus in Britain	
450		
MARCIAN (E) 450–457	Patrick's *Letter* c. 450	*Richborough* c. 450
AVITUS (W) 455–456		Coroticus, Clyde, c. 450
Aegidius in Gaul 455–464	Northern Irish sees c. 459	Massacre c. 458.
LEO I (E) 457–474		Aelle, South Saxons
		Second Migration to Brittany c. 459
460		
Icel of Angel c. 460/480?	HILARY 461–468	AMBROSIUS AURELIANUS
Syagrius in Gaul 464–486	Faustus at Riez 462–c. 495	c. 460–c. 475
ANTHEMIUS (W) 467–472	Ibar, Enda, Kebi in Rome c. 465	*AILLEL MOLT* 464–482
		ANGUS of Munster c. 465–492
470		
ZENO (E) 474–491	Sidonius of the Auvergne 470–479	ARTHUR c. 475–c. 515
Odovacer ends western emperors 476	Docco died c. 473	
480		
CLOVIS (Franks) 481–511	Illtud's school c. 480–c. 510	Portsmouth c. 480
Soissons 486	Brigit c. 480–524	Cerdic c. 480–c. 495
		Migration of Angel kings c. 48
		LUGAID 482–505
490		
ANASTASIUS 491–518	Abban and Ibar, Abingdon, c. 498	Irish attacks on Britain 495/51
THEODORIC in Italy 493–526		*Badon* c. 495. Partition.
500		
Poitiers 507	Benedict of Nursia c. 500–c. 542	Demetia recovered c. 500/510
Gaul becomes France		Dal Riada Scots c. 500
End of main Elbe cemeteries		Dyfnwal, Clyde, c. 500
		MAC ERCA 505–532
510		
SONS OF CLOVIS 511–561*	Dubricius c. 510–c. 540	*Camlann*, Arthur killed, c. 51
JUSTIN I 518–527		
520		
Beowulf c. 520/550	Samson c. 525–c. 563	Vortipor c. 515–c. 540
JUSTINIAN 527–565		MAELGWN c. 520–551
530		
Africa reconquered 533, Italy 533–544	Finnian of Clonard c. 530–551	Saxon migrations from Britain to Europe c. 530/550
THEUDEBERT (East Franks) 533–548	Gildas' book c. 538	*TUATHAL* 532–548
540		
Bubonic plague 543–547	Kentigern exiled c. 540	Eliffer of York c. 540/560
THEUDEBALD (East Franks) 548–555	Columba, Derry 544	Morcant, Clyde, c. 540/560
	Cadoc c. 545–c. 580	Gabran, Dal Riada, 541–560
	Brendan's voyages 545/560	*DIARMAIT* 548–564
		Plague 547–551

ABROAD	THE CHURCH ABROAD	THE CHURCH IN THE BRITISH ISLES
550	Radegund at Poitiers 550–587 PELAGIUS I 555–560	David c. 550–589 Comgall founded Irish Bangor 558
560 CLOTHAIR killed Chramn and CONOMOR 560 BRUNHILD 566–613 JUSTIN II 565–578 Lombards in Italy 568		Daniel at Bangor, Menai c. 560–584 Columba at Iona 563–597 Gildas in Ireland 565
570 TIBERIUS 578–582	Gregory of Tours 573–594 PELAGIUS II 578–590	Gildas died 570 Kentigern, Glasgow, c. 575–c. 603
580 MAURICE 582–602		Aedan of Ferns c. 585–627
590	GREGORY the Great 590–604 Columban in Gaul and Italy 595–615	Augustine Archbishop of Canterbury 597–604
600 PHOCAS 602–610		
610 HERACLIUS 610–641		
620 PEPIN I Mayor 624–639	HONORIUS I 625–640	Edwin baptised 625
630 DAGOBERT I 630–638 Arabs took Damascus 634, Jerusalem 637		Aedan of Lindisfarne 635–651
640 Arabs in Egypt 640, Persia 642, Africa 647 GRIMOALD, Mayor, 642–656	Eligius bishop 640–659	Hilda of Whitby c. 640–680

BRITAIN	IRELAND	THE ENGLISH
550		
RHUN of Gwynedd 551–580?		CYNRIC took Salisbury 552
BRIDEI, Picts, 554–584		AETHELBERT of Kent 555–61
560		
PEREDUR, York, c. 560–580	*AINMERE* 565–569	IDA, Bamburgh, c. 560–c. 570
RIDERCH, Clyde, c. 560–c. 600	*BAETAN* c. 569–588	*Wibbandun* 568; Ceawlin
CONALL, Dal Riada, 560–574		and Cutha beat Aethelbert
570		
URIEN of Reged c. 570–c. 590		*Bedcanford* 571
Arthuret 573		*Dyrham* 577
AEDAN, Dal Riada, 574–609		
580		
MOURIC, Glevissig,	*AED* m. Ainmere	ADDA, etc., Bernicia,
c. 580–c. 615	588–601	c. 570–588
Caer Greu 580. PEREDUR killed		AELLE occupied York?
Tintern c. 584		AETHELRIC 588–593
590		
Lindisfarne c. 590		CEAWLIN killed 593
OWAIN of Reged c. 590–c. 595		AETHELBERT supreme
Catraeth 598?		c. 593–616
		AETHELFERTH 593–617

	NORTHERN ENGLISH	SOUTHERN ENGLISH
600		
Degsastan 603	AETHELFERTH in York 604	
610		
Chester c. 613	EDWIN 617–633	CYNEGILS, West Saxons, 611–643
620		
		PENDA 626–655
630		
Catwallaun killed Edwin 633	OSWALD 634–642	
640		
Penda and Welsh killed Oswald 642	OSWY 642–670	CENWALH, West Saxons, 643–672

ABROAD	THE CHURCH ABROAD	THE CHURCH IN NORTHERN BRITAIN AND IRELAND
650 EBROIN, Mayor, 656–681	Fursey died 649	
660 Arabs took Syracuse 664		Synod of Whitby 664
670 Arabs besiege Constantinople 673–675	Killian of Wurzburg c. 670–689	Wearmouth founded 674 Caedmon died c. 678
680 PEPIN II, Mayor, 681–714		Bede at Jarrow c. 681–735 Adomnan, Iona, 686–704
690	Willibrord, Frisia, 695–739	
700 Arabs in Spain 710 CHARLES MARTEL 714–741 *Poitiers* 732 PEPIN III 741–768	Boniface of Mainz killed 755 Alcuin of York and Tours 766–804	
800 CHARLEMAGNE, 768–814		

*SONS OF CLOVIS		
THEODORIC I,	East Franks, 511–533	
CHLODOMER,	Orleans, 511–524	
CHILDEBERT,	Paris, 511–558	
CLOTHAIR I,	Soissons, 511–561	
	Orleans, 524–561	
	East Franks, 555–561	
	Paris, 558–561	

THE CHURCH IN SOUTHERN BRITAIN	THE NORTH	MERCIA AND THE SOUTH
650		
	Oswy killed Penda 655	
	OSWY supreme 655–658	WULFHERE 658–675
660		
Theodore Archbishop of Canterbury 669–690	Plague 664	Second *Badon*; Morcant killed 665
670		
Barking, Chertsey founded 675	EGFERTH 670–685	West Saxon underkings 672–c. 682
Aldhelm c. 670–709	*Trent* 679	AETHELRED 675–704
680		
	ALDFRITH 685–705	CEADWALLA 685–688
	Ferchar, Dal Riada, 680–696	INE 688–726
690		
		WIHTRED, Kent, 691–725
700		
	Pict and Scot wars	Coenred 704–709
	Northumbrian civil wars	Ceolred 709–716
		AETHELBALD 716–757
		OFFA 757–796
		First Scandinavian raid 789
800		
	KENNETH MacAlpine 830–860 united Picts and Scots	EGBERT, West Saxon, 802–839
		RHODRI MAWR, Wales, 844–877
		ALFRED 871–?900

SUMMARY OF EVENTS

350–400. The Imperial Government, under pressure on the Rhine and Danube, kept the garrison of Britain under strength. Britain prospered, in spite of occasional raids. Christianity prevailed by the end of the century.

400–450. The Rhine frontier broke, 406/407. The emperor Constantine III, a Briton, cleared the barbarians from Britain and Gaul, but was suppressed by the legitimate emperor, Honorius. The Goths took Rome, 410. Honorius told the British to govern and defend themselves, legitimising local emperors. The British repelled foreign enemies, but divided in civil war. Vortigern (c. 425–c. 458) employed Saxons, or English, to defeat the Picts, barbarians beyond the Forth; he neutralised mainland Ireland and reduced Irish colonists in western Britain. The British nobility, led by Ambrosius the elder, rebelled against Vortigern and the Saxons; Vortigern enlisted more Saxons, who rebelled against both parties, c. 441, and destroyed Roman British civilisation. After heavy fighting, the political leaders of the British were assassinated, and much of the surviving nobility emigrated to Gaul, c. 459.

450–500. A national resistance movement of the citizens (*Cymry*) was initiated · by Ambrosius Aurelianus the younger, c. 460, and triumphed under Arthur at Badon, c. 495. The English remained in partitioned areas, chiefly in the east. The political forms of the Roman Empire were revived, but its economy had been destroyed.

500–550. The central government disintegrated with the death of Arthur (c. 515). Numerous generals became warlords of regions, Maelgwn of North Wales the most powerful among them, and provoked the resentment of civilians of all classes. A monastic reform movement on a mass scale freed the church from dependence upon the warlords; it spread to Ireland, and also prompted a massive migration to Brittany. Bubonic plague ravaged the mediterranean and also Britain and Ireland, 547–551.

550–600. The second Saxon, or English, revolt permanently mastered most of what is now England, destroying the remnants of the warlords. By 605, Aethelferth of Northumbria and Aethelbert of Kent were between them supreme over all the English. Kent was converted to Roman Christianity, 597. Columba of Iona established Irish monastic Christianity among the Picts, and among the Scot or Irish colonists of Argyle, 563–597.

600–650. The empire and Christianity of Kent collapsed, 616. Northumbrian supremacy, 617–642, was overthrown by Penda of the Mercians, with Welsh allies. The monastic impetus faded in Wales but renewed its vigour among the Irish.

650–800. The Mercian kings held empire over the southern English; the Northumbrian monarchy lost authority after 700. The Northumbrians and Mercians accepted monastic Christianity from the Irish, and the English and the Irish carried it to Europe north of the Alps. Its practices conflicted with those of Rome. Archbishop Theodore, from Tarsus (669–690), presided over the fusion of native monastic and Roman episcopal Christianity among the English; the Irish and the Welsh conformed later. Scandinavian raids began in 789, and sovereignty over the English passed from the Mercian to the West Saxon kings early in the 9th century.

ABBREVIATIONS
used in the Notes

AC	*Annals of Clonmacnoise* translated C. Mageoghagan (1627) from an original of c. 1408, now lost; ed. D. Murphy, Dublin 1896
ACm	*Annales Cambriae* Rolls 20, 1860; YC 9, 1880, 152; MHB 830; *Nennius* ed. Morris forthcoming; cf. Welsh Literature, Bruts
ACR	Sir Cyril Fox *The Archaeology of the Cambridge Region* Cambridge 1923, rev. 1948
AI	*Annals of Inisfallen* (1092) ed. S. MacAirt, Dublin 1951
AIM	*Anecdotes from Irish Manuscripts* ed. Bergin, Best and others, Halle 1907
ALE	*The Ancient Laws and Institutes of England* ed. B. Thorpe, London 1840
Ant.	Antiquity 1927–
Ant.Jl.	Antiquaries Journal 1921–
Arch.Jl.	Archaeological Journal 1845-
ASH	*Acta Sanctorum Hiberniae I* ed. J. Colgan, Louvain 1645, reprint Dublin 1948
AT	*Annals of Tigernach* (1088) ed. W. Stokes RC 16, 1895, 375–419: 17, 1896, 6–33; 119–263; 337–420: 18, 1897, 9–59; 150–198; 267–303; 374–391
BB	G. Baldwin Brown *The Arts in Early England*, especially vol. 3, London 1915
BBCS	Bulletin of the Board of Celtic Studies 1921–
BCS	*Cartularium Saxonicum* W. de Birch, 3 vols. London 1885–1893; Index of Persons 1899
BG	Procopius *de Bello Gothico* ed. Teubner, CSHB, Leob etc.
BM	British Museum
Brev.Ab.	*Breviarium Aberdonense* Aberdeen 1509–1510; facsimile London 1854
CArch	Current Archaeology 1967–
CASP	Cambridge Antiquarian Society Proceedings 1840–
CGH	GENEALOGIES *Irish* M. A. O'Brien *Corpus Genealogiarum Hiberniae* vol. 1 Dublin 1962
CIIC	*Corpus Inscriptionum Insularum Celticarum* ed. R. A. S. MacAlister, 2 vols. Dublin 1945–1949
CLH	Ifor Williams *Canu Llywarch Hen* Cardiff 1936
CPNS	W. J. Watson *The History of the Celtic Place-Names of Scotland* Edinburgh 1926
CPS	*Chronicles of the Picts and Scots* ed. W. F. Skene, Edinburgh 1867
CS	W. F. Skene *Celtic Scotland* 3 vols. Edinburgh 1876–1880
CT	Ifor Williams *Canu Taliesin* Cardiff 1960
CTh	*Codex Theodosianus* ed. T. Mommsen, Berlin 1905, reprint 1954
DB	*Doomsday Book* ed. Farely, London 1783; ed. with translation, Morris, Chichester 1973–; facsimiles, Ordnance Survey, Southampton 1861–1864; many county translations in VCH; and others elsewhere
ECMS	*The Early Christian Monuments of Scotland* ed. J. Romilly Allen and J. Anderson, Edinburgh 1903
ECMW	*The Early Christian Monuments of Wales* ed. V. E. Nash-Williams, Cardiff 1950
EHD	*English Historical Documents I* ed. D. Whitelock, London 1955
EIHM	T. F. O'Rahilly *Early Irish History and Mythology* Dublin 1946
EPNE	*English Place Name Elements* A. H. Smith EPNS 25–26 Cambridge 1956
EPNS	*English Place Name Society Survey* by counties, Cambridge 1924–
FAB	W. F. Skene *Four Ancient Books of Wales* 2 vols. Edinburgh 1868
HL	*Historia Langobardorum*
HE	*Historia Ecclesiastica*
HF	*Historia Francorum* and other works ed. Gregory of Tours

ABBREVIATIONS

HH	Henry of Huntingdon *Historia Anglorum* Rolls 74, 1879; MHB 689; ARS
HMC	Historical Monuments Commission
HWL	T. Parry (translated H. I. Bell) *A Hisotry of Welsh Literature* Oxford 1962
IANB	A. L. F. Rivet (ed). *The Iron Age in Northern Britain* Edinburgh 1966
ITS	*Irish Texts Society* Publications, with English translation on facing pages, Dublin 1899–
IWP	Twynn Williams *An Introduction to Welsh Poetry* London 1953
JRSAI	Journal of the Royal Society of Antiquaries of Ireland 1870–
Kenny	J. F. Kenny *The Sources for the Early History of Ireland I*, Ecclesiastical (all published), New York 1929, reprint Dublin 1969
LBS	S. Baring-Gould and T. Fisher *The Lives of the British Saints* 4 vols., London, 1907–1913
Lec.	*Yellow Book of Lecan* in Trinity College Dublin; *Great Book of Lecan* in Royal Irish Academy
Leeds Corpus	E. T. Leeds *A Corpus of Anglo-Saxon Great Squareheaded Brooches* Oxford 1949
LL	*Liber Landavensis* J. G. Evans *The Book of Llan Dav* Oxford 1893
LRE	A. H. M. Jones *The Later Roman Empire* Blackwell, Oxford 1964
M	MARTYROLOGIES of
	Donegal ed. J. H. Todd and W. Reeves, Dublin 1864
	Gorman ed. W. Stokes, London 1895
	Oengus the Culdee ed. W. Stokes, London 1905 (often called the *Felire of Oengus*)
	Tallaght ed. R. I. Best and H. J. Lawlor, London 1931
MHH	*Miscellanae Hagiographica Hibernica* ed. C. Plummer (*Subsidia Hagiographica* 15) Brussels 1925
Mon.Ang.	W. Dugdale *Monasticon Anglicanum* 3 vols. London 1655–1673; ed. 2., 6 vols., London 1817–1830
OIT	K. H. Jackson *The Oldest Irish Tradition; a Window on the Iron Age* (Rede Lecture) Cambridge 1964
P and P	Past and Present 1952–
PP	F. T. Wainwright (ed.) *The Problem of the Picts* Edinburgh 1955
Phases	Eoin MacNeill *Phases of Irish History* Dublin 1920
PSAS	Proceedings of the Society of Antiquaries of Scotland 1852–
RC	Revue Celtique 1870/72
RIB	*The Roman Inscriptions of Britain* ed. R. G. Collingwood and R. P. Wright, Oxford 1965
RS	Record Society
Sal.	*Vitae Sanctorum Hiberniae e codice Salmanticenso* ed. C. de Smedt and J. de Backer, Brussels, 1887; ed. W. W. Heist, (*Subsidia Hagiographica* 28), Brussels, 1965. (References are here given to the columns)
SANHS	Somersetshire Archaeological and Natural History Society Proceedings 1851–
SC	*The Saxon Chronicle* Rolls, 23, 1861, ed. B. Thorpe; MHB 291; ed. J. Earle, Oxford 1865; revised C. Plummer, 2 vols. 1892–1899; D. Whitelock and others, text London 1952, translation 1961; translated G. N. Garmonsway, Everyman's Library 1953
SCSW	E. G. Bowen *The Settlements of the Celtic Saints in Wales* Cardiff 1954
SEIL	R. Thurneysen and others *Studies in Early Irish Law* Dublin 1936
THSCymm	Transactions of the Honourable Society of Cymmrodorion 1892/3–
Tischler	F. Tischler *Der Stand der Sachsenforschung* (35 Bericht der Romisch-Germanischen Kommission) 1956, 21 ff.
TT	*Trias Thaumaturga* (Patrick, Brigit, Columba) ed. J. Colgan, Louvain 1647
TYP	*Trioedd Ynys Prydein* ed. B. Bromwich, Cardiff 1961; cf. WHR Special Number 1963, 82
VSH	*Vitae Sanctorum Hiberniae* ed. C. Plummer, Oxford 1910
WBT	Gwynn Williams *The Burning Tree* London 1956
ZCP	Zeitschrift fur Celtische Philologie 1897–

NOTES

8 Pagan Ireland (pp. 142–163)

142.1 PATRICK: *Confessio* 46.

142.1 TOLD SEPARATELY: in the following narrative it has proved necessary to repeat the accounts of many events, and sometimes the comments made upon them, since they are viewed from a different standpoint in the context of the history of the Irish or the British, the English or the Northerners.

143.4 GENEALOGIES: see **G** Introduction, and **G** 1.

144.2 ANNALS: see **A** Introduction. The main European source seems to have been a Latin translation, no longer extant, of Eusebius' Chronicle, with continuations, fuller than the translation by Jerome which has been preserved (see BICS 19, 1972). This text was also a main source of Bede's Chronicle, since he and the Annals quote from it independently, and occasionally reproduce passages that are otherwise preserved only in the Armenian translation of Eusebius. Irish notices are said to have been collected from the 6th century onward. Most of the apparent inconsistencies are due to comments incorporated from corrupt genealogies or to mistakes, usually identifiable, in the European sources. Except for the Inisfallen Annals, most printed texts are faulty, and fail to distinguish the body of the MSS they reproduce from glosses added thereto.

145.3 MAELGWN . . . IDA: Nennius 62, cf. 61; 63.

146.1 SAINTS' LIVES: see **E** Introduction and p. 164 below.

146.1 EVIDENCE OF . . . DEDICATIONS: outlined by Bowen SCSW 6 ff., cf. **D**.

146.1 ARGUMENTS: cf. e.g. Simpson *Celtic Church* and Owen Chadwick SEBH 173 ff.

146.1 CHURCH OF MARTIN: Gregory of Tours, sensitive to the conventions of his own day, is careful to describe the church as 'the church which Briccius built over Martin'.

146.1 NINIAN: see p. 337 below. Bede's statements are explicit; it is most improbable that Ninian, devoted to Martin's then rare advocacy of monastic discipline and preaching to peasants and barbarians, could have avoided visiting Tours on his return from Rome in the 390s, and spending some time with Martin.

146.2 LOCAL . . . TRADITION: a clear instance is St. Asaph, formerly Llanelwy, the monastery on the river Elwy. The conventions of the medieval founders of the see did not permit a cathedral to be dedicated to a river; it was therefore given the name of a saint who was already widely honoured locally, but who was not, like others, the national saint of a Welsh kingdom.

146.2 NATIONAL TRADITION: Irish Norse brought Columba to Iceland, and Patrick and Brigit to Cumberland, and sometimes elsewhere in England; for the few dedications in England to Welsh and Armorican saints, see p. 370 below and map 28, p. 393 below. It is noteworthy that dedications to the numerous major or local saints of Normandy, Brittany and Flanders are not found in lands settled by lords from these territories after the Norman conquest.

147.1 KING LISTS: see **K** 1; martyrologies also supplement Saints' Lives, see **E** Introduction.

147.3 PREHISTORY: the main sources are *Lebor Gabala Erenn* (The Book of the Invasions of Ireland), the substance of whose tradition was known to Nennius, and to Cormac mac Cuilenan (**G** IMC 490 note) in the 9th century; Keating's

History of Ireland 1635; and the Annals. LG incorporates some 136 poems older than itself, varying in length up to about 150 lines. The synchronists supply dates, which the Annals repeat.

147.3   ANTIQUARIES: cited Keating 1, 5, 4 (ITS 1, 149). The 'Just Canon' is the Old Testament.

147.3   I LIKE NOT: CS p. 9.

147.3   NOT GENUINE HISTORY: Keating 1, 5, 4 (ITS 1, 147), cf. AT (Tigernach) 307 BC (RC 16, 1895, 394) *omnia monimenta Scottorum usque Cimbaed incerta erant.* Cimbaed, whose reign is dated 307–279 BC in the Annals, was the legendary founder of the Ulaid dynasty of Emain; recent excavation has shown that the great ceremonial mound of Navan (Emain, near Armagh), was constructed at a radio carbon date of 245 BC, $+$ or $-$ 50 years, cf. C. Arch. 22, 1970, 304 ff., where the date given needs slight adjustment. Tigernach accepts the historical reality of the Ulaid heroes, but rejects their mythological predecessors; recent discovery tends to confirm rather than to challenge his judgment.

148.2   BRONZE AGE . . . ROUTES: e.g. JRSAI 75, 1945, 94, fig. 6, cauldrons with conical rivets, a dozen by the Tyrrhene Sea, 4 about the headwaters of the Rhine and Danube, 10 in Denmark and Sweden, 7 in Ireland and 1 in Wales.

149.2   PTOLEMY: his account of Ireland is conveniently set forth in the Ordnance Survey's Map of Roman Britain, p. 20; cf. O'Rahilly EIHM, 1 ff., see **M.**

149.3   CRUITHNE: held to have been powerful in the distant past, cf. e.g. AI, AT (**A** 172 AD) 'Seven kings of the Cruithne ruled Ireland before Conn'; Tuathal's predecessor Elim was regarded both as king of Ireland and as king 'of the Domnann' LG 9, 95 (para. 593a) (ITS 5, 311), etc.

149.3   CRUITHNE . . . IDENTITY . . . LANGUAGE: change of language need not imply change of national identity; a modern Jones or Williams does not cease to be Welsh because he speaks English and bears a name of English origin.

150.1   JACKSON: OIT 44–45 note.

151.3   TUATHAL: extensively treated in AC 50–54, Keating 1, 39 (ITS 2, 243), LG 9, 95 (para. 593 ff.) (ITS 5, 309).

151.5   AGRICOLA: Tacitus *Agricola* 24, in 81 or 82 AD.

155.2   CAERNARVON: RIB 430; the repair of a ruined aqueduct implies rebuilding after disuse.

155.2   BENNE BRIT: see **A** 217 and note thereto; cf. also CGH 403 LL 328f 11, 14; Keating 1, 41 (ITS 2, 272), etc. The name is a corruption rather than an invention; invented foreigners were normally given Irish names, as 'Fergus the king of Spain's son', AC 59 etc.

155.3   CORMAC: see **A** 217–257, with note to 257; cf. also especially AC 60 ff., Keating 1, 43 ff. (ITS 2, 298 ff.) etc.

155.3   OBSOLUTELY: AC 60.

155.3   ALBA: see **L.**

156.1   REACHTAIRE: Keating 1, 43 (ITS 2, 306).

156.1   FINN: see especially **A** 257 note.

156.1   WISE, LEARNED: AC 60.

156.3   INSCRIPTIONS 244–264; of Philip (244–249) RIB 327 (Caerleon), 882–883 (Papcastle), 915 (Old Penrith); of Gallus (251–253) 2057–8 (Bowness-on-Solway); of Valerian (253–258, in Britain) 316, 334 (Caerleon), 913 (near Carlisle), 2042 (Burgh-by-Sands); of Postumus (258–268) 605 (Lancaster, dated 262/266).

156.4   COIN HOARDS: see **R.**

157.1   PLUNDER . . . SEVERN: see **R.**

157.2   AMARGEIN: e.g. Keating 1, 43 (ITS 2, 304); cf. Plummer VSH clxiii 6.

157.3   EMAIN: the ceremonial mount at Navan, p. 151 above, remained important for several centuries after 300 BC. The hill top of Armagh, 2 miles away, was fortified at a radio carbon date of AD 310, + or — 80 years, cf. CArch. 22, 1970, 308, where '5th century' is mistaken. Cf. 147.3 above.

157.5   CRIMTHANN: The Southern Irish texts do not refer to the Picts of north Britain; cf. **G** IML.

158.1   DIN TRADUI: **T** Cormac, and **L**.

158.1   CAIRPRE: see **G** IMW.

158.1   DERGIND: CGH 196 R 148a 31; see **L**. Inscriptions, CIIC 488, 489, 492, 493, 494.

158.1   AENGUS: see **G** IML.

158.2   UI LIATHAIN: see **G** BD and IML (especially CGH 228 R 151b 37 Lec.).

158.2   NENNIUS 14: *filii autem Liethan obtinuerunt in regione Demetorum et in aliis regionibus, id est Guir Cetgueli, donec explusi sunt a Cuneda et a filiis eius ab omnibus Brittannicis regionibus.*

158.2   CORMAC: see **T**.

158.2   EOGAN ALBANACH: see **G** IML.

158.2   MUNSTER: see **P** Builc.

158.2   LEINSTER: the peninsula of Lleyn, by Caernarvon, may take its name from the Laigin of Leinster; cf. also the later campaigns of Illan of Leinster (see **E** Brigit and p. 168 below), possibly fought in support of compatriots who had settled earlier in Britain.

159.2   NIALL: see **G** IN. King of Alba, king of the western world, CGH 122 R 136 b 27, b 23; king of the western world, invaded the kingdom of Letha (Letavia, Llydaw, see **L**), meaning Europe in general, or specifically Gaul, as here, and especially Brittany, LG 9, 114 (para. 612; ITS 5, 348).

160.1   CORCC: see **G** IMC, cf. **A** 439 Senchus Mor, FM etc.; Keating 1, 3 (ITS 1, 122–124), etc. Eoganacht genealogists legitimised his sovereignty by marrying him to Crimthann's sister Mongfind, whose other connections place her generations earlier, and make her the wife of Eochaid.

160.1   ULAID, LEINSTER: see **A** and **G**.

160.2   NIALL'S SONS: see **G** INA; *Eriu* 13, 1942, 92; Hogan *Onomasticon* Cenel, Tir, Ui etc.

160.3   NAMES: the fundamental discussion remains MacNeill's *Early Irish Population Groups* (PRIA 29 C, 1911/12, 59 ff.) cf. *Eriu* 3, 1907, 42 ff.

160.3   PATRICK: *Confessio* 41, cf. 52; *Ep. ad Coroticum* 12.

161.2   MUIRCHU 9: *imperator barbarorum regnans in Temoria, quae erat caput Scotorum, Loiguire nomine, filius Neill, origo stirpis regiae huius pene insolae.*

161.2   ADOMNAN: 1, 36, adding *deo auctore ordinatus.*

161.2   BRIAN BORU: Book of Armagh 16 v° *ego scripsi id est Calvus Perennis, in conspectu Briain imperatoris Scotorum.* Brian plainly authorised and accepted a title written under his eyes. The scribes name translates Mael Suthain, **G**.

161.3   ADOMNAN: Comgall, Cormac 3, 17; Columbanus 3, 12.

161.4   GLOSSES: e.g. *Cenel Conaill Cernaig*, Great Book of Lecan 190, Book of Leinster 312, cited Hogan 218; *Clann Cathair Mair* CGH 78 R 125 a 50, in contrast with the normal usage of e.g. CGH 358 LL 318 b 60 *Ic Cathair Mor condrecat Hui Falgi 7 Hui Enechglais . . . 7 Hui Crimthaind 7 clanda Cathair archena*, cf. e.g. CGH 44 R 121 a 19 ff., where Cathair is made ancestor of families named from persons elsewhere dated to the early 5th century; *Cenel Rochada* CGH 139 R 140 b 46. Such associations are not made in the main pedigrees or their headings.

162.1   BEC: AC 550.

162.1   ALL SUBJECTS: Ultan 66 (TT 534). The Life is early.

9 Christian Ireland (164–176)

164.1   SAINTS' LIVES: see **E** introduction.

164.1   COULANGES: *La Monarquie Franque* 9–12, cited Stokes *Lismore Lives* xci–xcii; cf. also JTS 17, 1966, 347 ff.; *Christianity in Britain* 65 ff.

164.2   SUPPRESSED . . . DOCTRINE: e.g. Jocelyn of Furness complained, *vita Kentigerni* prologue, that his sources were full of 'solecisms' and also *relatu perverso et a fide averso*; he took pride in his attempt, in rewriting them, *barbarice exarata Romano sale condire*, and tried to restore *sana doctrina*. Serious study cannot rest content with poking fun at Jocelyn's pretentious style and boundless ignorance of the times he described; the need is to get rid of the 'Roman salt' and 'sound doctrine', and to seek out the 'barbarisms' and 'perversity' that Jocelyn was unable to suppress.

164.2   GARRULITY: *Britannica garrulitate*, Vitalis of Fleury *vita Pauli Aureliani* ASS prologue, cf. RC 5, 1881/3, 415.

164.2   UNCOUTH . . . NAMES: *absona . . . barbara Britonum nomina*, Vitalis of Fleury, cf. note above, cf. AB 1, 1882, 209. The nature and extent of the omissions and alterations may be observed, since a version of the original which Vitalis abbreviated is extant.

165.1   HISTORICAL CRITICISM: the starting point of criticism is the comparison between those Lives that survive both in their original form, or in an early version that reproduces much of its names and content, and in 12th century or later recensions. The Lives of Samson, p. 357 below, and of Paul Aurelian, cf. note 164.2 above, are among the most important of those so preserved. Such comparison demonstrates how medieval editors actually altered their originals and disperses subjective speculation about what was or was not 'forged' or invented. No such comparison has yet been systematically undertaken.

166.1   ENDA: see **E** and p. 352 below.

166.2   CIARAN SAIGIR: *vita* (VSH) 18.

166.2   CIVIL VIOLENCE: Prisoners freed, e.g. *vitae* Ciaran Clonmacnoise 19; Colman Elo 24; Adomnan 1, 11. Cruelties, e.g. the tossing of a murderer's child, which survived to Viking times as *gall-cherd*, Macnissi (Sal.) 9; Cainnech 34, etc. Execution, e.g. Fintan 17, cf. Ruadan p. 170 below. Opposition to war e.g. Tigernach (VSH) 10, where the glory of the saint's deception was that 'the enemy army was put to flight without hurting anyone and without being harmed itself'. Comgall startled contemporary notions of justice by sentencing a slave girl, convicted of trying to poison her mistress, to be freed both of her slave status and of her prison, to spend the rest of her life in perpetual penance. Other saints, however, became patrons of their people, whose military victory their prayers ensured.

166.2   VORTIGERN'S DAUGHTER: see **E** Foirtchern, and p. 65 above. The surviving notices report that Foirtchern, whose name is an Irish transliteration of the British Vortigern, was the son of Fedlimid, son of Loegaire, and of the daughter of an unnamed British king. Since she gave her son the alien name of Vortigern, it is probable that in the original version of the tale he was her unnamed royal father; for the surviving fragments are unaware that there was a British king so named. Foirtchern became a notable ecclesiastic, particularly active in South Leinster, and his name subsequently passed into common use for a short period, especially in the south, since he was the principal teacher of Finnian of Clonard, the father of Irish monasticism. The name is not recorded in Ireland before his time, and soon after disappeared.

166.3   PATRICK . . . POPE . . . BISHOP: see pp. 64 and 348.

167.4   OCHA: cf. MacNeill *Phases* 190 ff., 231 ff. Though the Annals and Genealogies do not support the view that *derbfine* succession already obtained generally in the 5th century, the battle secured Ui Neill kingship.

168.2   DAL RIADA: see p. 180 below, also **L**, and **G** IDR.

168.3   ILLAN: see **G** ILD. *Novemque certamina in Britannia prospere egit* Ultan *vita* Brigit 90 (TT 538); variant *octosque* Animosus 2, 12 (TT 551).

168.3   CATWALLAUN: see **G** BGG.

168.3   SERIGI: (Triad 62, etc.) see **P**.

168.4   DEMETIA, CORNWALL: see **G** BB, BD; **P** Theodoric, and p. 125 ff. above.

168.5   MAC ERCA . . . LIVED AT PEACE: the numerous featureless battles entered in **A** 530, 531, appear to derive from a saga, whose date should be 6th or 7th century, since the source is given as Cennfaelad (**E**); and are entered for convenience in the Annals at Mac Erca's death. The only other wars noted by the Annals are dated before his accession.

169.2   REIGN OF TUATHAL: *Secundus vero ordo . . . ab extremis Tuthayl Maylgairb temporibus* Catalogus 2, confirmed by very many individual accounts.

169.3   DIARMAIT . . . BRIGIT: Ultan 64 (TT 534).

169.3   CIARAN: *vita Columbae* (O'Donnell), 44 (TT 396; ZCP 74).

169.4   DERRY: the traditions are summarised in Reeves' *Adomnan* 160. The Annals' date agrees with the tradition that Derry was founded immediately after the death of Mobhi Clarainech (**E**).

170.2   RUADAN: *vita* 15–18; AC 85–88.

170.2   PEACEFUL KING: *vita* Ruadan 17, *Rex enim defensor patrie pacificus erat, adiutor ecclesiarum et pauperum, verax in sermone, equus in iudicio, et firmus in fide.*

170.2   ULAID POET: Beccan, *M. Oengus*, prefaces, pp. 6 and 14.

170.2   HIS OWN SON: Book of Leinster 358, Book of Lismore 94 b, cited Stokes *Lismore Lives* xxvii; *M. Donegal* April 5.

170.3   BRITISH KING: perhaps Peter or Arthur of Demetia, see **G** BD; the powerful Rhun of Gwynned is less likely to have feared Irish threats.

171.1   COUNTRY SECURE: *vita* Ruadan 17, *Ego firmavi regiones, et pactum firmum feci in omni loco, ut pax firma ecclesiis et plebibus esset ubique. Ego bonum defendo secundum legem Christi; vos autem malum operamini, defendentes reum mortis. De parva enim multa surgent.*

171.1   PRICE: the author of the Life understood an ordinary compensation, and resumes his own jejune narrative, and inferior Latinity, with a story of miraculous horses who acquitted the payment.

172.1   COLUMBAN HOUSES: Reeves *Adomnan* 276 ff. lists 37 Irish and over 50 Scottish houses. The list is not exhaustive, but is likely to include some later offshoots which claimed personal foundation; see Map 26, p. 371.

172.2   FINNIAN'S BOOK: the story is told many times, and is here cited from *vita Columbae* (O'Donnell) 2, 1 (TT 408 (misnumbered 402)–409), ZCP 168; see also **E** Columba, Finnian of Moville.

172.4   CURNAN: Annals 560; *vita Columbae* (O'Donnell) 2, 2 (TT 409), ZCP 168; the lost Book of Sligo, cited Egerton MS 1782, *Silva Gadaelica* 79, translation 84, cf. Stokes *Lismore Lives* xxviii; and other versions.

173.1   CUIL DREMHNI: *vita Columbae* (O'Donnell) 2, 3 (TT 409), ZCP 170 ff., cf. **A** 561, etc. The essential facts are reported by Adomnan, see **E** Columba, and p. 377 below.

173.2   BRENDAN OF CLONFERT: see p. 384 below.

174.2   COLUMBA . . . CROWN: cf. p. 169 above and *Betha Coluim Chille* (Stokes

Lismore Lives 749), 'By inheritance his was the natural right to the kingship of Ireland, and it would have been offered him if he had not put it from him for the sake of God.'

174.2 THRONE OFFERED: vita *Columbae* (O'Donnell) 1, 44 (TT 396) *sceptrum antequam offeretur abrenunciavit*; 'it was offered many a time but he refused it' ZCP 74.

174.3 SYNOD . . . EXCOMMUNICATED: Adomnan *vita Columbae* 3, 3 etc.

174.3 LASRIAN: *vita* 31 (VSH) *Sanctus vero Columba visitavit sanctum Lasrianum, confessorem suum, post bellum de Cul Dremni, petens ab eo salubre consilium, quomodo post necem multorum ibi occisorum benevolenciam Dei . . . mereretur accipere. Beatus igitur Lasrianus . . . imperavit illi ut tot animas a penis liberaret quot animarum causa perdicionis exatiterat; et cum hoc ei precepit ut perpetuo moraretur extra Hiberniam exilio.* Exile did not of course preclude frequent visits to Ireland; it forbade permanent residence.

174.4 GILDAS: see p. 379 below.

175.1 CAIN ADOMNAN: ed. Meyer; cf. Kenney 245; SEIL 269 ff.

175.4 MONASTIC UPSURGE: see pp. 357 below.

176.2 KING . . . BORN IRISH: Aldfrith, cf. p. 196 below, and G ENB.

10   The Dal Riada Scots (177–185)

177.1 SCOTLAND: see Maps 2, 10–12, 26 (pp. 47, 179, 187, 189, 371), and L Atecotti, Caledonii, Circinn, Fortrenn, Miathi, Picts, Scots, etc. The principal collection of the sources is still the work of W. F. Skene, more than a hundred years ago, especially in CPS and CS; selections thereof are translated, with some supplementation, by Anderson ESSH. Much of Skene's interpretation is coloured by the assumptions of his day; but since no comparable comprehensive history of early Scotland has since appeared, any discussion of the formation of the Scottish nation must admit a considerable debt, directly or indirectly, to the body of evidence which Skene assembled and used.

177.2 ATECOTTI: the official 4th century spelling of the *Notitia Dignitatum* means 'the very ancient peoples', see L.

180.2 IRISH LEGEND: Watson CPNS 213 ff. summarises a number of the main stories.

180.2 BEDE: HE I, I, *Brittania . . . Scottorum nationem in Pictorum parte recepit, qui duce Reuda de Hibernia progressi . . . a quo . . . hodie Dal Reudini vocantur, nam lingua eorum 'daal' partem significat.*

180.2 FERGUS . . . DAL RIADA: see G IDR and p. 168 above.

180.3 TWO TEXTS: *Senchus Fir nAlban*, History of the Men of Alba (Skene CPS 308) see Q; T. *Cethri prim cenoil*, The Four Chief Dynasties, (Skene CPS 316) see G IDRF 590 Gartnaid; cf. p. 451 below.

180.3 COWALL, GOWRIE: see L Dal Riada.

180.4 PICT RECORDS: see K P and p. 191 below.

181.1 IONA: granted by Conall, A 574; by Bridei and the Picts, Bede HE 3, 4.

181.2 IONA . . . BURIAL PLACE: *Bethu Adomnan*, cited CPS 408 cf. MHH 179, 2 (AIM 2, 10 ff.; *Celtic Review* 5, 1908, 97 ff.)

181.2 NINIAN, KENTIGERN, COLUMBA: see Map 26, p. 371.

181.4 SEPARATE PORTIONS: *ri Aodhan na n-iol-rann* (Duan Albanach, CPS 60); the verses single out the particular distinction of each king, and therefore imply their author's view that Aedan was the first to unite the portions, to master the Cinel Loarn and Cinel Angus.

182.1 CONSECRATE AEDAN: Adomnan 3, 5.

182.3 DRUM CEAT: see L.

182.4	PEACE...BRITISH: Aedan may have attacked the Clyde after Columba's death, see **G** IDRF 560 Aedan.
183.3	DOMNALL: see **G** IDRF and **A**.
183.3	FIFE: Skene CPS 315–316, variant note 7.
183.3	CUMMENE: Adomnan 3, 5.
183.4	GLEN MURESON: cf. Skene CS 1, 249.
184.2	CUMMENE: Adomnan 3, 5.

11   The Picts (pp. 186–199)

186.1	PICTS: see **L**, cf. especially Chadwick *Early Scotland* 1 ff. and Isabel Henderson *The Picts*.
186.3	KING LISTS: see **K** P.
186.3	INSCRIPTION: RIB 191 *Lossio Veda ... nepos Vepogeni, Caledo*, cf. Vepoguenech, placed about the first half of the third century in the king lists, see **K** P.
188.2	PLACE NAMES: Map 11; Watson CPNS surveys Celtic, but not English or Norse names. 'Scotland north of the Forth' (206 ff.) is treated as a single unit, but the survey is almost entirely confined to districts east of the Great Glen. Four isolated Pictish place names opposite Skye suggest a garrison whose names endured; a few stones in Caithness, the islands and southern Scotland are probably memorials of lords and colonists in the years of Pictish supremacy.
188.3	DUNS AND BROCHS: see **M**, and Map 12. Many contained Roman objects of the early Empire but, unlike other native sites in Scotland, none has any of the late Empire; cf. *Britannia* 1, 1970, 202, cf. 210, 212; see **M**. See especially IANB 111 ff.; *Ant.* 39, 1965, 266; PPS 31, 1965, 93; *C.Arch.* 2, 1967, 27; 12, 1969, 5.
188.3	ORKNEYS: not part of Pictland, but situated 'beyond the Picts' (*ultra Pictos*), Nennius 8; their king was a subject foreign tributary of the Pict king Bridei, p. 193 below.
190.4	OTHER INDICATIONS: e.g. various confused Irish traditions, backed by Tacitus (*Agricola* 11) 'the red hair and huge limbs of the Caledonians proclaim their German origin; the dark complexions and the frequency of curly hair among the Silures (of Monmouthshire)... justify the belief that their ancestors crossed from Spain and settled there'. Excavation has confirmed the tradition of migration from Spain to South Wales, some two thousand years before Tacitus' time, and thereby adds weight to his comment on the more recently arrived Caledonians. Tacitus uses 'Caledonia' as a general term for all north Britain; the dated evidence of the brochs and their situation suggests that in his time their builders were the dominant power in most of northern Britain. At the time of their arrival in Britain it is probable that the larger part of the Germanic peoples still dwelt in Scandinavia. See **L**.
190.4	SOME OTHER CONQUERORS: e.g. the Normans, in England, France and Italy, and the Bulgarians, among the Slavs of the eastern Balkans, etc.
190.5	ATECOTTI: see **L**, and p. 177 above.
190.5	ABORIGINES: they are unlikely to have been concentrated in a single area. Communities who cling to a dying language are often isolated from each other by considerable distances, as, for example, the pockets of Slavonic speaking peoples who survived into modern times in widely separated regions of Germany.
191.1	OGAM: see p. 422 below.
191.1	STONES INSCRIBED IN OGAM: ed. MacAlister *MacNeill Essays* 184 ff., cf.

Diack *Inscriptions*, see **O**. Of 17 such Ogam stones, 7 are in the Orkneys and Shetlands, where brochs are numerous, but only 3 in Caithness and Sutherland, and none at all in Skye and the Hebridean area, where brochs are equally numerous. There are 3 in the Northern Pictish lands and 4 in the southern; none in the regions where duns are frequent. In addition, there are three similar inscriptions on knife handles, in Orkney, in the Hebrides, and in Norfolk (p. 57 above); but portable knives are not evidence of settlement. One stone from the Isle of Man may or may not belong to the same series.

Three of the inscriptions were added to Christian crosses, five to Pictish memorial stones, and can therefore hardly be earlier than the 7th or 8th centuries, if so early. But these stones cannot date the others, for date depends upon the origin of the script. The chief consideration is that its authors were familiar with Irish Ogam characters; but no Irish Ogams are known in the countries whence these inscriptions came, and only two are known anywhere in Scotland, both in Dal Riada, in Argyle. The most likely of the several possible origins of the script is therefore Irish Ogams inscribed on wood, by the earlier Irish population of north-western Scotland. The inscriptions appear on stone only in those regions where stone memorials were familiar.

If the symbols represent Irish letters, if the modern transcripts are secure, and if they represent a language at all, it is possible to detect Irish and Norse words for son and daughter, and some Pictish and Latin personal names; but it is also possible that all are an illiterate ornamental borrowing by persons who had seen Irish Ogams, but could not read or understand them. If the symbols do represent a language, the language is unknown, and attempts to 'translate' it have not succeeded.

191.3   BEDE: HE 3, 4.

191.3   NINIAN: see **E**, and p. 337 below; cf. Map 26, p. 371.

192.2   INHERITANCE: see **L**, Picts; land and property inherited through the woman, CPS 328; 126; 319; sovereignty through the woman, CPS 40; 45; 329. The Picts perpetuated customs that had been more widespread in pre-Roman Britain, and which also survived in other parts of northern Britain. Sovereignty through or of the woman is reported of the Iceni and Brigantes in Britain in the 1st century AD. In the 7th century the queen of Eigg exercised wide authority among the *Iardomnan*, M.Oeng. April 17; in the 6th century or earlier the Hebrides maintained a king who was denied marriage, children and personal property, Solinus (Irish version), ed. Mommsen p. 219, cf. Walter *Solinus*, especially p. 38, and Chadwick ES 92. Matrilinear inheritance still survives in parts of Asia, especially south-western India.

192.2   BRIDEI: see **P**.

192.2   PICTISH GRANDMOTHER: see **G** BGG.

192.3   RHUN: see **J** and **G** BGG.

193.1   BRIDEI'S ROYAL FORTRESS: Adomnan 2, 35.

193.1   BEDE: HE 3, 4 *venit ... Columba ... praedicaturus verbum Dei provinciis septentrionalium Pictorum ... gentemque illam verbo et exemplo ad fidem Christi convertit.*

193.1   ADOMNAN: 3, 3 *populorum ducem ad vitam*, cf. 3, 1 *animarum dux ad caelestem*; but Picts are one among several peoples in Adomnan's narrative, and are not the most prominent.

193.1   MAGI: Adomnan 2, 33–34, cf. **P** Broichan.

193.1   WINDS: Adomnan 2, 34.

193.1   LOCH NESS MONSTER: Adomnan 2, 27 *aquatilis bestia, bilua*, that bit and killed swimmers in the river Ness, below the Loch.

193.2   LORDS: e.g. at Urquhart, Adomnan 3, 14. Emchath was local, since his son Virolec was baptised *cum tota domu.*

193.3   ORKNEY KING: Adomnan 2, 42.

194.1   MEMORIAL STONES: Map 11, p. 187; see L Picts; cf. J.Romilly Allen and J.Anderson ECMS; Isabel Henderson *The Picts* 104 ff.; *Arch. Jl.* 120, 1963, 31, cf.118, 1961, 14; PSAS 91, 1957/8, 44; Wainwright PP 97; Cruden ECPMS.

194.1   STONES . . . DATE: a few of the earliest, e.g. Dunnichen, imitate 6th century Saxon saucer brooches too closely for coincidence.

195.1   PENTLAND . . . PEHTLAND: so Skene CS 1,238, without citation of evidence; cf. *Pettaland* (Pictland) for the Pentland Firth, between Caithness and Orkney, Watson CPNS 30.

195.2   AETHELFERTH'S SONS: his heir Osric was killed in an Irish battle shortly before Edwin's death A 631.

195.2   EANFRITH: Bede HE 3, 1.

195.3   ENGLISH KING: Talorcan filius Enfreth, see K P, cf. G ENB. It is likely that foreign-born Pictish kings who used Pictish names assumed them on their accession. Talorcan's English name is not recorded.

195.3   BEDE: HE 2, 5.

195.3   ENGLISH UNDER-KING: Beornhaeth (Eddius 19), apparently already in office on the outbreak of the revolt at the beginning of Egferth's reign.

196.1   BESTIAL NATIONS: Eddius 19.

196.1   WASTE . . . THE PICTS: Bede HE 4, 26.

196.1   ALDFRITH: see G ENB 650, and p. 176.

196.3   SCOTLAND: The most useful brief survey of Scottish history from the 7th to the 11th century remains that of Skene CS 1,240 ff., though much detail has since been corrected.

197.2   MORGAN: see G IDRL.

197.3   ALBAN: at the Battle of the Standard in 1138, the Scots from beyond the Forth *exclamant Albani! Albani!* HH 8, 9; cf. GESTA STEPHANI *Scotia quae et Albania dicitur*; Richard of Hexham *in fronte belli erant Picti*, Rolls 82, 3, 35 and 163.

197.4   EDINBURGH 960: CPS 365.

197.4   LOTHIANS 1018: Simeon of Durham *de Obsessione Dunelmi* 6.

198.1   DUNCAN KILLED: A AT (Tigernach) 379^2 (AD 1040) *Donncadh m Crinan, aird ri Alban, immatura etate a suis occisus est* ('Duncan mac Crinan, High King of Albany, was killed in youth by his own people'). Tigernach wrote within fifty years of the event.

198.1   MACBETH: see G IDRL.

198.3   WALTER OF OSWESTRY: cf. e.g. G.W.S.Barrow *Regesta Regum Scottorum* 1; for the genealogy see e.g. *Complete Peerage* 5, 391–2, Round *Peerage and Family History* 115 ff.; 129. Walter's grandfather was Flaald, brother of abbott Rhiwallon and son of Alan, steward of Dol; hence the later spread of the name Alan in England and Scotland.

12   British Supremacy (pp 200–224)

200.1   SOURCES: see pp. 143 and 164 above.

200.2   ARCHAEOLOGICAL EVIDENCE: is still much less in the midlands and the south than in the west and north; and little of it can yet be dated with confidence. 'Grass tempered' pottery, recently recognised, and provisionally dated to the Arthurian centuries, cannot yet be clearly interpreted; Celtic metalwork, listed by E. Fowler in *Arch. Jl.* 120, 1963, 135 ff., with an extensive bibliography, is reported from a number of southern and midland sites; but the import of British or Irish ornaments and craftsmen does not always imply a British or Irish population. Hanging bowl escutcheons with unequivocally Irish ornament, mostly of the 7th century, are known almost entirely from English graves, since they survive only in burials; in living use they are likely to have been at least as common among the Irish and British, and among the English they argue only the purchase of objects manufactured by Irishmen, who are as likely to have worked in Britain as in Ireland. Major British sites of the 5th and 6th centuries, outside the north and west, are few, and are at present most numerous in the Home Counties, cf. London, Colchester, Verulamium etc.

What is now known is surveyed in Alcock *Arthur's Britain* 142 ff. As yet the material is disjointed and of uncertain date, and there is not much of it. But since it has only recently begun to be recognised, it is likely that twenty years hence much more will be known, its dates more surely estimated, and that recognisable sites and objects will be more evenly distributed throughout Britain. They may well provide the most useful means of resolving many present uncertainties.

201.1	GILDAS' KINGS: 27 ff.
202.2	EMESA: *Novella Theodosii* 15, 2 (CTh. Vol. 2, p. 36).
203.3	PERHAPS OF GLOUCESTER: see **P** (Aurelius) Caninus.
203.3	VIOLATED HIS DAUGHTER: the offence was no more startling than many other dynastic marriages, e.g. Radiger's with his step-mother (p. 287 below) or the suggestion of marriage between Henry VII and his widowed daughter-in-law; but papal dispensation was less familiar in Gildas' time than a thousand years later.
206.4	ILL-STARRED GENERALS: *infausti duces* Gildas 50,1.
207.5	CAERWENT: see especially **E** Tatheus and **G** BMG.
208.1	GLEVISSIG, GLIVIS: see **G** BM and **L**.
208.1	PENYCHEN: see **E** Cadoc.
208.1	DEMETIA ... BORDER: *Venta provincia proxima eiusdem Demetiae* vita I Samsonis 1; *ultra Sabrinae fluminis fretum Demetarum sacerdotes* Aldhelm *Ep.* 4 (MGH p. 484), written from Malmesbury.
208.1	DUBRICIUS, TEILO: see **E**. David is freely called 'bishop' and 'archbishop' in the Lives; but no episcopal acts, comparable with those ascribed to Dubricius and Teilo, are related of him.
208.3	POMPEIUS, TURPILIUS: ECMW 198; 43. Cf. p. 251 below.
208.3	ILLTUD: see **E**.
208.3	CHEPSTOW: *vita Tathei* 4, see **E** Tatheus; the place is probably Portskewett.
208.3	CARRIAGE AND PAIR: Gildas *Ep.* 4 *habent pecora et vehicula vel pro consuetudine patriae vel sua infirmitate*, cf. *Ep.* 2. *vehiculis equisque vehuntur*.
210.1	DECANGI: Tac. *Ann.* 12, 32; Decanti ACm 822, cf. 812, cf. Degannwy by Llandudno, traditionally a royal centre of Maelgwn; Decangli, inscribed on lead pigs CIL VII 204–206; JRS 12, 1922, 283 15; cf. Tegeingl (Flintshire). It is possible but not probable that these spellings relate to two distinct adjacent peoples; cf. **L**.
210.2	WANSDYKE: see **L**. The frontier work included stretches evidently wooded in the 5th and 6th centuries, where it was not necessary to dig a dyke.
210.2	CATO: see **G** BC.
210.3	GREAT KINGS: e.g. Amlaut, Kassanauth, see **G**, index.
211.1	CARADOC VREICHVRAS: see **G** BLS.

211.1   SILCHESTER: see p. 137 above.

211.1   SILCHESTER DYKES: *Ant.* 18, 1944, 113, cf. 17, 1943, 188; cf. *Berks. Arch. Jl.* 54, 1954, 50.

211.2   ENGLISH TEXTS: SC.

211.3   CALCHVYNYDD: See **G** BLC, and **L**.

211.3   CATRAUT: see **G** BLC.

211.3   VERULAMIUM: cf. p. 137 above.

211.4   LONDON, COLCHESTER: see p. 137 above. The latest relics of British London are an *amphora* (wine or oil jar) imported from the eastern mediterranean, probably in or about the 6th century *Britannia* 1, 1970, 292 (where note 127 corrects the text), and several others excavated earlier, but first recognised after this discovery. The exact dating of these vessels is still uncertain.

211.4   ARTHUR'S CAMPAIGN: Nennius 56, see p. 111 above.

211.4   LINDSEY: one of its early 7th century rulers is said to have borne the British name of Caedbad, of **G** EL.

211.4   POETS: see **T** and p. 241 below.

212.1   WROXETER: see p. 241 below.

213.1   GENEALOGIES: especially **G** BA, BN. For Coel, see note 121.2, Cuill.

213.3   DEIRANS: **G** END 430 Soemil, see p. 77 above.

213.5   YORK CEMETERIES: see **S**.

214.2   GERMANIANUS . . . KINGDOM: see **G** BNM.

214.3   YEAVERING: see p. 320 below.

214.4   REGED: see **L**.

214.4   DENT: *regio Dunotinga* is one of four districts of north-western Yorkshire overrun by the English in or before the 670s, Eddius 17. The passage is overlooked in EPNS WRY 6, 252, where the early spellings Denet(h) are rightly related to a British *Dinned* or the like, and Ekwall's derivation from a non-existent British equivalent of the Old Irish *dind*, hill, is properly dismissed. EPNS does not observe that Dent was, and still is, the name of a considerable region, and that the village is still locally known as Dent Town, in contrast with the surrounding district of Dent. The physical appearance of the village is still strikingly unlike that of any other in the Yorkshire Dales, and it has been aptly described as a 'Cornish village stranded in the Dales.' *Regio Dunotinga* plainly takes its name from a person named Dunawt, Latin Donatus, as does the district of Dunoding in Merioneth, named from another Dunawt, son of Cunedda. See **L**.

214.4   SAMUEL: see **G** BN and **E** Cadoc.

215.2   GUALLAUC: his memory caused later parents in the area to name their children Wallace.

215.3   KENTIGERN: see **E**. Cambria, Jocelyn 11; Morken, Cathen, Jocelyn 22; see **G** BA, BN.

215.3   MANAU: see **L**.

215.3   DYFNWAL: see **G** BA; **J**.

216.3   WELSH ACCOUNT: see **J** and **Q**.

216.3   ELIDYR: see **G** BNR.

216.3   RHUN: see **G** BGG, and p. 192 above.

216.3   BRIDEI: see p. 193 above.

216.4   LLYWARCH . . . PASSIVE: Triad 8, cf. **G** BNR.

217.2   CYNDDELW: references assembled in TYP 502.

218.2   ARDERYDD: see **G** BN 560 Gwendoleu.

219.1   CELIDON: Nennius 56, cf. **T**; see **L**.

219.2   URIEN: see **G** BNR; see p. 232 below.

219.2   ROYAL RESIDENCE: Llwyfenydd, near the Roman fort of Kirkby Thore, by Penrith; see **L**.

219.3   CERETIC: Muirchu 28 cited p. 416.4 below.

219.3   MAELGWN: Gildas 34 *auscultantur . . . laudes . . . propriae . . . praeconum ore ritu Bacchantium concrepante*, cf. p. 416.4.

220.1   DINAS POWYS: Coed Clwydgwyn cf. **G** BB 530 Clytwin and p. 431 below.

220.3   MAELGWYN . . . TRIBUTE: e.g. Maelgwn imposed a tribute of a hundred cows and a hundred calves on each pagus; his *exactores* collected them in Glevissig, with a force of three hundred men, *vita Cadoc* 69.

220.4   LAWS . . . OF WALES: see **J** and p. 445.

220.4   ROMAN: see Jones LRE, especially 672 ff.; cf. 258–259 and 449 ff., and the texts there cited.

220.4   EROGATOR MILITARIS ANNONAE: cf. e.g. the texts cited in Du Cange, *Erogator*.

221.2   CAIS etc.: see p. 460 below. The evidence is briefly surveyed by W.Rees in *Angles and Britons* 148; cf. G.W.S.Barrow *Northern History* 4, 1969, 1 ff. It will be better understood when the texts, including the Yorkshire documentation, have been more fully studied. Random observation suggests that survivals of British administration were not confined to the north. *Gwestva*, tribute of food to the king, was reported in Flintshire in the 11th century, as *hestha* (DB 269 b (Cheshire FM 7); in the East Riding, as *hestcorne* oats, and as *hestra(st)la* or *hest(e)rasda*, horse fodder (Mon. Ang. 2,367; 1,170; HY 1,298); and, in the 13th century, as *ghestum*, loaves, in Northamptonshire (Northants. RS 5,793) and in Somerset (Archaeological Institute, Salisbury volume, 1851, 208; Somerset RS 5,83, cf. 89.90.93; cf. HMC Report 12, 1, 288, 329; SANHS 20, Supplement 67). I owe the references to *ghestum* to the kindness of Mr R.E.Latham. The obligation survived elsewhere without the name, cf. e.g. BCS 612 (Taunton, AD 904) 'one night's supplies (*pastus*) for the king and his kenneler and eight dogs, and nine nights' supplies for his falconers, and whatever the king may desire to convey thereof with waggons and horses to Curig (?) or Wilton'.

221.5   GILDAS: 1, 2 ff., quoting *Ecclesiastes* 3, 7.

222.1   MONKS: cf. chapters 18–20 below.

222.2   PLAGUE: see **M**.

222.3   TRADE: see p. 441 below.

223.1   EGYPTIAN SAINT: cf. p. 441 below.

223.2   PARTITION: see p. 134 above.

223.2   IRISHMEN: see **E** Abban, Columba of Terryglass and p. 386.

223.2   BRITISH . . . AMONG . . . ENGLISH: see **E** Gwenael, Winwaloe, and p. 314.

223.2   GIDEON: Gildas 70, 3; cf. 72, 3.

223.3   AFRICA: Corippus *Iohannidos* 3, 388–389 (p. 36 cf. xvi), *Gentes non laesit amaras Martis amica lues*.

13   British Collapse (pp. 225–248)

225.1   SAXON REVOLT: cf. p. 293 below.

225.1   CYNRIC: see **G** EW.

225.2   CEMETERIES: see **S**.

226.2   CIVIL WARS: the most likely cause of conflict between Winchester and Salisbury is a division of the *civitas* of the Belgae between the heirs of a former ruler, possibly Caradauc Vreichvras, cf. pp. 211 above, and 293 and 324 below.

226.2   CEAWLIN, CUTHA: see **G** EW, cf. p. 293 below.

227.1   GLOUCESTER ... POPULATION: BCS 60, cf. Finberg ECWM 158 ff.; p. 497 below.

227.2   FETHANLEA: see **L**; the name might be a misreading of *Feranlea*, any of the several places now called Fernley or the like, which include the old name of Hereford HW 282.

227.3   MAEDOC: *vita* (VSH) 17 see **E**.

227.3   FINNIAN: *vita* (Sal.) 8 see **E**.

228.1   BOULDERS: the story might suggest to the unwary that it was borrowed from Bede's account of Germanus' Alleluia victory (p. 62 above). But Irish tradition knew Germanus only as Patrick's teacher; the point of the story is not borrowed, and battles in Wales are commonly fought among hills; it is not therefore prudent to assume the influence of Bede.

228.2   CADOC ... PRAYED THE LORD: *vita Cadoc* 25, cf. **E**.

228.2   MOURIC: see **G** BM.

228.2   LLANCARFAN, LLANDAFF: see **T** Gospel Books.

228.2   THEODORIC: see **G** AC, BM and pp. 126 ff. above.

228.3   KING THEODORIC: LL 141–142.

229.1   BROCKWEIR: see **L**.

229.1   SIGBERT: Bede HE 3, 18.

229.2   AXMINSTER: *Beandun*, Bindon SC 614, see **L** and p. 307.

229.2   IDON: LL 123 see **G** BMG.

229.3   DUMNONIA: cf. p. 302.

230.1   BADON ... MORCANT: see p. 309 below.

230.2   UNTIL 775: see **G** BM. The reigns of a father and son for 110 years, from 665 to 775, are unusually long; but not unduly longer than those of Louis XIII and XIV of France, 105 years, or of Attalus I and II of Pergamon, 104 years. Queen Victoria's last surviving child died 107 years after her mother's accession to the throne.

231.2   RECORD OF THE ENGLISH: see **T** SC; cf. p. 317 below.

231.2   WELSH POEMS: see **T**.

231.5   IDA: see **G** ENB.

231.5   NENNIUS: 62, see **G** ENB.

232.2   TALHEARN: Nennius 62.

232.3   URIEN OF ECHWYD: CT 3, 1–4; 7–11; 27–30, translated IWP 28.

232.3   ECHWYD: possibly Solway, see **L**.

233.4   TERRITORIES ... SPLIT: see **G** ENB, cf. note 234 below.

233.4   CAER GREU: ACm 580, see **G** BN Peredur, ENB Adda.

233.4   GWGAUN: see **G** BN.

234.1   AELLE: see **G** END; Bede *Chronicle* 597.

234.2   ULPH: CT 7, 11–12; 29.

234.2   FFLAMDDWYN: see **G** ENB sons of Ida, Aethelric; **G** BNR Owain, Urien.

234.2   FOUR ARMIES: CT 6, 10; the Bernician forces were still organised in four armies at Catraeth, *Gorchan Tudfwlch* CA 1296 ff.

234.2   ARGOED LLWYFEIN: CT 6, translated WBT 29, PWP 18; see **L**.

234.3   URIEN'S ELEGY: CLH 3 (FAB 359, 259).

234.3   PILLAR OF BRITAIN: *Post Prydein* CLH 3, 16, cf. **T** 5, bracketed with **Pabo**, father of Dunaut, and Cynvelyn Drysgl of Edinburgh, cf. **G** BN.

234.3   HUSSA: Nennius 63. The text is early, using the 7th century spelling **Urbgen** for Urien.

234.3   METCAUD: Lindisfarne, A 635 (Metgoit); cf. **L**.

235.1   FIACHNA: Fiachna Lurgan, see **G** IUA 570/580 note.

235.3   WHEN OWAIN: CT 10, 11 ff., translated Parry HWL 3, cf. IWP 27; EWP 65.

236.2   THE HEAD I CARRY: CLH 3, 8; 30–31; cf. 46; 51; 53; 56; 59.

237.2   CATRAETH: see **L** and **A** 598.

237.2   DEIRAN TREACHERY: CA 198–201 'The treacherous Deirans asked "Is there a Briton truer than Cynan?"' **L**; Jackson *Ant.* 13, 1939, 27; *Gododdin* **A** 18.

237.3   MEN WENT TO CATRAETH: CA 33 (372–375); 31 (361–2); 58 (670–674); 60 (689–694); Jackson *Gododdin* **A** 33; 31; 56; 59.

238.1   MAEL UMA: see **G** INE 570/580, IDRF Aedan note.

238.1   BEDE: HE I, 34.

238.2   DEIRA: see **G** END Aelle; the statement of SC that Aelle died in 588 is formally denied by Bede and other earlier texts.

238.2   CHESTER: Bede HE 2, 2 cf. **A** 614.

239.1   CONTEMPLATED CONQUEST OF NORTHUMBRIA: see p. 301 below.

239.2   CLYDE: see **G** BA.

240.2   GWYNEDD: see **G** BGG Cadman, Catwallaun, etc.

240.2   VESTIGES OF POEMS: BBCS 7, 1933, 24, cf. TYP 294.

240.2   MEVANIAN ISLANDS: Bede HE 2, 5, cf. 2.9; see **L**.

240.3   PENDA: see **G** EM and pp. 302 ff. below; one tradition held that he was first attacked and subdued by Catwallaun, another that Catwallaun married his sister or niece.

240.3   EDWIN KILLED: the campaign apparently involved two battles, near Welshpool and Doncaster, see **L** Meicen, Hatfield.

240.4   MERIONETH: Idris, see **A** and **G** BGM.

241.2   OSWALD IN WESSEX: SC 635.

241.2   CYNDDYLAN: see **G** BCW.

241.2   MAES COGWY: see **L**.

241.2   GAIUS CAMPUS, WINWAED: see **L**.

241.3   CYNDRWYN: Triad 60, his son Gwiawn at 'Bangor Orchard'.

241.3   CYNDDYLAN: CLH II, 3 and 4.

241.3   WROXETER: CArch. 4, 1969, 84; 23, 1970, 336; 25, 1971, 45; where however the word Germanic is misleading.

242.2   MAES COGWY: CLH II, III.

242.2   OAKEN COFFIN: CLH 13, 1; 25 ff.

242.3   MY HEART IS AFLAME: CLH 13, 42 ff.

243.1   LUITCOET: see **L**.

243.1   MORFAEL: see **G** BCL and p. 308 below.

243.2   OSWY . . . RAIDED: ACm 656.

243.2   TRIBAL HIDAGE: see **T** and p. 492.

243.2   WULFHERE'S FORD: DB f. 259 d, Shropshire IV, last entry, cf. HW 195.

244.1   CYNDDYLAN: CLH II, 6; 15–16; 18; 27; 29; 31; 66; 69; 71–72; 85; 87. EWP 46.

245.2   WREKIN: CLH II, 81, 'Once I looked from Dinlle Wrecon, Down upon the land of Freuer'. Freuer is represented as the sister of Cynddylan.

246.1   BROKEN SHIELD: CLH II, 55–56.

14 Brittany (pp. 249–260)

249.1   ARMORICAN BRITISH: see **L** Llydaw and **G** A.

249.1   SAINTS' LIVES: see **E** introduction, and p. 164.

249.2   MANUSCRIPTS: many of the published texts were discovered by a deliberate search conducted by French scholars in the Bibliothèque Nationale, the libraries of Fleury, St. Germain-des-Prés, and other houses, chiefly between 1880 and 1914; further search in such libraries offers the most likely chance of finding unpublished texts that concern Britain and Brittany.

249.2   PERTINACIOUS ENQUIRY: *Cartulary of Quimperlé*, preface, pp. vi–ix.

249.2   LE GRAND ... TEXTS: including Breviaries and *Propria*, service books, in manuscript, or printed in the 16th and 17th centuries for the use of particular houses, which were also extensively consulted by Baring-Gould LBS; full publication is likely to add to knowledge; see **T**.

249.2   LE GRAND: see **E** introduction.

249.2   CHARTERS: see **C**.

250.1   GREGORY OF TOURS: see **E**.

250.1   PILGRIM: see p. 383 below.

250.2   MANY REGIONS: Nennius 27.

251.2   SECOND MIGRATION: cf. pp. 38 and 90 above.

251.3   BRITISH COUNTS: Greg. Tur. HF 4, 4 *nam semper Brittani sub Francorum potestatem post obitum regis Chlodovechi (511) fuerent, et comites non reges appellati sunt.* The language of the Lives is normally precise, using *rex* for 5th century rulers, *comes* for 6th-century rulers.

251.3   THIRD MIGRATION: for its date and nature see especially p. 364 below.

251.4   CONOMORUS, RIWAL: see **G** A; the most important of the 6th-century emigrant leaders was probably Arthmael (see **E**), but little is known of him.

251.4   CARADAUC: see **G** BLS.

251.4   RIWAL ... FROM OVERSEAS: *vita Winnoci,* cf. LBS 1, 297 note 3; cf. also *vitae Leonori, Tudwal*; see **G** ADW.

251.4   FRACAN: *vita Winwaloe* 1, 2.

252.2   HORSE RACE: *vita Winwaloe* 1, 18; cf. **E**.

252.4   PAUL TRAVELLED: *vita Pauli Aureliani* 15, cf. **E**.

253.2   ROSCOFF ... POTTERY: discovered by the late Professor J.B.S.Haldane.

253.3   BACAUDAE: see pp. 8 and 90 above.

253.4   VICTOR: *vita Pauli Aureliani* 15, cf. 19 *rex Philibertus istam mihi regionem sub suae potestatis conditione ad regendam tradidit.*

256.1   CYNAN: see **G** AG, AV.

256.1   DANIEL, BUDIC, THEODORIC etc.: see **G** AC and p. 130.

256.2   MACLIAVUS: Greg. Tur. HF 5, 16, cf. **G** AV.

256.3   MACLIAVUS, CONOMORUS: Greg. Tur. HF 4, 4; cf. **G** AC.

256.3   CONOMORUS: *iudex externus* in Armorican tradition, *vita I Samsonis* 1, 53; *vita Leonori*, a foreign ruler, in contrast with the immigrants who had forsaken their homes in Britain; to those in Britain, Armorica was also *externae gentis regio* (vita Pauli Aureliani 9). His kingdom is approximately located by the Life of Paul Aurelian, whose father took service in Glevissig, but whose ancestral estates lay on the Channel coasts and within the dominion of Conomorus. Conomorus' royal centre is explicitly located at Castle Dore by the Norman poets, see references in *P and P* 11, 1957, 15–16. No evidence locates him in South Wales, as THS Cymm. 1953, 47 ff., cf. TYP 446.

257.1   BANHEDOS ... MARCUS: *vita Pauli Aureliani* 8; variant reading *Bannhedos*.

257.1   DRUSTANUS: CIIC 487, corrected JRIC n.s.I, 1951, 117, *His iacit Drustanus Cunomori filius*; the name *Drustanus*, no longer legible, is restored, chiefly from earlier readings. It recalls Pictish Drust, but is rare, cf. Columba's pupil Drostanus, abbot of Deer, *Book of Deer* p. 91, who is however said to have been son of an Irish Coscrach, *Brev. Ab.* PH 19 d. The Tristan of the legends is transformed into a nephew of Mark and given alternative fathers, Rivalen in Brittany, Tallwch in Wales; both names are late additions, not related to the realities from which the legend originated.

257.3   CHRAMN: Greg. Tur. HF 4, 20 cf. 21, death of Clothair; cf. *vita Samsonis* (AG) 14–15; the AG Life of Samson concentrates upon events in Brittany; the early *vita prima* and its derivatives deal chiefly with events in Britain.

258.2   BURIED AT CASTLE DORE: *vita Pauli Aureliani* 8.
258.4   THEODORIC: Greg. Tur. HF 5, 16, cf. **G** AC, BM and p. 228.
258.4   WAROC: see **G** AV.
259.2   IUTHAEL, HAELOC etc.: see **G** ADe.
259.2   MALO: see **E**; the principal life is a 9th-century text, using 7th-century sources.
259.3   IUDICAEL, IUDOC, WINNOC: see **G** ADe, and **E**.
259.3   MEVEN: see **E**.
259.4   FITZALANS, STUARTS: see p. 198 above.

15 English Immigrants (pp. 261–292)

261.1   HOMELAND: see **S**.
261.2   GERMANIC LEGEND: especially the poem *Widsith*, notably lines 18 ff. and 57, and *Beowulf*.
261.2   OCEAN PEOPLES: see **F**.
261.4   MIGRATION: the fundamental survey of the texts is Thomas Hodgkin *Italy and her Invaders*. Lucien Musset *Les Invasions; les Vagues Germaniques* summarises more recent thinking. The viewpoint is Roman. From the barbarian standpoint the fullest study is L. Schmidt *Allgemeine Geschichte der Germanischen Völker*. There is no comprehensive survey of the archaeological evidence.
262.2   CHAMAVI: Eunapius, fragment 12.
264.3   SCANDINAVIA: *vagina nationum* Jordanes *Getica* 4.
264.3   OTHERS: e.g. the Burgundians, whose name is preserved in Bornholm and elsewhere.
264.3   GERMANIC NATIONS: the nearest equivalent to a comprehensive map of barbarian Europe is the *Grosse Gesamtkarte* in Eggers *Römische Import*; though it excludes sites that have no import, few areas had none, and the blanks on the map are usually devoid of native as well as of imported finds.
264.4   LANGOBARDI: Cassius Dio 71, 3, 1a; see **F**.
265.2   EORMENRIC: see PLRE I, Ermanaricus.
265.2   JUTLAND . . . DEPOPULATED: see **F** and **S**.
265.3   OFFA: see **G** EM.
266.3   HENGEST: see **G** EK. Hengst and Hors mean 'Stallion' and 'Mare', evidently the nicknames, and perhaps the ensigns of the two leaders. One genealogy suggests that Hengest's name may have been Aethelbert. Bede HE I, 15 says that the name of Hors was to be seen on a monument in East Kent. What was seen was doubtless the remnant of a Roman inscription erected by a [CO]HORS; if so, the place was probably Reculver, the only place in Kent or in southern Britain where a cohort was stationed in the period when such inscriptions were commonly erected.
266.3   BEOWULF: see **T**; Hengest, lines 1068 ff.
266.3   FINN'S BURG: see **T**.
267.5   GRAVE GOODS: see **S** and p. 32 above.
268.2   ROUTES: they were a particularly unhappy handicap to the sensitive and perceptive studies of E. T. Leeds; in other hands the concept often verged upon the absurd.
269.3   CRUCIFORM AND SAUCER BROOCHES: cf. p. 32 above.
270.2   THE NATION: Bede HE I, 15.
270.2   HE KNEW: Bede HE 5, 9.
272.1   ENGLISH: Nennius 56, cf. p. 106 above.
272.1   PROCOPIUS: BG 4, 20.

272.2   ICLINGAS: see **G** EM.

272.3   NAME OF ICEL: in Sussex a few Icel names, together with Cutha names and great squareheaded brooches, suggest some East Anglian settlement in the later 6th century, cf. Map 20, p. 295. Personal names in Cutha are numerous at all periods, but, on the evidence so far published by EPNS, are relatively infrequent in place names outside the districts overrun by the Eslingas; the most noticeable other Cutha region is in northern Mercia.

273.2   ESLINGAS: see p. 110 above.

273.4   ENGLISH IN EUROPE: Map 16; see **S** and the particular peoples and regions in **F**. Pagan English burials are said to have been found in Poland, and a Slavonic origin has been claimed for some urns found in England.

274.1   EVERY OARSMAN: Sidonius *Ep.* 8, 6, 13 *Saxones ... archpiratas ... ita ut simul omnes imparent parent, docent discunt latrocinari.*

274.2   CORSOLDUS: see p. 92 above.

274.2   ODOVACER: see **P** and p. 91 above.

276.1   PRESSURES: exactly defined and keenly remembered in the native tradition of the continental Saxons, e.g. *Translatio S. Alexandri* 1, reporting that their ancestors had been continually obliged to defend their living space (*spacia*) against four named enemies who pressed upon them, *a meridie Francos ..., a septentrione vero Nordmannos ..., ab ortu Obroditos ..., ab occasu Frisos.* The *Obroditi* were Slavs, the *Nordmanni* Danes.

278.1   DANISH INVASION: Greg. Tur. HF. 3, 3, cf. the Latin sources printed in Chambers *Beowulf* 3–4, cf. pp. 381 ff. Frisian territory, though not settled by Franks, seems to have been a *pagus* of the Frank kingdom before5 20, see **L**.

278.2   DANES: see **F**.

278.3   SLAVS: see **F**. The main difficulty in the interpretation of the evidence is that the same grave goods are often given quite different dates by modern German and modern central European scholars. Identical pots are sometimes assigned to the 7th or 8th centuries if they are excavated in Baltic lands and published in Germany, to the 5th and 6th centuries if they are excavated by the Danube and there published. Until a thorough comparative study is available, it is only possible to observe that the Danubian dates are based on the evidence of associated Roman objects, while the north German graves have no such evidence. The Danubian material justifies the conclusion of, e.g. Preidel (*Slawische Altertumskunde* 2, 14 ff.) that Slav graves begin in the 4th century, and that the 'Prague Type', and related pottery vessels, were 'dominant' during the 5th and 6th centuries, rare thereafter. They are markedly absent from 7th century southern Slav sites. Such vessels are quite common in north Germany; though it is theoretically possible that their manufacture might have begun later and continued longer in the north, such a hypothesis cannot be maintained until decisive evidence is clearly demonstrated. The dating at present given by different scholars in different countries, and the reasoning upon which it is based, is discussed in **F**.

278.4   HAMBURG CEMETERY: Tischler *Sachsenforschung*, plate 29, p. 85, cf. H. Jankuhn *Geschichte Schleswig-Holsteins* 3, 1957, 100, citing local publications. The view that the large vessel there illustrated seems to be a normal Slavonic Prague Type, and that the smaller vessels are imitations of late Roman provincial wares, is endorsed by Czech scholars conversant with these vessels, who have been kind enough to look at the illustration. Present conditions preclude a more precise pursuit of the opinions expressed.

279.1   PROCOPIUS: especially BG 2, 15, 1 ff.; 3, 35, 16; see **F** Slavs.

279.3   AGRICULTURAL TECHNOLOGY: it is sometimes schematically pretended that a 'slash and burn economy' is necessarily more 'primitive' than the cultivation of lands already cleared. But the opening up of virginal lands commonly requires greater application and a technology as 'advanced' as inherited cultivation, or more so; 'slashing and burning' is the most suitable technique for the clearance of lightly wooded lands. It may only be dismissed as 'primitive' when it is not followed by continuing cultivation. The nature of Slavonic agriculture in Bohemia and the Baltic lands will be better understood when adequate comprehensive and comparative study has been directed to excavated Slavonic objects; to old Slavonic words for tools; and to Slavonic place names. Circumstances have tended to inhibit such study.

280.1   STIRRUP . . . HORSE COLLAR: cf. p. 437 below.

280.3   MAP 8: Partition, p. 134 above.

281.2   PROCOPIUS: BG 4, 20.

281.2   BURIALS: see S.

281.3   SMALL PEOPLES: most are mapped on the Ordnance Survey's *Map of Dark Age Britain*.

282.1   BERNICIANS . . . FOUR PEOPLES: cf. pp. 233–234 above.

282.3   NEW IMMIGRANTS: see S.

283.2   ANGLIAN CHRONICLE: cf. Liebermann MGH SS 28, 11. Differently excerpted by Henry of Huntingdon and *Flores Historiarum*, both under the year 527. In the reconstructed text below, the words common to both are printed in capitals; those excerpted by Henry only are in italics, and those excerpted by the *Flores* only are in Roman type.

> VENERUNT *multi et saepe* pagani DE GERMANIA ET OCCUPAVERUNT EST ANGLIAM (id est regionem illam quae Orientalium Anglorum regio dicitur) *et* quorum quidam MERCIAM invadentes bella cum Brittonibus plurima peregerunt SED *necdum sub uno rege redacta erant. Plures autem proceres certatim regiones occupabant, unde innumerabilia bella fiebant,* quoniam PROCERES *vero* eorum *quia* ERANT MULTI NOMINE CARENT.

I am grateful to my former pupil, Dr. Wendy Davies, for drawing my attention to the significance of the *Flores* entry, cf. **T**.

283.3   MEDRAUT: see p. 140 above.

284.1   ALAMANNIC GRAVE GOODS: see S.

284.1   ALMONDBURY: EPNS WRY 2, 256.

286.3   GILDAS: 92, 3.

286.4   HERPES: it is possible that some of the Kentish objects catalogued in the British Museum as from Herpes did not come from there; but probable that most did; cf. Delamain *Herpes*.

287.1   PROCOPIUS: BG 4, 20; see **T** and **F**.

287.3   BOULOGNE: Map 19A, and notes thereto; cf. *Cartularium Sithiense*, c. AD 850; see **N** Place Names.

287.3   BROOCHES: said to have been in Boulogne Museum before 1940; none are known to have survived the war.

287.3   EGWIN: Fredegarius 4, 55, cf. 4, 78, see **P** Aigynd.

288.2   NORMANDY . . . VILLAGE NAMES: Map 19B and notes thereto; see especially *Annales de Normandie* 10, 1960, 307 ff.; 13, 1963, 43 ff.; cf. **N** Place Names.

291.1   SAXONS . . . OF BAYEUX: Greg. Tur. HF 5,26; 10, 9.

291.2   SAXON PEOPLE: *Translatio Sancti Alexandri* 1; cf. Adam of Bremen 1, 4 *Saxones primo circa Rhenum sedes habebant [et vocati sunt Angli] quorum pars inde veniens in Brittaniam Romanos depulit; altera pars Thuringiam oppugnans tenuit illam regionem.*

291.2   DATE 531: Greg. Tur. HF 3, 7.

291.2   HADELN: *Annales Regni Francorum* AD 797. '*Haduloha . . . ubi Oceanus Saxoniam alluit*' beyond the Weser, but not beyond the Elbe, therefore the region now called Hadeln, cf. **F**.

291.3   SAXONS REBELLED: Greg. Tur. HF 4, 10 cf. 4, 14.

291.3   ROUGH POTTERY: Tischler *Sachsenforschung* 79.

291.3   BUTTL NAMES: see Map 17, p. 277.

292.2   THURINGIA . . . ANGLIAN POTTERY: Map 16, p. 275, and notes thereto. The Anglian grave goods of the Czech and East German museums have not yet been sufficiently studied to determine their date; it may prove possible to distinguish two movements, from the lower Elbe in the 5th century, and from Britain in the 6th century. Most of the stray English grave goods in Hungary, Albania and elsewhere in the Balkans (see **S**) seem to be 6th century, matched in cemeteries in Britain, but not on the Elbe.

292.2   -LEBEN NAMES: see Map 17, p. 277. The names clearly remained in use for some time, into the earlier stages of German conquest of Slav territory.

292.2   SAXONS AND LANGOBARDS: Greg. Tur. HF 4, 42; 5, 15, cf. Paul the Deacon HL 2, 6; 3, 5–7. Since the Suevi were installed before the death of Clothair in 561, these Saxons left their homes earlier.

16   English Conquest (pp. 293–316)

293.1   CYNRIC, CEAWLIN, CUTHA: see **G** EW; cf. p. 225 above.

293.3   CUTHWULF: the story that he was Ceawlin's 'brother' is confined to guesses in late genealogies and insertions into the later texts of SC.

293.3   PLACE NAMES: see **G** EW 560 Cutha, and Map 20, p. 295.

293.3   CUTTESLOWE: now commonly spelt Cutslow, cf. *Ant.* 9, 1935, 96 and EPNS Oxfordshire 267.

293.3   ESLINGAS: see p. 110 above.

294.1   GEWISSAE: see **L**. The word probably means 'confederates', either a federation of different English peoples, whose burial rite attests a mixed origin, or else translating *foederati*, the status accorded to them by the British. Their ornament demonstrates that they included many immigrants from the Saxon country on the left bank of the Elbe estuary, whose descendants in time predominated (cf. p. 324 below), and, in contradistinction to the Mercian Angles, consented to be known by the collective national name of Saxons, which their British neighbours applied to them, as to other English immigrants.

296.1   ILCHESTER: see **S** and Map 21.

296.1   GLASTONBURY: William of Malmesbury *de Gestis Regum* 1, 27–28, in 601; Morfael, in or about 655, see p. 243.

296.1   CANNINGTON: *ST 25 40*, MA 8, 1964, 237; *Christianity in Britain* 195.

296.2   INDEPENDENT MONARCHY: see **G** E and **T** Anglian Chronicle, cf. p. 283 above.

296.3   EAST ANGLIAN WARS: see p. 283 above.

298.1   UFFINGAS: see **G** EA.

298.1   SQUAREHEADED BROOCHES: see **S**.

298.2   CREODA: see **G** EM.

298.2   TRIBAL HIDAGE: see **T** and p. 492 below.

299.2   WYE . . . 584: see p. 227 above.

299.3   KENTISH . . . MIDLANDS: e.g. Leighton Buzzard, Chamberlain's Barns Pit II, which endured, and Totternhoe (Dunstable), Marina Drive, which did not long survive, *Arch. Jl.* 120, 1963, 161; *Bed. Arch. Jl.* 1, 1962, 25; together with many of the sites listed *Arch. Jl.* 120, 190, beside others which contain Kentish material but are less specifically Kentish.

300.3   PIONEERS: see Map 22, p. 305. The latest pagan burials, most of them of the early 7th century, extend into a few concentrated regions, between Bernicia and Deira; in the Peak District; in the border lands between the West Saxons and the Mercians, about the Cherwell and the Cotswolds; on the south-western borders of the West Saxons; and on the edges of the Weald. Pagan English burials have not been reported from the British lands of the north-west midlands, allied with the Mercians, though some Cheshire place names ending in -*low* (burial mound), preceded by an English personal name, suggest some colonisation in the 7th century, perhaps beginning at the end of the 6th century, cf. p. 310.2 below.

301.2   BISHOP IN YORK: Bede HE 1, 29 cites a letter of Gregory the Great, dated 22 June 601, elevating Augustine to metropolitan status, and adding,

> we wish you to appoint and send a bishop to York, provided that if the city and its neighbourhood receive the Word of God, he also may conse-crate 12 bishops, and exercise metropolitan authority.

301.3   HUMBER AND ... BEYOND: Bede HE 1, 25 says that in 597 the *imperium* of Aethelbert extended 'as far as the Humber, the great river that divides the southern and northern English'; on Aethelbert's death in 616 he describes the frontier as 'the river Humber and its adjacent borders' HE 2, 5. In both passages the language is careful; the reason for the variation may be that in the meantime Aethelbert lost all or part of Lincolnshire, to Aethelferth.

301.4   GOLDEN AGE: Bede HE 2, 16.

302.3   EDWIN AND THE WEST SAXONS: Bede HE 2, 9; SC 626.

302.4   EDWIN AND WALES: see p. 240 above.

302.4   PENDA: see p. 240 above.

302.4   OSWALD ... SEVERN: see **A** 635 and p. 240 above.

302.4   ENGLISH REBELLION: **A** 636 *congregacio Saxonum contra Osualt*.

302.4   ATBRET IUDEU: Nennius 64–65, see **L** Giudi (probably Stirling). The word *atbret* is British, 'older than ... Primitive Welsh, and therefore not later than the seventh century', Jackson *Celt and Saxon* 38; cf. also **L** Winwaed.

303.2   PICTS AND SCOTS: Bede HE 2, 5.

303.2   PICTISH KING: Talorcan son of Enfrith **A** 656, see p.195 above; **K** P; **G** ENB; son of Oswy's elder brother, he had by Anglian law a better claim to the Northumbrian throne than Oswy himself.

303.2   ENGLISH UNDER-KING: see p. 195 above.

303.2   CLYDESIDE KINGS: see **G** BA.

303.2   EGFERTH: made Mercia tributary, before the death of Wulfhere (675), Eddius 20; constrained by archbishop Theodore to make peace after a disastrous battle on Trent in 679, where his young brother Aelfwin was killed, possibly at Elford *SK 18 10* near Lichfield, perhaps *Aelfwin's Ford*; Bede HE 4, 21; **A** 679; cf. Eddius 24.

303.2   EGFERTH ... IRELAND: Bede HE 4, 26; **A** 684, in Breg (eastern Meath north of Dublin).

303.2   EGFERTH ... PICTS: Bede HE 4, 26, **A** 685, SC 685. He was killed at Lin Garan, Nennius 57; at Dun Nechtain, **A**; Nechtansmere, Simeon of Durham HDE 9; Dunnichen *NO 51 48* near Forfar, north of Dundee, cf. **L**.

303.3   AETHELRED ... NO CIVIL WAR: he faced and survived one major rebellion, **A** 692, 'battle against the son of Penda', which is probably not a doublet of the 679 entry; his enemy is more likely to have been Ine of Wessex than a relative or a Welsh invader.

303.3   EGBERT: he asserted Wessex independence in 803, and subdued Mercia twenty years later. 'The great battle between Egbert, king of the West Saxons and Ceolwulf, king of the Mercians, at *Cherrenhul* between Oxford and Abingdon, which Egbert won', Leland *Itinerary* (Toulmin Smith 2, 151), cf. *Ant.* 9, 1935, 99, probably preserves in Latin the full text of SC 823 (821) 'Ceolwulf was deprived of the kingdom.' The Saxon Chronicle dates the completion of the conquest of Mercia to 829, but Mercian independence was briefly re-asserted in the following year.

307.3   LATEST PAGAN BURIALS: there was no sharp and sudden end to the old funeral rites. Clothed burial lasted in some areas throughout the 7th century, and beyond. Some of the dead, especially wealthy women and young girls, were buried in their best clothes, with their finery. But in most of large midland and southern cemeteries the pagan convention that deliberately buried objects intended for use in the after life declined after the conquest and was almost entirely discontinued early in the 7th century. Strong evidence indicates the date at which weapons, emblems of office, pottery vessels and the traditional jewellery of ordinary women ceased to be normal in graves. The great royal barrows of the south, and some of the warrior graves of the Peak District, are securely dated to about the 630s by continental coins and ornament; the decorative styles of objects found in these tombs are slightly later than the latest normally observed on humbler brooches and ornaments in the large cemeteries, but not much later. Most pagan cemetery burial ended a generation or more before the coming of Christianity. Pagan burial was not ended by conversion, but by the causes that made easy conversion possible; the grip of the old beliefs upon men's minds was already weakening before the Mercian and West Saxon kings were baptised.

307.4   BEANDUN: see **L**. Bindon, Devon, unlike Bindon, Dorset, and Bindon, Somerset, probably derives from *bean dun*, 'bean hill', EPNS Devon 636; cf. Hoskins WEW 8.

308.2   GLEVISSIG: see p. 228 above.

308.2   MORFAEL: see **G** BCL (H 25) and p. 243 above.

308.2   PENSELWOOD: see **L**. The suggestion that the battle was fought near Exeter and that the British withdrew northward towards Bridgwater (Hoskins WEW 15) is possible, but not probable.

308.3   POSBURY CAMP: *SX 80 97*, 'Possebury' in the 13th century, EPNS Devon 406.

309.1   CORNISH BISHOP: HS I, 674, cf. **E** Petroc.

309.1   BODMIN: HS I, 676 ff., cf. **T** Gospel Books.

309.1   DUNGARTH: ACm 875.

309.2   MORCANT: cf. p. 230 above; *moritur*, died, is commonly used of death in battle, e.g. ACm 558 (for 560) *Gabran . . . moritur*; 580 *Gurci et Peretur moritur*.

309.2   INE . . . MERCIAN SUPREMACY: In 701 Aldhelm secured the confirmation of the Pope's privileges for Malmesbury by both Aethelred and Ine; they
came to an agreement, and so concluded, that whether it were peace or war between Saxons and Mercians . . . the monastery should be ever in peace.

Aethelred signed first, as *Myrcena kyncg*, followed by Ine, *Wessexena cyng* BCS 106, end. In the 680s Wiltshire estates had been granted by Mercians alone (e.g. BCS 58, cf. 54); Ceadwalla and Ine had revived Wessex, but not thrown off Mercian supremacy. Coenred, who granted land near Shaftesbury in 704, could have been either king of the Mercians, or Ine's father, BCS 107.

310.1   ELISEG: ECMW 182 cf. **G** BP; *necxit hereditatem Povo[i]s [et recepit ?] per VIIII [annos ?] e potestate Anglorum in gladio suo parta in igne.* The grammar is too eccentric for exact translation, but the meaning seems clear.

310.2   DERBYSHIRE: see Map 22, p. 305.

310.2 NORTHUMBRIAN BORDER: the early place names of Cheshire and south Lancashire are chiefly Mercian rather than Northumbrian. Peaceful settlement of some Mercian English in allied Welsh lands may have begun quite early, for early in the 7th century a Welsh churchman was said to have been disturbed by Englishmen shouting 'Ker gia, ker gia!' at their hunting dogs on the upper Severn, far beyond lands yet conquered, *vita Beuno* 8. But extensive settlement is unlikely before Wulfhere's accession, cf. p. 300.3 above.

310.3 BEDE . . . ENGLAND: cf. e.g. for the territory *regio Anglorum* HE 3, 8; *Anglorum provinciae* 3, 3; cf. *Brettonum provinciae* 2, 2; for their dominion, *Anglorum regnum* 3, 24; 4, 26, etc.; for the population, *Anglorum populi* 1, 25; *natio Anglorum* 2, 2; 4, 26; *gens Anglorum* 2, 2; 3, 3; and *gentes Anglorum* 2, 3. These are samples of normal usage. 'Anglia' does not occur. 'Engelonde' in BCS 738, dated AD 939, may or may not belong to the original text.

311.1 CYMRY: cf. p. 41 above.

311.2 SAXONIA: cf. p. 41 above.

311.2 ANGLI SAXONES: first used in the later 8th century, in Europe, by Paul the Deacon *Historia Langobardorum* 4, 22, about 790, cf. Willibald, *Anglorum Saxonumque vocabulo*, vita Bonifatii 4 (11), about 760. *Angul Saxones* is common in 9th-century charters, usually in Latin, but found no wider popularity; Latin variants were used by Florence of Worcester and a few other medieval writers, citing from West Saxon usage.

311.2 WEST ANGLI: and *Suth Angli*, used consistently by the chronicler Aethelweard, himself a prince of the West Saxon dynasty, as substitutes for West and South Saxons; but the substitution would not work for East and Middle Saxons, since East and Middle Angles already existed; it found few imitators.

312.4 ALDHELM: Bede HE 5, 18 cf. Aldhelm *Ep.*4 (also excerpted HS 1,202).

313.1 CONBRAN: Combran BCS 169 (745), Cumbran SC 755, possibly a nickname, 'the Welshman', more probably the name Conbran, cf. LL index, LL 122 etc.

313.1 CATWAL: BCS 186.

313.2 HENRY I: *Consuetudo West Sexe* (70) 5, Liebermann *Gesetze* 1,588; cf. J.

313.3 LAET: the German word *litus*, or variants, including the *laeti* imported into Roman territory, denoted dependent cultivators, usually foreign, often conquered natives. The *laeti* of Kent were probably British; so Stenton ASE 300, cf. 311, and most who have studied the evidence in context.

313.3 DUNWALD, DUNWALLAUN: BCS 160, 175, 192 (about 747–772), cf. 332 (811) and 254 (788).

313.3 WELHISC: BCS 45, 72 (679, 688).

313.3 MABAN: Bede HE 5, 20, cf. Jackson LHEB 295[1].

313.3 MALUINUS: BCS 250.

314.1 NUNNA: very rare among the English, but a normal late Roman and British name, cf. Nonn(ita), mother of David, cf. E; Nunechia, wife of the early 5th-century British *magister militum* Gerontius G BC 380; Nunechius, the name of two bishops of Nantes, Duchesne *Fastes* 2, 365; 367; and of a *comes* of Limoges, Greg. Tur. HF 6, 22; Ninian, cf. E and p. 337, called Nynia by Bede, Nyniga by Alcuin.

314.2 CHAD: etc., from British Catu–, Jackson LHEB 554.

314.2 CAEDMON: Bede HE 4, 24, Welsh Cadfan, Jackson LHEB 244, etc.; cf. p. 421 below. Bede does not say that he was a 'cowherd', 'humble', or a 'lad'. He was 'elderly', *provectioris aetatis*, before he composed verses or entered a monastery. He had previously attended English-speaking dinner parties, where the *cithara*, 'guitar', or 'harp', was passed round in turn, but always left before his turn came, returning 'to his own house'. But on the particular night when his gift came to him, it fell to him to guard the stables (*stabula iumentorum*), for which he received payment from the steward, apparently of the monastery, next morning. The word *iumenta* means draught animals, oxen, horses or mules, who pull carriages or carts; not 'cows'. They were a valuable property, and the duty of night guard clearly went by rota; adequate guard against thieves plainly required a number of people under a responsible person. The implication of Bede's words is that landowners undertook the duty in turn, supplying a guard from their dependents; Bede does not indicate whether the obligation fell upon all landowners, English and Welsh, or upon Welshmen only. It was an imposition likely to fall on men of Welsh status; Caedmon's name was Welsh, but his language was English, at least in his later years; there were doubtless many Welshmen born who normally spoke English, but were held to the legal status of their birth.

314.2   PENNINES ... STRATHCLYDE: *vita Cadroe* 17, Colgan ASH 497 and Skene CPS 116. In the early 950s Dyfnwal of the Clyde (see G BA) escorted Cadroe to meet the envoy of Eric Blood-Axe, king of York, *usque Loidam civitatem, quae est confinium Normannorum atque Cumbrorum*, 'as far as the city of Leeds, which is the border between the North Men and the Cymry'. The place could not be the Lothians, also called *Loidis*, Skene CS 1,241 note, which was not a *civitas* and was far from Eric's borders. The place name and other evidence for the British reconquest of the Pennines in the earlier 10th century is discussed by Kenneth Jackson, *Angles and Britons* 72 ff. Dyfnwal's short-lived reconquest, however, extended far to the south and west of the border there indicated; his suzerainty over remote and inaccessible Yorkshire dales implies the survival of a considerable Welsh-speaking population until the Norse settlement of the later 10th and earlier 11th centuries. That settlement was thorough enough to enable modern Norwegians to understand conversation in broad Yorkshire concerned with agricultural and topographical terms; what remained of Welsh speech and custom in Yorkshire was evidently extinguished after the devastation of the north by William I in 1069, except possibly in Dent.

314.2   WILFRED: lands, Eddius 17.

314.2   BRITISH ADMINISTRATION: see p. 221 above.

314.2   BRITISH LAND TENURE: R.C.Shaw *Post-Roman Carlisle* 55 ff.

314.2   WILFRED ... VILLAGE: Eddius 18. Wilfred was in pursuit of a boy whom he claimed for his monastery, whose parents had fled to a British village to save the child. Wilfred was at *On Tiddanufri*, probably Tideover *SE 32 49*, in Kirkby Overblow, south of Harrogate; the British village was perhaps nearby Walton Head EPNS WRY 5, 43.

314.2   WALLERWENTE: the 'North People's Law' *North leodalage*, Liebermann *Gesetze* 1,460, cf. EHD 1,433; see J.

314.3   LONDON: VI Athelstan (*Iudicia Civitatis Lundoniae*) 6, 3, cf. IV Athelstan 6, 3.

314.3   CAMBRIDGE GUILD: Thorpe ALE 1,258, DAS 610, see J; translated Kemble SE 1,514, and, less accurately, EHD 1,557, with the strange suggestion that *Wylisc* means 'servile'. It does not. For the meaning of *wealh*, see p. 315 below.

314.3   BEANE: SC 913 *Beneficcan*, interpreted as *Bene fychan*, 'Little Beane' in Welsh, probably rightly, cf. Jackson LHEB 567. Many English rivers have Welsh names; but the retention of the Welsh adjective *fychan* argues that Welsh was commonly spoken when the English first settled by its banks, about the beginning of the 7th century, and perhaps for some time thereafter.

314.3   NORFOLK: Winnold House *TF 68 03* at Wereham, cf. Tanner 355 and *Norfolk Archaeology* 5, 1859, 297 ff., preserves the name of Winwaloe (see E) and incorporates much of the medieval monastic buildings. It was the site of a major fair on Winwaloe's day, March 3, until the late 18th century, superseded by Downham Market (*TF 61 03*) fair on the same day.

The cult of Winwaloe in Norfolk was not confined to Wereham. He is said to have had a church in Norwich (LBS 4, 361) and a widespread Norfolk weather rhyme on the windy first days of March runs

> First come David, then come Chad,
> Then come Winnell roaring mad.

The rhyme is cited LBS 4, 360; Arnold-Foster SCD 2,284. A radio broadcast request in the late 1950s elicited half a dozen versions, with slight variants, still known in different parts of Norfolk. David and Chad are extensively venerated in Britain on March 1 and 2; the observation of Winwaloe's day on March 3 is recorded only in Norfolk, and in Wales, Cornwall and Devon.

314.3   HERTFORDSHIRE: Wynnel's Grove *TL 41 35* in Cokenach, astride the boundary between Nuthampstead and Barley parishes, was *capella Sancti Winwaloei* in the 13th century, *Registrum de Walden* (BM Harleian MS 3697) folio 189, printed Dugdale *Mon. Ang.* 1, 462–3; traces of what may be the chapel are visible in the wood, but have not yet been excavated. A stretch of the Icknield Way near Royston was called *Wynewalestrete* c. 1470, EPNS 175.

Both Wereham and Cokenach were granted to St. Winwaloe's Abbey at Montreuil-sur-mer in Picardy about the end of the 12th century. At first sight these grants might seem to be the reason why Winwaloe became patron of the places granted. But the late acquisition of a small dependent priory is insufficient to explain the wide and persistent honouring of Winwaloe's name in Norfolk; and in Hertfordshire the grants refer to the chapel, with its monks, as already in existence at the time when the grant was made, while the grantor's son undertook to maintain it in good repair. Moreover, a late name for a little chapel cannot by itself explain the local name for a major Roman and prehistoric highway five miles distant.

No medieval reason explains or links the grants of the two sites, remote from each other, to a foreign abbey without other English connections. The likely cause is that at the time of the grants both houses already bore the name of Winwaloe, but were doubtless in deep decay. The Life of Gwenael, Winwaloe's successor at Landevennec in Brittany, states that in or about the 590s he visited Britain and founded one or more houses; several are known in Wales and the west (see E), and they may have included Wereham and Cokenach, named, as often, in honour of the founder's teacher and master.

314.3   GUTHLAC: Felix *vita Guthlaci* 34. A band of Britons fired the monastery in a dawn attack, and wounded the saint who was wakened from a 'light sleep'. The incident was not an 'unquiet dream', nor were the British 'devils in disguise', as Colgrave, *Felix* 185 (for the translation, see *Ant.* 8, 1934, 193); Guthlac lived among British neighbours, for, at Crowland, he was a 'pattern to many a Briton', Cynewulf III c. 140 Kennedy p. 268.

314.3   11th CENTURY: BCS 991 and Ramsey Chronicle, cited H.C. Darby, *Ant.* 8, 1934, 194.

314.3   CAEDMON: see p. 314.2 above.

315.3   CAMBERWELL: the well from which the place is named has been excavated and found to be Roman British.

315.3   WEALH . . . SERF: EPNS 1 i 18 (1924).

315.3   SPECULATION: EPNE 2, 242–3 (1956).

315.4   WEST SAXON TEXTS: the texts are cited and discussed by H.P.R. Finberg *The*

Agrarian History of England, vol. 1,2 ch.1; to whom I am indebted for permission to read the manuscript before publication.

315.4   INE: 23, 3.

315.4· WALL, WOOD: EPNE 2, 241; 244. These names are however far fewer than *wealh-tun*.

17   English Monarchy (pp. 317–334)

317.1   BEDE . . . EMPIRE: HE 2, 5, cf. p. 329; Aethelbert of Kent *imperavit* all the English *provinciae* south of the Humber; and was the third to hold such *imperium*. Bede adds details only of the Northumbrians, evidently commenting on a list already recognised. Its existence emphasises that the concept that the English should have one over-king who held 'empire' over all Britain was already established in the 7th century.

317.1   SAXON CHRONICLE: 827 (829), repeats the list, on Egbert's conquest of Mercia, adding Egbert, and gives these rulers the title *Bretwalda*, 'ruler of Britain', adapting the Welsh *Gwledic* (p. 206 above).

318.1   ANGLES: **G** EM and p. 265 above.

318.1   SAXONS . . . NO KING: Hucbald *vita Lebuini* 4.

318.1   FRANKS . . . EXASPERATED: e.g. *Annales Laurissenses* AD 798 *perfidissimos primores Saxonum*.

318.2   OESC: see **G** EK.

320.1   LEODE: Laws of Aethelbert 2.

320.1   REFERENDARIUS, GRAFIO: BCS 4; 5. The witness-lists are older than the body of the text; 'Hocca grafio' in 4 has been misunderstood by the copyist of 5, and turned into two persons, 'Hocca comes' and 'Grafio comes'.

320.2   FOUR LEADERS: cf. p. 233 above.

320.3   YEAVERING: publication forthcoming; the excavator, Brian Hope-Taylor, has kindly allowed me to give this short description; cf. p. 214 above.

321.3   GOODMANHAM: see p. 390 below.

322.2   SUTTON HOO, BROOMFIELD, TAPLOW: see **S**.

323.1   TAEPPA'S KINGDOM: the location of his tomb argues that his territory included south Buckinghamshire. Its splendour implies a wider kingdom. The then English settlements, whose ornament resembles that of the Taplow region, extended eastward along the Thames bank. Taeppa's 'Norrey' may therefore have been coterminous with Surrey, including the future Middlesex. In the poorly recorded conflicts that followed Aethelbert's death, Edwin of Northumbria overran Mercia and Wessex, and his ally Redwald was dominant in the south east, probably through most of the 620s; it is possible that Taeppa then took London from the East Saxon allies of the enfeebled Kentish kingdom. It is also possible that the king buried at Broomfield was an East Anglian, temporarily installed as ruler of the East Saxons under Redwald's suzerainty; alternatively, it might be that Taeppa was himself an East Saxon, but since all known East Saxon kings, except Offa, bore names beginning with S for almost 200 years, the alternative is less likely.

The evidence does not suffice to determine the origin of Taeppa or the precise limits of his kingdom; but the magnificence of his tomb demonstrates that he was a great king who ruled north of the Thames in a generation when the history of the region is not known, between the collapse of the Kentish empire and the consolidation of Mercian control. Whatever the vicissitudes of the London region (cf. p. 493.1 below) in these years, East Saxon control was probably reasserted by the middle of the 7th century; the weak record and uncertain dates of the East Saxon kings are discussed by Plummer, Bede, 2, 176; cf. **G** EE.

323.3   FRONTIER PEOPLES: the term chiefly applies to the western districts of the Mercians and the West Saxons, and to the Bernicians in the north.

323.3   ANGLIAN CHRONICLE: p. 283 above, and **T**.

323.4   SAXON CHRONICLE: see pp. 103 and 317 above; cf. **T** and **G** EW.

324.2   WEST SAXON RULERS: the older national name was *Gewissae* (p. 294 above), probably meaning 'confederates' (see **L**). It may have originated when Ceawlin and Cutha organised the separate southern English settlements into a single nation in the 570s and 580s, but was more probably the earlier name of the Berkshire English of the middle Thames about Abingdon, who began as an amalgam of immigrants from different parts of the continental homeland, who used differing burial rites, and ornament, and were also *foederati* of the British. They were known to the British as Saxons, as were all other English, and are first known to have used the collective term Saxons of themselves in the preamble to Ine's laws in the 690s, though the same laws describe the individual members of the population as English (p. 41 above). Thereafter 'West Saxon' was the common and usual national name, though for centuries the old name Gewissae occurs as an occasionally literary variant in Bede, Asser and elsewhere.

324.3   WESSEX: the territorial name Westsexe is rarer than the ethnic term West Saxons. The adjective 'West' was required when other kingdoms also accepted the name Saxon. The English of the former *civitates* of the Trinovantes and Regnenses are also first recorded as East and South Saxons in the 690s (BCS 81, 87, 78 ff.), those of the London region as Middle Saxons in 704 (BCS 111). All four names were well established by Bede's time. The extant late copies of the 'Tribal Hidage' (p. 492 below) use the terms Wessex, Essex and Sussex; since they are unacquainted with the term Middlesex, their usage may date back to the original of the document, probably drafted about 661. The name Saxon may have been first and most readily accepted by the Gewissae, since ornament that derives from continental Saxons of the lower Elbe is plentiful among the first immigrants, and continental Saxon political notions won acceptance in later generations (cf. note 324.4, Power of the Overking, below); but ancestry cannot explain the name of the East Saxons, whose archaeology and traditions have little to do with the continental Saxon area. A more compelling reason to accept a national name used by the British was doubtless dislike of the masterful assertion of sovereignty by the Northumbrian and Mercian Angles over all the English, that pressed acutely upon the West Saxons from the 620s, upon the East and South Saxons from the 640s and 660s.

324.3   WESSEX ... FIVE ... KINGDOMS: SC 626; Bede HE 2, 9; cf. p. 302 above. See **G** EW and **L** Wessex. The charters and some SC entries locate the kingdoms and name many of their rulers. The evidence has not yet been sifted, and has sometimes been swept aside by the easy pretence that the names are 'spurious'; it indicates however that the regions were in substance the future counties of Berkshire, Hampshire, Wiltshire, Somerset and Dorset. These kingdoms emerged from the former Roman *civitates*, Berkshire from the Atrebates, Hampshire and Wiltshire from the division of the Belgae (cf. p. 226.2 above), Dorset from the Durotriges, Somerset from the portion of north-eastern Dumnonia subdued by the English in the late 6th century (see p. 294 above), extended westward by later conquest. The subjugation of the rest of eastern Dumnonia in the mid and late 7th century added the new region of English Devon, which may thereafter have formed an additional kingdom. Some boundaries shifted; notably, some southern Atrebatic territory was incorporated in Hampshire.

324.3   THREE ... KINGS: in 661, while Cenwalh was High King, SC notes the deaths, presumably in the course of Wulfhere's invasion of Wessex, of king Coenberth, father of Ceadwalla, and of Cuthred, son of Cynegils' contemporary king Cwichelm (SC 614–636). The wording of many of the charters, and of the pedigrees inserted into SC, suggest that each kingdom had its own hereditary dynasty; Cuthred may or may not have been ancestor of Cuthred, king in Berkshire and northern Hampshire in Ine's time, c. 700, (BCS 101, 102, 155 etc.) and of Cuthred, High King of Wessex 741–756.

324.3   OVERKINGSHIP DISCONTINUED: Bede HE 4, 12 'the under kings took over the government of the nation and held it divided between them for about ten years'. SC exploited a different tradition, that recognised a High Kingship continued, in name at least, by Cenwalh's widow for a year, by Aescwine from 674 to 676, and by Cenwalh's (grand)son Centwine from 676; Florence of Worcester (Appendix, *Genealogia regum West-Saxonum*, at 672, ed. Thorpe 1,272), on the authority of a *Dicta Regis Alfredi*, adds Aescwine's father Cenfus, from a tradition that evidently intended the dates 672–674. The variant traditions are not in conflict; it is likely that these rulers claimed the high kingship at or about these dates; Bede's words show that the claims did not then succeed.

324.3   OVERKINGSHIP REVIVED: by Centwine, who is said to have claimed it from 676. He was acknowledged as 'King of the West Saxons' by his Northumbrian contemporary Eddius (ch. 40) in 680/681, at the end of Bede's ten year period.

324.3   DIFFERENT DYNASTIES: the future form of the West Saxon monarchy was the result of a deliberate political decision taken at a particular time. The 60 years unbroken rule of a father and his son from 611 to 672 had threatened to establish the High Kingship permanently in one dynasty. In 672 the West Saxon magnates refused to perpetuate its supremacy. Though Centwine briefly regained his ancestors' title, he failed to re-establish his dynasty. Ceadwalla, the young son of a former regional king, soon 'began to contend for the kingship' (SC 685), and succeeded. Three years later he abdicated; the political pressures and personal motives which induced him to do so are not fully recorded. He was succeeded by Ine, the son of a regional king who was still alive. Nothing is recorded of the ancestry of his successors, save that none of them is said to have been the son of his predecessor before 839; and that one of them retained Hampshire, presumably his own kingdom, when deprived of the High Kingship (SC 757). The principle of an elective monarchy, whose conventions limited the choice of the supreme ruler to the kings of regional dynasties, closely resembles the practice of the Irish, who for centuries chose their High King from among the heads of the several Ui Neill dynasties in turn.

324.4   POWER OF THE OVERKING: the decision to abolish a permanent dynasty in 672 automatically restricted the High King's power. It marked the dominance of those who clung to the continental Saxon tradition of effective government by local rulers, and rejected the continental Anglian tradition, powerfully asserted in Britain by the Mercians, of a strong central monarchy. It coincided in time with the consolidation of Mercian supremacy over the southern English, and with the replacement of the old national name of Gewissae (see p. 324.3, Wessex, above) by the collective ethnic term Saxon, and was reached when the influence of monks trained in Ireland, familiar with Irish hierarchical kingship, was at its strongest throughout Britain.

324.4   DIFFERENT TEXTS: closer study is likely to suggest when the differences are no more than varying formulae, and when they imply differing political conceptions. Occasionally an underking is termed *minister*, e.g. BCS 60, whereby Aethelred of Mercia granted Gloucester, c. 680, to Osric and Oswald *duobus ministris meis nobilis generis in provincia Huicciorum*, though they are elsewhere regularly termed *reges*.

324.4   REX: still used of regional West Saxon kings of the later 8th century, cf., e.g., SC 757.

325.1   KINGDOMS . . . DETACHED FROM WESSEX: e.g. Wiltshire grants in 680–681 made to and by Cenfrith, *comes Mertiorum*, who is also called *patricius*, and *propinquus*, near relative, of Aethelred of Mercia, BCS 54, 58, 59.

325.2   MERCIANS: see **G** EM.

326.3   COLLECTING TAXES: cf. p. 460 below.

327.1   OSWY: William of Malmesbury *de Gestis Regum* 1, 50; he 'ruled (*praefuit*) the Mercians and the peoples of the other southern provinces', Bede HE 3, 24.

327.2   ALDHELM: e.g. BCS 108 *Ego Ine . . . rex cum consilio et decreto praesulis nostri Aldhelm*.

328.2   CHARTERS: see **C**.

329.1   EMPIRE: Bede regularly distinguishes the *imperium* of each over-king from his own *regnum*, e.g. HE 1, 25; 2, 5, cf. Plummer *Bede* 2, 43; 86. The Mercian charters and the 'Tribal Hidage' similarly distinguish between the *imperium* and the *regnum* of the Mercian kings; cf. Stenton ASE 234, and EHR 33, 1918, 433.

329.1   EMPEROR: BCS 289 *rector et imperator Merciorum regni*.

329.2   IRISH . . . IMPERATOR: Muirchu 9, cf. Loegaire, p. 161 above.

329.2   OSWALD: Adomnan *Columba* 1, 1 *totius Brittaniae imperator a Deo ordinatus*; earlier in the chapter *regnator Saxonum*, cf. p. 161 above.

329.2   BRIAN BORU: Book of Armagh, folio 16 verso, cf. p. 167 above.

329.2   ARMORICAN BRITISH: *vita Pauli Aureliani* 15, cf. p. 253 above.

329.3   BONIFACE: *Ep.* 78 *imperator vel rex* referring to Aethelbald, cf. *Ep.* 75. Aethelbald calls himself *gentis Merciorum regens imperium* in an original charter, BCS 162, ruling the empire held by the Mercian nation.

329.3   GWLEDIC: cf. p. 206 above.

329.3   BRETWALDA: cf. p. 317 above, and Athelstan's usage of *Brytaenwalda*, BCS 706, to translate *rector Britanniae* of BCS 705, dated AD 934.

330.2   10TH CENTURY: occasionally used by Athelstan, e.g. *basileus Anglorum simul et imperator regum et nationum infra fines Britanniae commorantium*, BCS 700, dated AD 934, exactly defining notions of the respective meanings of king and emperor; cf. also BCS 746.

330.2   EDRED: king and emperor, e.g. BCS 874, 882, 884; Caesar BCS 909.

330.2   AETHELRED: e.g. KCD 1308 *rex Anglo-Saxoniae, atque Nordhymbrensis gubernator monarchiae; paganorumque propugnator, ac Bretonum ceterarumque provinciarum imperator*.

330.2   GREEK TITLES: e.g. *basileus orbis Britannie* KCD 1283; *basileus Albionis* KCD 1279 cf. note 330.2, 10th century, above.

331.2   ALCUIN: see **E**.

331.2   ALCUIN . . . IMMENSE THREAT: *Ep.* 129, also printed HS 3, 509–511, cf. *Ep.* 17.

332.3   THREE PERSONS: Alcuin *Ep.* 174.

333.2   DAVID . . . JOAB: Alcuin *Ep.* 178.

333.2   PRESSURES . . . ADVICE: cf. Ganshof *Speculum* 24, 1949, 524. 'It was . . . owing to Alcuin that he (Charles) went to Rome . . . it was under the same influence that he accepted there the imperial dignity.' The story that Charles was taken by surprise when the Pope crowned him is unconvincing government propaganda, that could have deceived no one who knew what Alcuin had been advising, or had read his letters.

333.2   CHARLEMAGNE ... ROME: at the moment of his coronation Charles was not crowned 'western' emperor. He was crowned Roman emperor while the imperial throne in Constantinople was vacant. But the elevation of a new emperor in Constantinople made him and his successors western emperors.

333.2   ENGLISH PRECEDENT: English practice grew from past English, Welsh and Irish experience. Irish political practice was the main root of government by a High King over subordinate kings who acknowledged his precedence, but denied his authority. The circumstances of Europe prevented the emergence of a sovereign high-kingship on the English model and condemned the emperors to a high-kingship as weak as the Irish. For the next several centuries the main political relationships of European rulers, that are at present commonly classified as 'feudal', were of necessity obliged to reproduce many of the features of Irish government, which had underlain their formation at several removes. The study of 9th, 10th and 11th century Europe is impoverished if Irish experience, secular as ecclesiastical, is disregarded.

INDEX

Italic figures refer to the notes.

An asterisk (*) indicates a note on the name or word concerned

The letters f (*filius*) and m (*mac* or *map*) mean 'son of'; f. means 'following'.

Modern conventions on the spelling of names vary, and are often arbitrary; thus, Aethelbert or Ethelbert are nowadays equally familiar, Athelbert unfamiliar, but Athelstan prevails over Ethelstan or Aethelstan. The most recognisable form is normally used. Irish names are normally given in plain English spelling.